Family and Succession Law in New Zealand

Family and Succession Law in New Zealand

Third Edition

W.R. (Bill) Atkin

This book was originally published as a monograph in the International Encyclopaedia of Laws/Family and Succession Law.

Founding Editor: Roger Blanpain
General Editor: Frank Hendrickx
Volume Editor: Walter Pintens

Wolters Kluwer

Published by:
Kluwer Law International B.V.
PO Box 316
2400 AH Alphen aan den Rijn
The Netherlands
E-mail: lrs-sales@wolterskluwer.com
Website: www.wolterskluwer.com/en/solutions/kluwerlawinternational

Sold and distributed by:
Wolters Kluwer Legal & Regulatory U.S.
7201 McKinney Circle
Frederick, MD 21704
United States of America
E-mail: customer.service@wolterskluwer.com

Printed on acid-free paper

ISBN 978-94-035-4883-8

e-Book: ISBN 978-94-035-4614-8
web-PDF: ISBN 978-94-035-4624-7

Printed in the United Kingdom.

The Author

Prof. W.R. (Bill) Atkin, BA LLM (VUW), is a professor in the Faculty of Law at Victoria University of Wellington and has been the Faculty's Director of Postgraduate Studies. He has taught a wide range of subjects at undergraduate and postgraduate levels over many years, including Family Law, Law and Medicine, Torts, Welfare Law, Land Law and Law for Social Workers. He is a barrister and solicitor of the High Court of New Zealand.

He has written extensively, especially in the area of family law. In addition to being a member of the team which contributes to the *LexisNexis Family Law Service*, he has written *Relationship Property in New Zealand* (3rd edn, LexisNexis, Wellington 2018) and co-edited with Mark Henaghan *Family Law Policy in New Zealand* (now in its fifth edition). He is contributing editor of *Fisher on Matrimonial Property* (online) and is responsible for the titles 'Husband and Wife' and 'Family Property Arrangements' in the *Laws of New Zealand*. He is also a contributor to Todd (General Editor), *Todd on Torts* (8th edn, Thomson Reuters, Wellington 2019). He wrote the New Zealand monograph on social security law for the International Encyclopaedia of Laws. For ten years, he was General Editor of the International Society of Family Law's *International Survey of Family Law*, published annually.

He was a member of the Justice Department Working Group which in 1988 produced a report on *Matrimonial Property and Family Protection*. In 1990, he chaired the Ministerial Adoption Practices Review Committee which made important recommendations to the Minister of Social Welfare, and in 1992 he submitted a report to the Minister of Justice entitled *Personal Obligations of Support: Options and Discussion*. He was one of the two members of the Ministerial Committee on Assisted Reproductive Technologies, which reported to the Minister of Justice in 1994. The Human Assisted Reproductive Technology Act 2004 is in part based on recommendations in the Committee's report. He was on the Expert Advisory Group for the Law Commission's project on relationship property, which published its final report in July 2019, and the Expert Reference Group for the Independent Panel reviewing changes to the family justice system, which reported in May 2019.

The Author

Table of Contents

List of Abbreviations

AC	Appeal Cases
ALR	Australian Law Reports
All ER	All England Reports
B & Ald	Barnewall and Alderson
CA	Court of Appeal
Ch	Chancery
ChD	Chancery Division
ER	English Reports
Fam	Family
Family LR	Family Law Reports
FDR	Family Dispute Resolution
FRNZ	Family Reports of New Zealand
HC	High Court
Imp	Imperial Statutes
J	Justice
KB	King's Bench
LJ	Lord Justice
LT	Law Times
M & W	Meeson and Welsby
NZAR	New Zealand Administrative Reports
NZFLR	New Zealand Family Law Reports
NZLJ	New Zealand Law Journal
NZLR	New Zealand Law Reports
P	President (with reference to a judge)
P	Probate
PC	Privy Council
PD	Probate and Divorce
QB	Queen's Bench

List of Abbreviations

R	Rule
SC	Supreme Court
UK	United Kingdom

General Introduction

§1. General Background of the Country

1. New Zealand[1] is a nation made up of two main islands, the North and the South Islands, plus a host of smaller islands. It is surrounded by the Pacific Ocean and the Tasman Sea and is a two to three hours flight from its nearest large neighbour, Australia. The country was first settled by Polynesians in the eighth century. The first European visitor was Abel Tasman in 1642, but it was not until 1769 that the coastline was navigated thoroughly by the English explorer James Cook. Colonization, primarily from Britain, began in the nineteenth century.

2. A critical date in the country's history is 1840, when tribal leaders of the indigenous Maori people and representatives of Queen Victoria signed the Treaty of Waitangi. Although there is controversy over the exact meaning of the Treaty, in broad terms, the Māori retained control of their own affairs while ceding overall governance of the islands to the Crown. The country remained a British colony until 1907 when it became a Dominion. It is now a fully independent member of the British Commonwealth, and the British monarch serves as its head of state.

3. As of 31 December 2021, the estimated population was 5.13 million, approximately three quarters living in the North Island (including an estimated 1.7 million in the northern city of Auckland alone) and a quarter in the South Island. Auckland has attracted many people, especially from the Pacific area. As of the 2018 census, 70.2% of the population were of European origin with Māori making up the next largest grouping at 16.5%. Asians made up 15.1% and 8.1% identified as Pasifika.[2] While most of the population lives in urban areas, large tracts of land are farmed, and the rural sector has traditionally played a vital role in the nation's economy.

4. In the year to December 2021, there were 58,659 live births, as compared with 60,153 in 1990. There is now a trend towards later childbearing, with 30–34 being the most common age group for women having children. This compares with an age group of 20–24 in the early 1970s. The fertility rate in 2021 continued a trend of

1. Much useful demographic and other data can be obtained from the website of Statistics New Zealand: www.stats.govt.nz.
2. N.B. some people identified themselves as more than one ethnicity, so the figures do not add up precisely. The 2018 census was the first census to be trialled as online, as a result there was an 82% increase in non-respondents (from 5.5% to 10%) and concern over certain groups being underrepresented in the data set.

2004 (as amended). Second, under section 46E of the 2004 Act, they must have attended 'FDR', which in reality is a form of mandatory mediation. Various FDR providers and organizations, which sit outside the Family Court structure, are empowered to provide mediation. The rules governing the FDR process itself, including the place of children and who may attend, are scanty but, under section 11 of the FDR Act 2013, an FDR provider 'must make every endeavour to ... assist the parties to reach an agreement ... that best serves the welfare and best interests of all children involved in the dispute'. In 2021, legislation was passed to ensure that children have reasonable opportunities to participate in the mediation process.[7] This legislation is not yet in force as efforts are made to work out the best ways of implementing it. The parties must pay for the cost of mediation unless they satisfy the narrowly framed conditions for obtaining legal aid. Some exceptions to the mandatory mediation requirement exist. For example, FDR can be avoided if there has been violence, and if a case is urgent, then an application can be made directly to the Family Court. Somewhat counter-intuitively, lawyers for the parties were not usually allowed to appear in court on their behalf until the matter reaches a full hearing. This rule was repealed on 1 July 2020.[8] While in the past a lawyer was appointed automatically to represent the child, under section 7 of the 2004 Act as amended, the Family Court can make an appointment only if it 'has concerns for the safety or well-being of the child' and 'considers an appointment necessary'.

11. In August 2018, the Minister of Justice appointed an independent panel to 'consider the 2014 family justice reforms as they relate to assisting parents/ guardians to decide or resolve disputes about parenting arrangements or guardianship matters ... '. The independent panel delivered its report, *Te Korowai Ture ā-Whānau,* in May 2019.[9] The report made seventy system-wide recommendations, the principal recommendation being to bring together a range of already existing services under a new title of 'Te Korowai Ture ā-Whānau'. The report identified that the system had become too fragmented over time, and this was causing serious issues in access to justice. The panel envisioned that the new agency would sit over the system like a korowai (Māori cloak) and provide a variety of streamlined avenues for people to access the right family justice service at some of the most vulnerable moments of their lives. While legislation has addressed some of the report's recommendations,[10] much still remains to be implemented.

12. Matrimonial property laws have altered dramatically over time. The position inherited from Britain was that husbands owned the property of a marriage and the wife was incapable of doing so. This changed radically with the Married Women's Property Act 1884, which enabled a wife to own and deal with property as if she were unmarried. This meant that, in effect, spouses were treated as if they were

---

7. Family Court (Supporting Children in Court) Legislation Act 2021, amending s 11 of the Family Dispute Resolution Act 2014.
8. Family Court (Supporting Families in Court) Legislation Act 2020, s. 4.
9. Ministry of Justice, *Te Korowai Ture ā-Whānau: The final report of the Independent Panel examining the 2014 family justice reforms* (May 2019), available at www.justice.govt.nz.
10. Family Court (Supporting Families in Court) Legislation Act 2020 and Family Court (Supporting Children in Court) Legislation Act 2021.

strangers. However, as they were not normally income-earners, little was improved for most wives until the passage of the Matrimonial Property Act 1963. Under this legislation, power was given to the court to make awards with respect to property, notwithstanding the parties' legal and equitable interests. This approach was taken a stage further by the Matrimonial Property Act 1976, under which matrimonial property is normally divided equally between the parties. This Act underwent significant revision in 2001, including a name change. The Property (Relationships) Act 1976, as it is now called, currently applies to de facto relationships, civil unions,[11] and widowed parties, in addition to married and divorced couples. The Law Commission issued a major report in 2019 in which it recommended significant changes to the current law.[12] As a follow-up project, the Law Commission was asked to look at the law of succession and especially its interrelationship with the 1976 Act. Its final report was released in December 2021 and is awaiting the government's response.[13] Special laws relating to the family home date back to the Family Homes Protection Act 1895, under which homes registered under the Act enjoyed some protection from creditors. Tax advantages and access to cheap government housing finance encouraged more use to be made of this law and its successor, now found in the Joint Family Homes Act 1964. Many of these benefits no longer apply (e.g., death duties or taxes were abolished in the early 1990s and 'gift duty' in 2011), and the legislation is no longer used to the extent it was in earlier decades.

13. New Zealand's law on children has often been ahead of many parts of the world. New Zealand was a leader of the British colonies when it passed legislation for the adoption of children: the Adoption of Children Act 1881. The current law, the Adoption Act 1955, is often thought to be out-of-date, especially in the light of the practice of 'open adoption', but access to details about birth parents is dealt with by the Adult Adoption Information Act 1985. In June 2021, the Ministry of Justice released a review of adoption law and sought submissions from the public.[14] Further consultations are planned for mid-2022. New Zealand law has allowed for the legitimation of children upon the marriage of their parents since 1894, although a similar rule had existed from 1860 where a child was born to a European and a Māori – the Half-Caste Disability Removal Act 1860 – surely a far-sighted, even if narrowly defined, piece of legislation for its day. The Status of Children Act 1969 completed the process of removing the legal stigma attached to illegitimacy, so that from that time onwards children have been, for virtually all legal purposes, treated the same whether born in or out of wedlock.

14. Under the Infants Guardianship and Contracts Act 1887, a mother was able to apply for custody of her children. The court was required to have regard for the welfare of the child, the parents' conduct and their wishes. On divorce, the court

11. Civil unions, available to couples of both the opposite and the same-sex, were created by the Civil Union Act 2004. The Act came into force on 26 Apr. 2005.
12. Law Commission *Review of the Property (Relationships) Act 1976* (NZLC R143, 2019).
13. Law Commission *He arotake i te āheinga ki ngā rawa a te tangata ka mate ana | Review of succession law: rights to a person's property on death* (R145, Wellington, 2021).
14. Ministry of Justice *Adoption in Aotearoa New Zealand Discussion document* (Wellington, 2021).

could declare that a party at fault was unfit to have custody. The welfare of the child became the first and paramount consideration under section 2 of the Guardianship of Infants Act 1926. That Act also provided that the court was not to take into account a father's claim that he had common law rights which were superior to those of the mother, or a similar claim by the mother. The mother had an equal right to apply to the court for custody. Today, the paramount principle is found in sections 4 and 5 of the Care of Children Act 2004 (which replaced the Guardianship Act 1968). The court can take conduct into account only in so far as it is relevant to the child's welfare. The child's views are relevant irrespective of the age and maturity of the child. The court is not permitted to discriminate between the parents simply on the grounds of gender.

15. The history of childcare dates back to the early colonial era. From the 1860s, legislation enabled the government to provide for neglected children. The Neglected and Criminal Children Act 1867 provided for 'industrial schools' to which neglected, indigent and delinquent children could be sent. The number of children left destitute appears to have risen with the gold rushes which took place in the 1860s. The emphasis shifted over time from institutional to non-institutional care, and the law was updated and codified in the Child Welfare Act 1925. This was replaced by the Children and Young Persons Act 1974 and then by the Children, Young Persons and Their Families Act 1989. The latter Act's name was changed in 2017 to Oranga Tamariki Act 1989 or Children's and Young People's Well-Being Act 1989 (most commonly referred to by the Māori version), a change accompanied by a number of system-wide changes recognizing the special needs of Māori within the system.[15] The 1989 Act represented a radical change in perspective. It endeavoured to ensure that children in need of care and protection are cared for within the wider family network rather than being placed in foster care or in a residential institution. The key decision-making body is the so-called family group conference, although in a minority of cases, where the family group cannot reach a satisfactory solution, the court may grant orders concerning the child. Several reports have criticized the operation of the Act, especially in respect of Māori children,[16] and further changes are likely. A Bill before Parliament, the Oversight of Oranga Tamariki System and Children and Young People's Commission Bill Legislation Bill, establishes an Independent Monitor of the Oranga Tamariki System, and also abolishes the Children's Commissioner and replaces that office with a Children and Young People's Commission. Public submissions on the Bill have been critical, especially regarding the abolition of the Children's Commissioner, and the form of the legislation may well change. Another development is the Royal Commission of Inquiry on Abuse in Care, which began in 2018. This is about historical abuse in both state and faith-based institutions.[17]

15. 'Oranga' can be broadly translated as 'welfare' or 'health', and 'Tamariki' is the Māori word for 'children' or 'youth'. The broader reforms came into effect on 1 Jul. 2019: Children, Young Persons, and Their Families (Oranga Tamariki) Legislation Act 2017.
16. For example, Waitangi Tribunal *He Pāharakeke he Rito Whakakīkinga Whāruarua: Oranga Tamariki Urgent Inquiry* (Wai 2915, 2021).
17. https://www.abuseincare.org.nz.

16. The Family Proceedings Act 1980, which changed the law on divorce, coincided with the creation of the Family Court. This major development is discussed in a subsequent section.

17. The law relating to succession is more straightforward. The United Kingdom Wills Act 1837 applied in New Zealand from colonization until it was replaced by the Wills Act 2007. A major revision of the law on intestacy occurred with the passage of the Administration Act 1879 Amendment Act 1885. This Act placed widowers in the same position as widows with respect to intestacy, a change which was consequential upon the enactment of the Married Women's Property Act 1884 (*see* above, paragraph 12). The law is now found in the Administration Act 1969 and has been extended, first to surviving de facto partners and then to civil union partners. New Zealand was one of the first countries to empower the court to make orders affecting testamentary dispositions. The Testator's Family Maintenance Act was passed in 1900 and allowed wives and children who had not been adequately provided for in the deceased's will to apply for some provision out of the estate. The courts soon developed a test based on the testator's moral duty.[18] Legislation enacted during the twentieth century extended coverage to other members of the family, although it did not cover unmarried partners until reforms were passed in 2001. The law is now found in the Family Protection Act 1955. Another novel development was the Law Reform (Testamentary Promises) Act 1949, which enabled anyone, not necessarily a member of the family, to seek provision from the estate, so long as the applicant could show that there had been a promise to leave something in the will in return for services provided to the deceased. As noted above (paragraph 12), the Law Commission has reviewed aspects of succession law.[19]

§3. Sources of Family and Succession Law

I. Constitution

18. New Zealand has no formal written Constitution, but instead has a collection of documents and conventions which form the constitutional threads of the nation. Of these, one of the most significant is the New Zealand Bill of Rights Act 1990. This Act is not an entrenched statute and cannot as such be used to strike down other legislation which is inconsistent with it. Although no provisions of this piece of legislation explicitly relate to family and succession rights, it has been invoked in several such cases. For example, the clash between the child's right to life and the parents' right to freedom of religion was critical in the Court of Appeal

18. For example, *see In re Allardice, Allardice v. Allardice* (1910) 29 NZLR 959 and *In re Allen, Allen v. Manchester* [1922] NZLR 218.
19. Law Commission *He arotake i te āheinga ki ngā rawa a te tangata ka mate ana | Review of succession law: rights to a person's property on death* (R145, Wellington, 2021).

27. Succession cases must normally be heard by the High Court. However, jurisdiction under the Family Protection Act 1955 and Law Reform (Testamentary Promises) Act 1949 was granted to the Family Court in 1991. The court also has limited powers under the Wills Act 2007.

Part I. Persons

Chapter 1. The Status of a Person

§1. Definition of a Person

28. The question of the definition of a 'person' has rarely been considered under New Zealand law. Section 29 of the Interpretation Act 1999 states, '"Person" includes a corporation sole, a body corporate, and an unincorporated body.' Section 31 states that 'In an enactment passed or made before the commencement of this Act, words denoting the masculine gender include females.' A natural person is a 'person' from birth until death.

29. Unborn children have no legal status.[31] In one anomalous case, a Family Court judge held that an unborn child who had reached a stage of development where it was able to survive independently of the mother could be made the subject of an order that the child was in need of care and protection.[32] This case conflicts with other British Commonwealth precedents,[33] but gains some support from a decision of a High Court judge in a case where a pornographic film was going to be made of a mother in labour and giving birth.[34] The judge held that there was jurisdiction to place an unborn child under the guardianship of the court but that this would only be done in rare cases.

30. Certainly, for the purposes of New Zealand's abortion laws, the unborn child has no status.[35] Historically, however, abortion has been a crime in New Zealand, only recently abolished by the Abortion Legislation Act 2020, noted later in this paragraph. Section 182 of the Crimes Act 1961 provided that anyone 'who causes the death of any child that has not become a human being in such a manner that he or she would have been guilty of murder if the child had become a human being'. This was subject to exceptions contained in section 187A of the same Act. These exceptions (now repealed) included:

---

31. *Wall v. Livingstone* [1982] 1 NZLR 734; (1982) 1 NZFLR 417 (CA) and *Right to Life New Zealand Inc v. Abortion Supervisory Committee* [2012] NZSC 68; [2012] 3 NZLR 762.
32. *In the matter of Baby P (an unborn child)* [1995] NZFLR 577.
33. For example, *Paton v. British Pregnancy Advisory Service Trustees* [1979] QB 276.
34. *Re an Unborn Child* [2003] 1 NZLR 115, Heath J.
35. *Wall v. Livingstone* [1982] 1 NZLR 734; (1982) 1 NZFLR 417 (CA).

- where the continuance of the pregnancy would have resulted in serious danger to the mother;
- that there was a substantial risk that the child if born would be 'seriously handicapped';
- that the pregnancy was the result of sexual intercourse between the 'prohibited degrees';[36]
- the pregnancy was the result of sexual intercourse with a dependent family member;[37]
- the woman or girl was defined as 'severely subnormal'.[38]

Whether or not to carry out an abortion is left to the judgment of a registered medical practitioner.[39] There also exists an Abortion Supervisory Committee comprised of three people, two of whom must be medical practitioners. This committee is to supervise, review, monitor and issue licences relating to abortion law. In 2019, the Abortion Legislation Bill 2019 was introduced and given the royal assent on 23 March 2020. The Bill decriminalized abortion and reformed the Contraception, Sterilisation and Abortion Act 1977. The most significant change is the ability for women to be able to seek an abortion without restrictions within the first twenty weeks of their pregnancy. Following the twenty-week period, the women must seek a medical practitioner who will assess the mental and physical well-being of the women. The medical practitioner may thereafter perform an abortion if he or she believes it to be appropriate in the circumstances.

31. In the context of New Zealand's accident compensation scheme, it has been held that a stillbirth as a result of medical error is an injury to the mother rather than a separate injury to the unborn child.[40] Another accident compensation case held that the continuation of a pregnancy following a misdiagnosis could be considered a treatment injury affecting the mother.[41] The mother in this case applied to the court arguing that the continuing development of the foetus constituted a 'treatment injury'. This was because the practitioners had failed to detect spina bifida lesion on a developing foetus: had they detected the abnormality, the mother would have terminated the pregnancy. As a consequence, all physical consequences arising out of the pregnancy were held to be covered by New Zealand's accident compensation scheme.

32. For the purposes of birth registration, birth includes a stillbirth.[42] A 'stillborn child' is a dead foetus that either weighed 400 grams when it was issued from

36. *See* Part II, Ch. 1.
37. *See* Crimes Act 1961, s 131.
38. *See* definition in Crimes Act 1961, s 138.
39. Contraception, Sterilisation, and Abortion Act 1977, s 32 and 33.
40. *Harrild v. Director of Proceedings* [2003] 3 NZLR 289 (CA).
41. *Cumberland v. Accident Compensation Corporation* [2013] NZCA 590, [2014] 2 NZLR 373.
42. Section 2, Births, Deaths, Marriages, and Relationships Registration Act 1995. The Births, Deaths, Marriages, and Relationships Registration Act 2021 is not yet in force but contains the same definition.

its mother or issued from its mother after the twentieth week of pregnancy. However, apart from the notification of the stillbirth to the authorities, the stillborn child does not have any other legal status. While the legal status of illegitimate children was at one time equivocal, the legal differences between children born inside and out of wedlock have been removed by the Status of Children Act 1969.

33. While at one stage in the history of the common law, slaves lacked legal personality, slavery has been abolished in New Zealand. Section 98 of the Crimes Act 1961, based on the Slave Trade Act 1824 (UK) and the Slave Trade Act 1843 (UK), makes dealing in slaves a serious offence.

34. While a person who has died has no status as a person, the personal representative is able to take various actions on behalf of the deceased person, including suing and defending suits.[43]

§2. CAPACITY

35. The capacity to marry and testamentary capacity are discussed elsewhere.[44] In general, the capacity of persons is affected by such factors as age, maturity, illness and disability. The starting point is that there is a presumption that people are capable and competent to look after themselves and their affairs.[45] Where a person lacks capacity, wholly or partly, to look after financial and property matters, the Family Court can appoint a manager to act on the person's behalf.[46] In doing so, however, the court must make the least restrictive intervention possible, and the court's order may, therefore, be tailored to the particular needs of the person concerned rather than giving the manager unrestricted powers.

36. The law also has provisions relating to the personal care and welfare of someone whose capacity is limited. The Family Court must be satisfied that the person wholly or partly lacks the capacity to understand and foresee the consequences of personal decisions, or alternatively is unable to communicate decisions (as in the case of some stroke victims). The lack of capacity may arise from a wide range of circumstances, in some instances, for example, because of congenital intellectual disability, mental illness, senility or accident. Each case must, however, be considered on its own merits. Where appropriate, the court can make a specific order, for example, about accommodation, employment or health matters. Controversial examples of the latter include orders for sterilization,[47] enforced feeding of an anorexia sufferer[48] and birth by caesarean section.[49] Other court orders have involved

---

43. *See* further Part IV, Ch. 1, s. 3, II and Ch. 4, s. 1.
44. *See* Part II, Ch. 1, s. 2 and Part IV, Ch. 2, s. 1, respectively. *See* generally I Reuvecamp et al *Mental Capacity Law in New Zealand* (Thomson Reuters, Wellington, 2019).
45. Sections 5 and 24, Protection of Personal and Property Rights Act 1988.
46. Sections 25 and 31, Protection of Personal and Property Rights Act 1988.
47. *Re H* [1993] NZFLR 225 and *R v. R* [2004] NZFLR 797.
48. *Re CMC* [1995] NZFLR 538.
49. *In the matter of V* [1997] NZFLR 718.

Chapter 2. Registration of Civil Status

§1. The Registrar

43. Official registration of births, adoptions, marriages, civil unions and deaths is covered by the Births, Deaths, Marriages, and Relationships Registration Act 1995 (the Births, Deaths, Marriages, and Relationships Registration Act 2021 has been enacted but is mostly not yet in force). Overall control is vested in the Registrar-General with the help of a Deputy Registrar-General.[64] Several Registrars are also appointed around the country, and many of the day-to-day tasks are delegated to these officials.[65]

§2. Registers and Certificates

44. When the mother of a new baby (including a stillbirth) is admitted to hospital, the hospital must give notice of the birth within five days.[66] Otherwise, preliminary notice of birth must be given by a medical practitioner at the birth, a midwife or else the occupier of the premises where the birth took place. One of the guardians of a child must notify a Registrar of the birth as soon as reasonably practicable, using the prescribed form.[67] The relevant information is then registered. Foundlings should be reported to the police who then notify the Registrar-General.

45. There is a complex set of rules relating to the registration of an unmarried father. Broadly speaking, the unmarried father will be registered if both mother and father agree, or if there is a court order determining the child's paternity. The decision of whether or not to register the father can be tested by appealing to the Family Court.

46. After a child has been adopted, the court granting the adoption order must inform the Registrar-General of the details.[68] Generally, the child's birth certificate is changed to insert the names of the adopting parents. There is, however, provision for the term 'adoptive parent' to be used if the adoptive parent of a person who has not reached 18 or an adopted person who has married or is aged 18 or over so applies.

---

64. Sections 79, 80, Births, Deaths, Marriages, and Relationships Registration Act 1995 (Births, Deaths, Marriages, and Relationships Registration Act 2021, part 5).
65. Section 81, Births, Deaths, Marriages, and Relationships Registration Act 1995 (Births, Deaths, Marriages, and Relationships Registration Act 2021, s 126).
66. Section 5A, Births, Deaths, Marriages, and Relationships Registration Act 1995 (Births, Deaths, Marriages, and Relationships Registration Act 2021, s 11).
67. Births are covered by ss 5–17 of the Births, Deaths, Marriages, and Relationships Registration Act 1995 (Births, Deaths, Marriages, and Relationships Registration Act 2021, part 2, subpart 2).
68. Adoptions are covered by ss 23–27 of the Births, Deaths, Marriages, and Relationships Registration Act 1995 (Births, Deaths, Marriages, and Relationships Registration Act 2021, part 2, subpart 3).

47. The Adult Adoption Information Act 1985 sets out procedures for the parties to an adoption to gain access to the original birth certificate.[69] The adopted person can take advantage of this only on reaching the age of 20, and both the adopted person and the birth mother can place vetoes on the release of information.

48. Birth certificates will record a person's sex. There is, however, provision for the Family Court to order a change of sex on the person's certificate.[70] The court must be satisfied that the person is over 18, has 'the gender identity' of the other sex and has undergone the necessary sex-change procedures. Expert evidence is required to support the application for a change of the birth certificate. In one case, the court allowed a change of sex from female to male even though the person still retained female genitalia.[71] Applications can also be made by a child's guardian where it is desired to change the child's sex. This may occur, for example, where the child suffers from a congenital problem which has given rise to some doubt about the child's sexual identity. Again, expert evidence must be presented to the court, and the child must have undergone, or be about to undergo, any reasonably necessary medical treatment.

49. Under the Births, Deaths, Marriages, and Relationships Registration Act 2021, section 23 and following (when it comes into force), the procedures change and a court order will not be necessary. A person aged 16 or over will be able to apply to the Registrar-General for registration of their nominated sex, 'specifying male, female or other sex or gender specified in regulations for the purpose of this paragraph as the person's nominated sex'. If aged 16 or 17, the application will have to have a guardian's written consent and a letter of support from a qualified third party confirming a belief in the applicant's preference and understanding of the consequences.

50. The responsibility of sending details of a marriage to a Registrar rests with the marriage celebrant, who has ten days after the solemnization of the marriage to do so.[72] Marriages solemnized overseas are generally not registered, but there are exceptions for overseas marriages of members of the armed forces, where a New Zealand diplomat in the overseas country forwards relevant information to the Registrar-General. When the Family Court orders a marriage dissolved or declares it a nullity, it must inform the Registrar-General who records the information appropriately. Convictions for bigamy are likewise to be recorded. These same rules are

69. *See* Part II, Ch. 5.

70. *See* ss 28–33, Births, Deaths, Marriages, and Relationships Registration Act 1995.

71. *'Michael' v. Registrar-General of Births Deaths and Marriages* (2008) 27 FRNZ 58. *See also Gordon v. Registrar General of Births, Deaths and Marriages* [2019] NZFC 10586 (change of gender from female to male of 17-year-old) and *Gordon v. Registrar-General of Births Deaths and Marriages* [2019] NZFC 10586, [2020] NZFLR 139 (under 18-year-old).

72. Marriages and civil unions are covered by ss 53–62 of the Births, Deaths, Marriages, and Relationships Registration Act 1995 (Births, Deaths, Marriages, and Relationships Registration Act 2021, part 2, subpart 5).

mirrored in provisions applying to civil unions.[73] These provisions are combined with marriages under the Births, Deaths, Marriages, and Relationships Registration Act 2021.

51. Deaths in New Zealand are to be registered.[74] This is generally not so for deaths occurring outside New Zealand, but there are exceptions for deaths on New Zealand aircraft and ships, where a New Zealand resident died in a place where the death could not be recorded, or where a member of the armed forces or the police serving as part of a United Nations force dies overseas. Nevertheless, a person may, for a fee, deposit an overseas death certificate with the Registrar-General, who may record the information accordingly.

52. Where a death has occurred, the person having charge of the body must dispose of it within a reasonable time and notify a Registrar of the death. The name of the doctor giving a medical certificate of death must be included. In certain circumstances, deaths are to be reported to the coroner.[75] These are primarily where the death appears to have been without a known cause, by suicide or unnatural or violent means, where the person was undergoing surgery, or where the person was incarcerated, for example, in prison or police custody. In these circumstances, the coroner may decide to hold an inquest.

73. *See* s. 62A–62G of the Births, Deaths, Marriages, and Relationships Registration Act 1995.
74. Deaths are covered by ss 34–53 of the Births, Deaths, Marriages, and Relationships Registration Act 1995 (Births, Deaths, Marriages, and Relationships Registration Act 2021, part 2, subpart 4).
75. Coroners Act 2006.

Chapter 3. Personality Rights

53. The phrase 'personality rights' is not used in New Zealand. People do, however, have important rights, most of them of recent origin and granted by statute.

54. One of the most important statements of rights is the New Zealand Bill of Rights Act 1990. This purports to affirm the country's commitment to the International Covenant on Civil and Political Rights, although the rights in the two documents are not identical. The rights in the New Zealand Bill of Rights Act 1990 are designed to protect individuals from the various branches of government and persons performing public functions. The Act is not supreme law. It can be amended or repealed by Parliament. Also, it is not an entrenched bill of rights and can be overridden by other statutes. The rights are also subject to 'such reasonable limits prescribed by law as can be demonstrably justified in a free and democratic society'.[76] The rights are as follows:

- the right not to be deprived of life;
- the right not to be subjected to torture or cruel treatment;
- the right not to be subjected to medical or scientific experimentation;
- the right to refuse to undergo medical treatment;
- the right to vote and stand for Parliament;
- the right to freedom of thought, conscience and religion;
- the right to freedom of expression;
- the right to manifestation of religion and belief;
- the right to freedom of peaceful assembly;
- the right to freedom of association;
- the right to freedom of movement and residence;
- the right to freedom from discrimination;
- the right of minorities to enjoy culture, religion and language;
- the right to be secure from unreasonable search and seizure;
- the right not to be arbitrarily arrested or detained;
- various rights for people who are arrested, detained or charged with offences;
- rights against retroactive penalties and double jeopardy; and
- the right to justice, including the observance of the principles of natural justice and a right of appeal.

55. Section 28 of the New Zealand Bill of Rights Act 1990 preserves all existing rights and freedoms not expressly set out in the Act. Thus, for example, there is a right to the protection of reputation, which has been a part of the law of defamation for a long time. There is also a right to privacy which is discussed below.[77] Where there has been a breach of one of the rights in the New Zealand Bill of Rights Act 1990, the person may seek damages.[78]

76. Section 5, New Zealand Bill of Rights Act 1990.
77. Paragraphs 61 and following.
78. *Simpson v. Attorney-General* [1994] 3 NZLR 667 (CA) (commonly known as *Baigent's Case*).

56. The ability of the courts to challenge legislation inconsistent with the New Zealand Bill of Rights Act 1990 was tested in *Taylor v. Attorney-General.*[79] On 15 December 2010, the Electoral (Disqualification of Sentenced Prisoners) Amendment Bill was given the royal assent. The effect of this Bill was to remove the right of prisoners to vote. Arthur Taylor, an inmate at Auckland Prison at the time, applied to have the court make a declaration of inconsistency saying that the removal of the right of prisoners to vote was inconsistent with the New Zealand Bill of Rights Act 1990. After the High Court held in favour of Taylor, the case was appealed to the Court of Appeal and then the Supreme Court, with both courts dismissing the appeal and allowing the declaration to stand. A declaration of inconsistency in New Zealand is a political tool more than a legal one, as Parliament is not legally obliged to change a law that has been declared inconsistent by the courts. With respect to the constitutional position of the Bill of Rights Act, the Chief Justice said:[80]

> Under New Zealand constitutional arrangements, saying whether the obligation of compliance has been met is inescapably a judicial function. I consider that the scheme of the New Zealand Bill of Rights Act means that modification of content of rights contained in the Act is unlikely to be accomplished by inconsistent action but will generally need legislative amendment of the New Zealand Bill of Rights Act itself. That does not affect the ability of Parliament to legislate inconsistently with the New Zealand Bill of Rights Act. A declaration by the High Court that it has acted inconsistently with a right does not impede the freedom of action of Parliament.

57. A Bill before Parliament will require the Attorney-General to notify Parliament of a declaration of inconsistency, and the responsible minister must report the government's response to Parliament.[81]

58. Following the above judgment on voting rights, the Waitangi Tribunal released *He Aha I Pērā Ai?* (Why is it like this?).[82] This report concluded that the removal of the rights of prisoners to vote not only was a breach of the rights contained in the Bill of Rights Act but also disproportionately affected Māori as they make up a disproportionately high percentage of the prison population. This was a serious breach of both the Treaty of Waitangi and New Zealand's obligations under the United Nations Declaration on the Rights of Indigenous Peoples. The right of prisoners to vote was restored in 2020 but only for those serving a sentence of less than three years of imprisonment.[83]

79. [2015] NZHC 1706.
80. *Attorney-General v. Taylor* [2018] NZSC 104, [2019] 1 NZLR 213 at [103], per Elias CJ (Citations omitted).
81. New Zealand Bill of Rights (Declarations of Inconsistency) Amendment Bill.
82. Waitangi Tribunal *He Aha I Pērā Ai: The Māori Prisoners' Voting Report* (Wai 2870, 2019).
83. Electoral (Registration of Sentenced Prisoners) Amendment Act 2020, s 7, inserting s 86A into the Electoral Act 1993.

59. Another important piece of legislation is the Human Rights Act 1993. The Act prohibits discrimination on a number of grounds. These grounds, found in section 21 of the 1993 Act, are as follows:

(1) For the purposes of this Act, the prohibited grounds of discrimination are
- (a) sex, which includes pregnancy and childbirth;
- (b) marital status, which means the status of being;
  - (i) single; or
  - (ii) married, in a civil union, or in a de facto relationship; or
  - (iii) the surviving spouse of a marriage or the surviving partner of a civil union or de facto relationship; or
  - (iv) separated from a spouse or civil union partner; or
  - (v) a party to a marriage or civil union that is now dissolved, or to a de facto relationship that is now ended;
- (c) religious belief;
- (d) ethical belief, which means the lack of a religious belief, whether in respect of a particular religion or religions or all religions;
- (e) colour
- (f) race
- (g) ethnic or national origins, which includes nationality or citizenship;
- (h) disability, which means –
  - (i) physical disability or impairment;
  - (ii) physical illness;
  - (iii) psychiatric illness;
  - (iv) intellectual or psychological disability or impairment;
  - (v) any other loss or abnormality of psychological, physiological, or anatomical structure or function;
  - (vi) reliance on a guide dog, wheelchair, or other remedial means;
  - (vii) the presence in the body of organisms capable of causing illness;
- (i) age ...
- (j) political opinion, which includes the lack of a particular political opinion or any political opinion;
- (k) employment status, which means;
  - (i) being unemployed
  - (ii) being a recipient of a benefit under the Social Security Act 2018 or an entitlement under the Accident Compensation Act 2001.
- (l) family Status, which means –
  - (i) having the responsibility for part-time care or full-time care of children or other dependents; or
  - (ii) having no responsibility for the care of children or other dependents; or
  - (iii) being married to, or being in a civil union or de facto relationship with a particular person; or
  - (iv) being a relative of a particular person:
- (m) sexual orientation, which means a heterosexual, homosexual, lesbian, or bisexual orientation.

(2) Each of the grounds specified in subsection (1) of this section is a prohibited ground of discrimination, for the purposes of this Act, if:
   (a) It pertains to a person or to a relative or associate of a person; and
   (b) It either:
      (i) currently exists or has in the past existed; or
      (ii) is suspect or assumed or believed to exist or to have existed by the person alleged to have discriminated.

60. Complaints about unlawful discrimination under the 1993 Act may arise in relation to discrimination in employment, partnerships, various professional and qualifying bodies, access to places, vehicles and facilities, the provision of goods and services, the provision of land, housing and other accommodation, and access to educational establishments. Complaints are made to the Human Rights Commission and, if not settled, can be taken to the Human Rights Review Tribunal. Under section 20I–20L of the Human Rights Act 1993, applications can be made against the government or persons or bodies fulfilling public functions claiming unjustified discrimination. This can include a declaration of inconsistency with respect to existing legislation. Such a claim has been made with respect to the Adoption Act 1955.[84] A declaration does not render the law unconstitutional but forces the government to report the matter to Parliament and indicate the government's response (*see* sections 92K, 92WA and 92WB of the Human Rights Act 1993).

61. For a long time, the common law provided no generic right to privacy, although causes of action such as defamation and trespass to land contain an element of the protection of privacy. In much more recent times, the New Zealand courts have accepted that there is a cause of action for breach of privacy.[85] According to the Court of Appeal, there are two fundamental requirements for interference with privacy:[86]

(1) the existence of facts in respect of which there is a reasonable expectation of privacy; and
(2) publicity given to those private facts that would be considered highly offensive to an objective reasonable person.

The court has accepted that there exists a defence of legitimate public concern. In the leading case, *Hosking v. Runting*, although the court accepted the existence of

84. *Adoption Action Inc. v. Attorney-General* [2016] NZHRRT 9, [2016] NZFLR 113, where the Tribunal issued a declaration that six provisions of the Adoption Act 1955 and one provision of the Adult Adoption Information Act 1985 were inconsistent with freedom from discrimination. No action has been taken to repeal these provisions.
85. *See* the leading Court of Appeal decision *Hosking v. Runting* [2005] 1 NZLR 1 *See also Tucker v. News Media Ownership Ltd* [1986] 2 NZLR 716, *Bradley v. Wingnut Films Ltd* [1993] 1 NZLR 415, *P v. D* [2000] 2 NZLR 591, *Andrews v. Television New Zealand* [2009] 1 NZLR 220, *Television New Zealand v. Rogers* [2008] 2 NZLR 277 (SC) and *Henderson v. Walker* [2019] NZHC 2184.
86. *Hosking v. Runting* [2005] 1 NZLR 1.

the tort, a remedy was declined that would have prevented a magazine from publishing photographs of the plaintiff's children taken in a public street. The plaintiff was a well-known broadcasting personality.

62. In a further development, a High Court judge held that liability might arise for 'intrusion upon seclusion'.[87] The facts involved the secret filming of a woman undressing and showering in her bathroom. The elements of this variation of the privacy tort are:

(a) an intentional and unauthorized intrusion;
(b) into seclusion (intimate personal activity, space, or affairs);
(c) involving infringement of a reasonable expectation of privacy;
(d) that is highly offensive to a reasonable person.

Just how far this formulation will extend remains to be seen.

63. Rather more important than the developments in the common law has been the passage of the Privacy Act 1993, replaced and updated by the Privacy Act 2020. The new Act keeps the principles-based framework of the original Act while updating the law to reflect the needs of the digital age. In broad terms, the Act provides for a set of 'Information Privacy Principles'.[88] These principles place limitations on the collection, use and disclosure of personal information, the underlying philosophy being that the person concerned should be fully informed of what is happening and should in most situations consent. There is, therefore, also provision, subject to some exceptions, for the person to gain access to any personal information, with an opportunity to correct any errors.[89] Complaints are made to the Privacy Commissioner.[90]

64. The Commissioner also has the power to develop codes for special purposes.[91] One of the most significant of these is the Health Information Privacy Code. One of the major exceptions to the general rule of non-disclosure of a person's health information is where disclosure is necessary to deal with a serious and imminent threat to public health or safety or to the life or health of the person concerned or of another individual. Where an individual is in a hospital, a general statement about the patient is allowed, unless the patient has expressly requested otherwise.

87. *C v. Holland* [2012] 3 NZLR 672, especially [94]–[97].
88. Privacy Act 2020, part 3, subpart 1.
89. Privacy Act 2020, part 4, subpart 2.
90. Privacy Act 2020, part 5, subpart 1.
91. Privacy Act 2020, part 3, subpart 2.

Chapter 4. Names

§1. Acquisition of the Surname

65. As a general rule, people can call themselves by whatever name they like, as long as no fraud is involved. For official purposes, however, a person will have a registered name.[92] Typically, in New Zealand, a person will have one surname and one or more first or other names. However, a person may bear one name only if this is required by the person's or the child's parents' religious or philosophical beliefs or cultural traditions. Prior to the passage of the Births, Deaths, Marriages, and Relationships Registration Act 1995, a guardian was entitled but not bound to register a child's surname. Registration of a surname along with one or more other names was made mandatory under the 1995 Act, unless the exception allowing for one name applies.

§2. Change of the Surname

66. Procedures are available for name changes.[93] Persons aged 18 or over or who are married or in a civil union can make a statutory declaration that their previous name has been abandoned or it is intended to be abandoned. Where this is deposited with the Registrar-General, the new name is to be included in the birth certificate.

67. The guardians of a child under 18 may also apply for a change to the child's name. If the child has reached 16, the child must consent to the name change. Controversy can arise where one guardian seeks a name change against the wishes of the other guardian. This may occur, for example, where the parents lived together but have separated. The mother may have resumed her maiden name or may have remarried taking on a new surname. The consent of the Family Court may be sought in this situation, but its consent cannot be regarded as automatic. The court will be careful not to harm the relationship between the child and the non-carer parent. However, the child may face embarrassment by having a different name from his or her regular parent, may have been using a new name for some time, or may be fully integrated into a reconstituted family.

68. The question of the names of children can also arise independently of a request to change the birth certificate. Where a child has been informally using a different surname, this may be challenged by the non-caregiving parent under the Care of Children Act 2004. Section 46R of that Act allows a dispute between guardians to be taken to the Family Court. In determining how to resolve this dispute, the

92. *See* ss 18–22, Births, Deaths, Marriages, and Relationships Registration Act 1995 (Births, Deaths, Marriages, and Relationships Registration Act 2021, s 13).
93. Births, Deaths, Marriages, and Relationships Registration Act 2021, part 2, subpart 6.

court must treat the welfare and best interests of the child as the paramount consideration.[94] In such cases, the most important consideration will often be that contained in section 5(f) of the Care of Children Act 2004 that 'a child's identity … should be preserved and strengthened'. Each case is intensely fact specific, but Judge Geoghegan summed up the general position of the New Zealand courts by saying:[95]

> A name is an important link to family history and to a child's identity. It should not be changed without there being a good reason to do so and without the Court being satisfied that it would promote the child's welfare and best interests … .

69. In a case where the maternal aunt and uncle had day-to-day care of a 3-year-old, a name change was allowed to reflect the reality of the parental situation.[96] This was deemed appropriate because the child would still have a connection with his mother by being in the care of her sister, and it was agreed that the child would take his father's first name as a middle name in order to maintain a relationship with his father.

70. An adopted child takes the surname of the adopting parents.[97]

71. A woman is not compelled by law to take her husband's surname although there is nothing to stop her from doing so by repute. Likewise, on dissolution of the marriage and even after remarriage to another man, the woman can retain her married name, revert to her maiden name or acquire another name by reputation. A married woman can change her surname formally by means of a statutory declaration in the same way that anybody can effect a name change with the Registrar-General. A married woman can also ask the Registrar-General to include the new name in the marriage records.[98] The position is the same with respect to civil union partners.

§3. First Names

72. Most of the rules relating to first names are similar to those for surnames. When it comes to registration, the Registrar may refuse to register a name if 'it is undesirable in the public interest'.[99] If the Registrar-General refuses to register a

94. Care of Children Act 2004, ss 4 and 5.
95. *E v. S* FC Waihi FAM-2006-063-367, 29 Jul. 2008.
96. *Chief Executive of the Ministry of Social Development v. Ware* [2016] NZFC 1481.
97. Section 16, Adoption Act 1955.
98. Section 62, Births, Deaths, Marriages, and Relationships Registration Act 1995 (Births, Deaths, Marriages, and Relationships Registration Act 2021, s 73). *See* s. 62G for a similar rule with respect to civil unions.
99. Section 18(4), Births, Deaths, Marriages, and Relationships Registration Act 1995 (Births, Deaths, Marriages, and Relationships Registration Act 2021, s 18).

name, an appeal may be made to the Family Court.[100] This usually arises where first names are in question. Thus, the use of 'Sir' as part of a child's name was refused because of the potential confusion among those people who are entitled to use the official title 'Sir' as a result of a royal honour.[101] However, 'Emperor' was permitted because any confusion in New Zealand would in this instance be negligible.[102]

73. In one case, a girl aged 8 was known as 'Talula does the hula from Hawaii' but had not had her birth registered. The judge placed her under the guardianship of the court in order to ensure that she was properly registered with a suitable name.[103] Under section 20 of the Births, Deaths, Marriages, and Relationships Registration Act 1995, the guardians may change a child's name within two years of birth (Births, Deaths, Marriages, and Relationships Registration Act 2021, s 67). Under section 84, the Registrar-General can correct clerical errors (Births, Deaths, Marriages, and Relationships Registration Act 2021, s 131). In a case that arose only after the parents had applied for a passport for their son, it was discovered that there was an inadvertent spelling error in the name. Contrary to the position of the Registrar-General, the judge held that the mistake could be corrected under section 84.[104]

74. Disputes over first names may also arise in cases between parents or cases between parents and foster caregivers. One example is where a boy, whom the mother had called Acorn, was held to be in need of care and protection and placed with foster parents. The latter got an order from the Family Court changing the boy's name, and this was upheld on appeal.[105] It was noted that the outcome of such proceedings turns on the child's welfare and more specifically whether the name would cause the child distress or disturb the child's welfare in some significant way. To similar effect was a case where a mother had named her daughter 'Pagan'. The permanent caregivers were raising the child as a Roman Catholic and sending her to a Catholic school. The name 'Pagan' invited 'ridicule and embarrassment' and was changed.[106] Another example is found in a case where a 9-year-old boy being raised in foster care was named 'Adonis'. He expressed a strong dislike for the name, and the court allowed a change to 'Apollo', being satisfied that it was in the boy's welfare and best interests.[107]

100. Section 18(5)–(8), Births, Deaths, Marriages, and Relationships Registration Act 1995. Subsection (8) sets out the criteria for a name being undesirable: causing offence to a reasonable person, unreasonably long, or including or resembling an official title or rank (Births, Deaths, Marriages, and Relationships Registration Act 2021, s 18(4)).
101. *Ojstersek v. Registrar-General* [1997] NZFLR 1006.
102. *Naidu v. Registrar-General* [1998] NZFLR 141.
103. *G v. K [Guardianship]* [2008] NZFLR 385.
104. *DJD v. Registrar-General of Births, Deaths and Marriages* [2011] NZFLR 713.
105. *C v. LT [Custody]* [2009] NZFLR 1098 per Gendall J especially at [66].
106. *ACP v. TJOM [Name change]* [2011] NZFLR 897 per Judge Burns. The application was made under s. 44 of the Care of Children Act 2004 (now s. 44R).
107. *Volevas v. Gore* [2015] NZFC 3749.

Chapter 5. Nationality

75. In New Zealand, the concept of nationality is largely bound up with that of citizenship. The primary source of the law is the Citizenship Act 1977 which replaced the British Nationality and New Zealand Citizenship Act 1948.

76. The following are the ways in which New Zealand citizenship can be acquired:

(1) By birth.[108] Subject to some narrow exceptions, everyone born in New Zealand from 1 January 1949 until 1 January 2006 is a New Zealand citizen. The exceptions relate to the children of diplomats from overseas countries and the children of enemy aliens in a part of the country under enemy occupation.[109] For persons born from 1 January 2006 onwards, the grounds for citizenship by birth are tighter. At least one of the parents must be a New Zealand citizen or be entitled to indefinite residence in New Zealand, the Cook Islands, Niue or Tokelau. However, a child abandoned in New Zealand whose parental identities are unknown will be a New Zealand citizen by birth.

(2) By descent.[110] Everyone born outside New Zealand from 1 January 1978 shall be a New Zealand citizen if either parent was a New Zealand citizen otherwise than by descent at the date of birth, or if either parent was a New Zealand citizen by descent and the person would otherwise be stateless. Such citizenship lapses, however, unless the person applies to have the citizenship registered within two years after turning 20. The rules for people born prior to that date are rather more complicated.[111] Between 1 January 1949 and 1 January 1970, citizenship by descent was acquired if the father was a New Zealand citizen at the time of birth. From 1 January 1970, descent could also be traced through the person's mother if she was a New Zealand citizen. However, anyone born before 1 January 1978 to a mother who was a New Zealand citizen otherwise than by descent can apply as of right for a grant of citizenship.[112] The 1977 Act also protects existing rights of citizenship.[113] It provides for those who were New Zealand citizens by birth or descent by virtue of the 1948 Act to retain that status.

(3) By grant.[114] Citizenship by grant may be authorized by the Minister of Internal Affairs under certain conditions:
   - The person is aged 16 or more (an exception for under 16-year-olds is mentioned later).
   - The person is of full capacity.

---

108. Section 6, Citizenship Act 1977.
109. No part of New Zealand has ever been under enemy occupation. The exceptions do not apply if the child would otherwise be stateless.
110. Section 7, Citizenship Act 1977.
111. Section 13, Citizenship Act 1977.
112. Section 10, Citizenship Act 1977.
113. Section 13, Citizenship Act 1977.
114. Sections 8–9B, Citizenship Act 1977. Note that there are some special rules for those residing in the Cook Islands, Niue or Tokelau.

- The person applies for citizenship.
- The person has been present in New Zealand for at least 1,350 days during the five years immediately prior to making an application and also has been in New Zealand for at least 240 days in each of the five years. These rather complex rules were introduced by the Citizenship Amendment Act 2005. An exception exists where 'there are exceptional circumstances particular to the applicant', but a minimum of 450 days residency during the twenty months prior to the application is still required.
- The person is entitled to remain in New Zealand indefinitely under the immigration laws.
- The person is of good character.
- The person has sufficient knowledge of the responsibilities and privileges attaching to citizenship.
- The person has sufficient knowledge of the English language. This requirement may be waived if it would cause undue hardship because of age, education or other personal reason.
- The person intends to stay residing in New Zealand or else will be working for the Crown, an international organization of which New Zealand is a member, or a New Zealand employer.

77. In certain situations, the above conditions are relaxed and, instead of being requirements, are matters which may be taken into account in determining an application for the grant of citizenship. These situations are:

- where the applicant is under 16;
- where either of the applicant's parents was a citizen by descent at the date of birth;
- where the grant would be in the public interest 'because of exceptional circumstances of a humanitarian or other nature relating to the applicant'; or
- where the person would otherwise be stateless.

It is not unknown for 'exceptional circumstances' to be used in situations where New Zealanders have had a child born overseas through surrogacy and wish to bring the child back to New Zealand.

78. The conditions for citizenship are also relaxed where the applicant is married to a New Zealand citizen. The period of ordinary residence is only two years and instead of an intention to remain resident in New Zealand, the spouse must have established and plan to maintain some association with New Zealand, apart from the marriage to a New Zealander.

79. Typically, on being granted New Zealand citizenship, a person will take an oath of allegiance to the monarch and to the laws of the country.

Chapter 6. Domicile and Residence

80. Domicile is a person's permanent or indefinite home. It is often an important factor in giving the New Zealand court's jurisdiction.[115] New Zealand has inherited the common law of England but has also modified the rules with the passage of the Domicile Act 1976. Everyone has a 'domicile of origin', which is acquired at birth. At common law, this could be abandoned by acquiring a 'domicile of choice'. If the domicile of choice was abandoned, then the domicile of origin could have been 'revived' until a new domicile of choice was acquired.

81. The doctrine of the revival of the domicile of origin has been abolished in New Zealand.[116] Section 9 of the 1976 Act enables a person to acquire a new domicile in another country (the language of 'domicile of choice' is not used) if the person is capable of having an independent domicile, is in the country and intends to live indefinitely in that country. So long as they have the mental capacity, persons are able to have an independent domicile on turning 16 but will keep their existing domicile until a new domicile is acquired.[117]

82. A child under 16 has the father's domicile if the parents are living together.[118] If they are not living together, then the child has the father's domicile if the child lives with the father, but this changes when the child shifts his/her home to the mother. In other situations where the parents are not living together, the child has the mother's domicile. A foundling has the domicile of the country where it was found (unless it later lives with one of its parents). The common law rule that a wife has the same domicile as her husband was abolished by section 5 of the Domicile Act 1976. This means that spouses may have different domiciles.

83. While 'domicile' has a fairly fixed meaning and a long common law history, the same is not true of residence. Nevertheless, various statutes use residence and its variants as a connecting factor for the purposes of private international law. For example, the Care of Children Act 2004, which incorporates the Hague Convention on child abduction, uses 'habitual residence' as the initial key to determine whether an abducted child should be returned. A person will be a habitual resident of New Zealand if he or she has a settled intention to remain living long term in New

115. A good example is an application for the dissolution of a marriage or a civil union. Under s. 37 of the Family Proceedings Act 1980, at least one of the parties must be domiciled in New Zealand. Another example is *Hanson v Frank* [2021] NZFC 279, [2021] NZFLR 375 where the wife sought a separation order under s 20 of the Family Proceedings Act 1980. Section 4 requires domicile or residence. The family resided in Oman, so the wife had to prove domicile. She successfully argued that New Zealand, as her domicile of origin, had not been replaced by any other jurisdiction such as Oman: she had not renounced her New Zealand citizenship and the parties owned property in New Zealand.
116. Section 11, Domicile Act 1976.
117. Sections 7 and 8, Domicile Act 1976.
118. Section 6, Domicile Act 1976.

Zealand. Unlike domicile, habitual residence may cease when a person leaves the country with a settled intention not to return; it is not necessary that a new habitual residence be acquired.[119]

84. 'Ordinary residence' is used, for example, in the Child Support Act 1991 as one of the factors which may enable financial support for a child to be sought from a liable parent. 'Ordinary residence' for the purposes of that Act is given a special statutory definition. It means a person's permanent place of abode, even if there is another such abode outside of New Zealand.[120] However, if the person is personally present in New Zealand for 183 days in aggregate during a twelve-month period, the person is deemed to be an ordinary resident of New Zealand.

85. 'Residence' is also a connecting factor, an example, where a 'marriage is void' declaration is sought.[121] In the absence of a special statutory definition, 'residence' does not have a fixed meaning. It can, however, be taken to mean voluntary physical presence in New Zealand with the intention of remaining, perhaps temporarily, for some settled purpose. It excludes tourists and visitors.[122]

119. Compare *S v. M* [1999] NZFLR 337. *See also Punter v. Secretary for Justice* [2004] 2 NZLR 28 (CA), *Basingstoke v. Groot* [2007] NZFLR 363 (CA) and *Re Adoption Application by KGC and TGC* [2007] NZFLR 851.
120. Section 218, Child Support Act 1991.
121. Section 29, Family Proceedings Act 1980. Domicile also gives the court jurisdiction.
122. *See The Laws of New Zealand* 'Conflict of Laws: Jurisdiction and Foreign Judgments', para. 106.

Chapter 7. Mentally Handicapped Persons

86. The law relating to the capacity of people with handicaps, including the Family Court's ability to appoint property managers and welfare guardians to act for people lacking capacity, has already been discussed.[123]

87. The law on the compulsory treatment of those with mental illness is found in the Mental Health (Compulsory Assessment and Treatment) Act 1992.[124] Broadly speaking, those who are 'mentally disordered' may be subjected to a month's compulsory assessment and treatment. Treatment can continue for a longer period only if there is an order from the Family Court. During the initial month, the person or various parties, including the person's principal caregiver, may challenge the compulsory action before the Family Court.

88. Where the court decides to make a compulsory treatment order, this should take the form of a 'community treatment order' unless the court considers that the person cannot be treated adequately as an outpatient, in which case the court makes an 'inpatient order'.[125] There is, therefore, a preference for people to be treated in the community rather than being institutionalized. Three months after a court order, and then every six months after that, a formal clinical review of each patient must take place.[126] The 'responsible clinician' undertaking the review must decide whether or not the patient is fit to be released from compulsory status. The test for determining whether someone is fit to be released is whether he or she is still 'mentally disordered': there is no further evaluation of whether the person should not be released, for example, in the public interest.[127] If the answer is in the negative, then the patient and various other parties are entitled to apply for a judicial review by the Mental Health Review Tribunal. Separate from this process is the ability of a judge of the High Court to undertake a judicial enquiry to determine whether a patient is being held illegally in a hospital.[128]

89. The Act includes a number of 'rights of patients'.[129] These include rights to information, respect for cultural and ethnic identity, language, religious and ethical beliefs, a right to treatment and to be informed about treatment, a right to be told of the visual or audio taping of an interview, a right to independent psychiatric advice, a right to legal advice, a right to company and seclusion, a right to receive visitors

123. *See* Part I, Ch. 1, s. 2 above.
124. *See* J. Dawson & K. Gledhill (eds) *New Zealand's Mental Health Act in Practice* (VUP, Wellington, 2013).
125. Section 28, Mental Health (Compulsory Assessment and Treatment) Act 1992.
126. Section 76, Mental Health (Compulsory Assessment and Treatment) Act 1992.
127. *Waitemata Health v. Attorney-General* [2001] NZFLR 1122 (CA) at paras. [57] ff. *See* s. 79(8), Mental Health (Compulsory Assessment and Treatment) Act 1992: 'If the Review Tribunal considers that the patient is fit to be released from compulsory status, the patient shall be released from that status accordingly.' 'Fit to be released' is defined in s. 2 as 'no longer mentally disordered and fit to be released from the requirement of assessment and treatment under this Act'.
128. Section 84, Mental Health (Compulsory Assessment and Treatment) Act 1992.
129. Sections 64–75, Mental Health (Compulsory Assessment and Treatment) Act 1992.

and make telephone calls and a right to receive and send letters and postal articles. Complaints that a right has been breached are to be made to district inspectors or official visitors who are independent appointees. District inspectors have to be lawyers.[130] A writ of habeas corpus may be used as a means of addressing a complaint of unlawful detention under the Act, but such cases would be of exceptional nature.[131]

90. The most important concept to be satisfied before any of the above procedures become relevant is whether a person is 'mentally disordered'. The key definition is in section 2(1) of the Act:

> 'Mental disorder', in relation to any person, means an abnormal state of mind (whether of a continuous or an intermittent nature), characterized by delusions, or by disorders of mood or perception or volition or cognition, of such a degree that it:
>
> (a) poses a serious danger to the health or safety of that person or of others; or
> (b) seriously diminishes the capacity of that person to take care of himself or herself; and 'mentally disordered', in relation to any such person, has a corresponding meaning.

91. An important limitation on the definition is found in section 4:

> The procedures prescribed by Parts I and II of this Act shall not be invoked in respect of any person by reason only of:
>
> (a) that person's political, religious, or cultural beliefs; or
> (b) that person's sexual preferences; or
> (c) that person's criminal or delinquent behaviour; or
> (d) substance abuse; or
> (e) intellectual disability.

The significance of section 4 is that it means that a person cannot be subject to compulsion simply, for example, because he or she is a homosexual, or has an intellectual handicap, or has antisocial religious beliefs.[132] Such a person may, however, be subject to the Act's procedures if there is other evidence which shows that he or she falls within the definition of 'mental disorder'.

---

130. Section 94, Mental Health (Compulsory Assessment and Treatment) Act 1992.
131. *B v. Auckland District Health Board [Mental disorder: habeas corpus]* [2011] NZFLR 454 (CA).
132. In *the matter of T* [1995] NZFLR 351, although the patient suffered from schizophrenia, it was held that his inability to look after himself arose from his habitual cannabis use, which brought s. 4 into play.

92. The definition of 'mental disorder' has been held to be a legal rather than a medical one.[133] It follows that proof of the relevant symptoms, rather than a psychiatric diagnosis, is required. As a result, personality disorders such as eating disorders may, depending on the circumstances, render a person mentally disordered. For example, a person suffering from bulimia who has mood swings is unable to make decisions about eating and has self-harm, and suicidal tendencies will likely be held to suffer from an abnormal state of mind, with disorders of mood, perception volition or cognition.[134] The Court of Appeal has noted that the Act does not refer to mental or psychiatric illness. The definition of 'mental disorder' uses 'words in ordinary use, although their application is heavily dependent upon the assessment of clinicians'.[135] The Court of Appeal also accepted that personality disorders might be 'an abnormal state of mind'. The Act avoids the distinction between 'mad' and 'bad'.

93. There must be a link between a person's abnormal state of mind and the second part of the definition. The second part requires either that the person has a seriously diminished capacity for self-care or is a serious danger to people. The second alternative has given the courts the most trouble. An early test which required proof of a demonstrable risk of serious physical violence has since been rejected as being too narrow. So, a sufficiently great risk of psychological or emotional harm is now enough.[136]

94. Persons who do not come within the definition of 'mentally disordered' may nevertheless have their liberty restricted by other means. A person may come under the mental health system via criminal justice procedures. For example, a person may be found not guilty by reason of insanity, or may be unfit to plead because of his mental condition.[137] Such a person is a 'special patient' under the mental health legislation. Further, Intellectual Disability (Compulsory Care and Rehabilitation Act) 2003 provides options for people with an intellectual disability who are charged with or convicted of an offence. Under section 45, the court can make a compulsory care order, based on a needs assessment of the person and a care programme that has been completed for the person.

133. *Re H* [1996] NZFLR 998.
134. As happened in *Re H*.
135. *Waitemata Health v. Attorney-General* [2001] NZFLR 1122 (CA) at para. [68], and *see* following paragraphs of the judgment. The patient had a history of assaults on women including sexual violation and had spent much of his life in hospital or prison.
136. *In the matter of D* [1995] NZFLR 28.
137. *See* Criminal Procedure (Mentally Impaired Persons) Act 2003, Part 2.

95. A person who is an alcoholic or a drug addict may be forced to undergo treatment under the Substance Addiction (Compulsory Assessment and Treatment) Act 2017. The Act provides the following definition for a 'severe substance addiction':[138]

> (1) is a continuous or an intermittent condition of a person that –
> (a) manifests itself in the compulsive use of a substance and is characterised by at least 2 of the features listed in subsection (2); and
> (b) is of such severity that it poses a serious danger to the health or safety of the person and seriously diminishes the person's ability to care for himself or herself.
> (2) The features are –
> (a) neuro-adaptation to the substance;
> (b) craving for the substance;
> (c) unsuccessful efforts to control the use of the substance;
> (d) use of the substance despite suffering harmful consequences.

Only those with such an addiction may be forced to undergo treatment. The Act also requires that such people have an impaired capacity to make informed decisions about treatment for their addiction, compulsory treatment is deemed necessary and appropriate treatment is available.[139] Such treatment must be a last resort and will only be necessary if voluntary treatment is unlikely to be effective.[140]

138. Substance Addiction (Compulsory Assessment and Treatment) Act 2017, s. 8. *See Shepperd v. Bay of Plenty District Health Board* [2018] NZFC 2115, [2018] NZFLR 684, *Waitemata District Health Board v. FP* [2019] NZFC 2830, [2019] NZFLR 80, and *McBride v. BB* [2019] NZFC 2596, [2019] NZFLR 87.
139. Substance Addiction (Compulsory Assessment and Treatment) Act 2017, s. 7.
140. Substance Addiction (Compulsory Assessment and Treatment) Act 2017, s. 10.

Part II. Family Law

Chapter 1. Marriage

§1. The Nature of Marriage

96. Marriage creates rights, duties and status upon spouses without many features of contract law being present to enforce the obligations. The principal piece of legislation governing marriage is the Marriage Act 1955 which, surprisingly, does not define marriage comprehensively. The courts have commonly accepted, however, that the old definition of marriage in *Hyde v. Hyde* [141] is the starting point. 'I conceive that marriage, as understood in Christendom, may for this purpose, be defined as the voluntary union for life of one man and one woman, to the exclusion of all others.'

97. In the modern age, this definition requires significant modification. The first modification of note is in light of the prevalence of divorce.[142] Another significant modification is in respect of same-sex marriage as a legislative amendment was enacted that gave a partial definition where 'marriage means the union of two people, regardless of their sex, sexual orientation, or gender identity'.[143] Indeed perhaps the only part of the *Hyde v. Hyde* definition that is still relevant is the concept of 'voluntary'. This requirement is discussed below (paragraphs 105 and following).

98. Prior to the legalization of same-sex marriage, Parliament created the concept of 'civil union', which is similar in many respects to marriage but is legally distinct. Both opposite and same-sex couples can enter into civil unions.[144] The relevant Act creating civil unions was passed very narrowly (65:55). By contrast, the Marriage (Definition of Marriage) Amendment Act 2013 passed easily some nine years later (77:44). The passage has resulted from a sharp decline in civil unions as perhaps the primary reason for a civil union is now irrelevant.

141. (1866) LR 1 P & D 130, 133.
142. *See* below, Part II, Ch. 2, for a discussion on divorce.
143. Marriage (Definition of Marriage) Amendment Act 2013. This effectively overrules the judgment of the court in *Quilter v. Attorney-General* [1998] 1 NZLR 523 (CA) which said that the Act did not allow same-sex marriage. It also makes the dicta in *Attorney-General v. Family Court at Otahuhu* [1995] NZFLR 57; (1994) 12 FRNZ 643, 643, regarding transsexual marriage irrelevant.
144. Civil Union Act 2004.

99. Other legislation that may impact marriage includes the following:

(1) The Births, Deaths, Marriages, and Relationships Registration Act 1995 (to be replaced by the Births, Deaths, Marriages, and Relationships Registration Act 2021).
(2) The Domestic Actions Act 1975.
(3) The Proxy Marriages Regulations 1958.
(4) The Marriage (Forms) Regulations 1995.
(5) The Marriage (Fees) Regulations 1995.
(6) The Family Proceedings Act 1980.

§2. The Capacity to Marry

100. There is a variety of factors which affect a person's capacity to marry. Persons will not be able to marry according to New Zealand law if they are within the 'prohibited degrees' of relationship if they are already married, if they are unable to consent by reason of duress, mistake, insanity or 'any other reason'.

101. The Second Schedule of the Marriage Act 1955 lists forbidden marriages, as follows (as amended by the Marriage (Definition of Marriage) Amendment Act 2013):

(1) A person may not marry the person's:
  (a) grandparent;
  (b) parent;
  (c) child;
  (d) grandchild;
  (e) sibling;
  (f) parent's sibling;
  (g) sibling's child;
  (h) grandparent's spouse or civil union partner;
  (i) parent's spouse or civil union partner;
  (j) spouse's or civil union partner's parent;
  (k) spouse's or civil union partner's grandparent;
  (l) spouse's or civil union partner's child;
  (m) child's spouse or civil union partner;
  (n) grandchild's spouse or civil union partner;
  (o) spouse's or civil union partner's grandchild.
(2) The prohibited degrees of marriage apply whether the relationships described are by the whole blood or by the half-blood.
(3) In this schedule, *spouse* and *civil union partner* include a former spouse or former civil union partner, whether alive or deceased, and whether the marriage or civil union was terminated by death, dissolution, or otherwise.

102. Section 15(2) of the Marriage Act 1955 provides that people within the degrees of affinity listed in the Second Schedule may apply to the High Court for consent to marry, and this consent may be granted provided that neither party contributed to the termination of a previous marriage of the other party. A court declined consent in the case of an adopted brother and sister as this was within the prohibited degrees of consanguinity, and the court, therefore, could not give consent.[145] Courtney J allowed the marriage of a father-in-law and daughter-in-law.[146] This was based primarily upon the impression conveyed through their affidavits that the relationship came about through genuine circumstances and involved mutual affection and respect, adding that none of their siblings/children objected to the union. The situation is somewhat different when adopted relations seek to marry. In *Re Barlow v. Hohaia* Gallen J held that the effect of section 16(2)(b) of the Adoption Act 1955 was that the legal fiction that an adopted person ceases to be the child of his/her birth parents that this did not apply for the purposes of marriage.[147]

103. The court has a wide discretion in determining whether to grant consent or not for the purposes of section 15(2), and this is always considered on the facts of the particular case. However, the following criteria are relevant to the granting of consent[148] as well as to whether either party has contributed to the dissolution of a previous marriage of the other party:

(a) the realities of the technical relationship of the applicants from the time the relationship first came into existence until the date of the application;
(b) what course is most likely to serve the best interests of public morality as it is likely to have been expressed in public opinion;
(c) whether the wish to marry springs from any ulterior motive; and
(d) the consequences, if any, for any children existing or yet to be born.

104. In all bigamous marriages, the second or subsequent marriage will be void. Even though to have a mistaken belief that the prior marriage has been lawfully dissolved is a defence to the criminal charge of bigamy, this is not the case in a civil action for bigamy. The only material fact for the court to consider is whether the first marriage has in fact and by law been terminated, not the parties' belief at the time of entering the second or subsequent marriage. The bigamy alleged in civil proceedings must be proved to a standard equating to the criminal one.[149] Sections 60 and 62F of the Births Deaths, Marriages, and Relationships Registration Act 1995 (Births, Deaths, Marriages, and Relationships Registration Act 2021, sections 65 and 66) prescribe the method of notification and manner of recording convictions for bigamy.

105. Arguably the largest category of void marriages is that in which there is an absence of consent. Where there is an absence of consent that affects the marriage,

145. *Re Thomson & Thomson* [1958] NZLR 580.
146. *Re Warahi* [2017] NZHC 115. *See also Re S and B [Marriage to Father-in-law]* [2012] NZFLR 531.
147. [1986] 2 NZLR 60.
148. *Re Hoskin and Pearson* [1958] NZLR 604, 607.
149. *Featherstone v. Featherstone* [1917] GLR 335.

the marriage will always be void. There are different types of absence of consent categories, and these will be discussed in order. The first category is that of insanity. In this situation, where either party to the marriage was so insane as not to understand the nature of the contract being entered into at the time of the ceremony, the marriage will be void. In all cases where insanity is alleged, there is a presumption of sanity, and the burden of proof lies upon the person alleging the insanity. The test to be applied in this situation was formulated by Singleton LJ in *In the Estate of Park*:[150]

> Was the [party] … capable of understanding the nature of the contract into which he [or she] was entering, or was his mental condition such that he was incapable of understanding it? To ascertain the nature of the contract a [person] must be mentally capable of appreciating that it involves the responsibilities normally attaching to marriage. Without that degree of mentality, it cannot be said that he [she] understands the nature of the contract. On the other hand, the mere fact that a spouse treats his [her] marital responsibilities lightly or is incapable of sustained effort or steady application after the fashion of men [women] who are eccentric does not amount to insanity.

This test should be applied in the case of drunkenness or drug addiction; the marriage will be void if the drunkenness or addiction induced the necessary degree of insanity or otherwise rendered the party incapable of understanding the nature of the contract of marriage.

106. The next example of an absence of consent is where there is a mistake. This will only succeed in two situations. The first is largely of historical interest as it would have been more common where clandestine marriages were arranged between the parties. It is where one party made a mistake about the identity of the other party, and this must result in a failure of that party to marry the person intended. A fraudulent misrepresentation will not vitiate consent unless it goes to the root of the consent. A woman fell in love with a Samoan man who had been deported from New Zealand. The man had assumed the identity of a dead person without telling the woman. It was held that the deception was no grounds for annulling the marriage, as the woman intended to marry the man in question.[151]

107. The second class of mistake that may result in an absence of consent is where one party is mistaken about the nature of the ceremony and does not realize that he or she is entering a contract of marriage. An example of this can be found in *Mehta v. Mehta*,[152] where there was a mistaken belief on the part of the wife that a Hindu marriage ceremony was a ceremony of religious conversion. If, however, each party realizes he or she is taking part in a form of marriage ceremony, no other type of mistake can make the marriage void. This was the case in *Fuller v. Draper* where the ceremony was ostensibly undertaken in order to provide photographs to

150. [1953] P 112, 127; [1953] 2 All ER 1411, 1430 (CA).
151. *NFH v. SV* [2007] NZFLR 428.
152. [1945] 2 All ER 690.

the groom's sick mother.[153] On the facts, the judge found that the couple intended to marry each other and understood what was involved in the ceremony; therefore, it was concluded that there was insufficient evidence to declare the marriage *void ab initio*. There have been dicta that a marriage entered into under a mistake may be ratified subsequently,[154] but it appears that on general principles such a marriage should be void *ab initio*.

108. The next category where an absence of consent may be found is where there is duress or fear on one party's part. The fear need not have been inspired by acts of the other party, but there are three requirements for the fear to exist. These are as follows:

(1) the fear must have been of a sufficient degree to vitiate consent;
(2) the fear must be reasonable; and
(3) the fear must arise from some external circumstance for which the applicant is in no way responsible.

This is elaborated by Simon P in *Szechter v. Szechter* [155] where he stated:

> It is, in my view, insufficient to invalidate an otherwise good marriage that a party has entered into it in order to escape from a disagreeable situation, such as penury or social degradation. In order for the impediment of duress to vitiate an otherwise valid marriage, it must, in my judgment, be proved that the will of one of the parties thereto has been overborne by genuine and reasonably held fear caused by threat of immediate danger (for which the party is not himself responsible) to life, limb or liberty so that the constraint destroys the reality of consents to ordinary wedlock.

109. The final class of case where there may be an absence of consent is 'for any other reason'.[156] This class may include 'sham' marriages, but this is highly debatable. Due to the political climate in New Zealand, this class of marriage may in fact be more prevalent than previously, as a married couple is entitled to state assistance in a number of situations where a single person is not (in particular, university students). A sham marriage has been described as one 'where the parties go through a form of marriage with the sole object of presenting themselves as married to the outside world with no intention whatever of cohabiting'.[157] Such a marriage will be valid unless there is some other real ground to the contrary. In many cases, however, parties will be unable to prove such things as mistake or duress.

153. *Fuller v. Draper* [2016] NZFC 7294, [2017] NZFLR 142.
154. *Valier v. Valier* (1925) 133 LT 830.
155. [1971] P 286, 297–298; [1970] 3 All ER 905, 915.
156. *McPherson v. Shepherd* (1984) 3 NZFLR 241.
157. *LexisNexis Family Law Service* (online, LexisNexis, Wellington) para. 1.11.

110. *M v. H* exemplifies the type of situation where a couple may enter a sham, but valid, marriage.[158] Both parties were students, and M was not entitled to a student allowance under the regulations then in force. The couple decided to marry as this would allow M to claim a student allowance, but at no point did they ever intend to cohabit or to have a sexual relationship. Neither saw the marriage as a lifelong commitment. Subsequently, M did not claim her entitlement to the allowance and came to deeply regret having entered the marriage contract. She then commenced court proceedings to declare the marriage void. The court found that M held a clear and lucid view of the reasons for the marriage and her intelligence and views on marriage generally meant that she understood the nature of the marriage contract. Therefore, despite the profound regret that she subsequently felt and in spite of the fact that the only witness called other than M was a psychologist whose opinion was that M had not consented to the marriage, an order declaring the marriage void was refused.

111. In *McPherson v. Shepherd,* the judge examined the 'or for any other reason' category.[159] In this case, a woman had married the respondent to help him out of a difficult situation, but it was held that she failed to give a valid consent because of her lack of sophistication, simple-mindedness and naivety.

112. In the context of consent, it is worth noting that in 2018 Parliament created a new offence of coerced marriage or civil union.[160] It includes situations that fall short of ostensibly being a marriage or civil union, as well as those where the ceremony was completed. Under the Births, Deaths, Marriages, and Relationships Registration Act 1995, sections 60 and 62A (Births, Deaths, Marriages, and Relationships Registration Act 2021, sections 65 and 66), the Registrar-General must be notified of convictions, which the Registrar then adds to the relevant record of a marriage or civil union.

113. The age of a person wishing to marry affects that person's legal capacity to marry. Section 17 of the Marriage Act 1955 provides that a marriage licence must not be issued or a marriage solemnized if either party is under 16 years of age on the date of notice required under section 23.[161] Section 17(2) used to state that no marriage was void by virtue solely of its failure to comply with the rule just mentioned. Subsection (2) was repealed in 2018,[162] bringing marriage into line with a civil union, which is invalid when an underage person is one of the parties.[163]

114. A minor aged 16 or 17 may not be issued a licence to marry unless the consent of the Family Court has been obtained under section 18 of the Marriage Act

158. *M v. H* [1996] NZFLR 241.
159. *McPherson v. Shepherd* (1984) 3 NZFLR 241.
160. Crimes Act 1961, s 207A.
161. *See* s. 3, The Formalities of Marriage.
162. Minors (Court Consent to Relationships) Legislation Act 2018, s 7.
163. Section 7, Civil Union Act 2004.

1955.[164] Prior to 2018, parents could consent, but that ability was removed. The judge must be satisfied that both parties to the marriage applied 'voluntarily, free of undue influence or coercion', that each understood 'the consequences of the application and wants the Judge to consent to the intended marriage', and that 'the intended marriage is in the party's interests'. Further, under subsection (5) the judge must take into account:

(a) the age and maturity of the party; and
(b) the party's views; and
(c) any views of the party's parents and guardians that can reasonably be ascertained; and
(d) any other information available to the court relevant to the party's application.

This tightening of the rules was linked to a concern about coerced or forced marriages. This was not the situation in a case where the court granted permission to marry.[165] The couple in question were expecting a child and wanted to marry before the birth. The father was under 18 and supported by the bride-to-be and members of the wider family. Although there were religious and cultural factors in play, these did not amount to undue influence. Other conditions were satisfied, so that, according to the court, the marriage could proceed.

§3. Formalities of Marriage

115. Prior to entering a marriage, one party to the proposed marriage must give notice in the prescribed form[166] to the Registrar. The Registrar is a statutory authority established for the purpose of registering births, deaths, marriages and civil unions. An applicant must make a statutory declaration that the particulars in the form are true, as well as stating that there is no lawful impediment to the marriage, and that the proposed marriage is not prohibited by section 15 of the Marriage Act 1955.[167]

116. Section 24 of the Marriage Act 1955 provides that, once the parties have given notice of the proposed marriage, the Registrar must issue a marriage licence to the person who gave the notice. The licence authorizes the marriage to take place at a named place within New Zealand where the marriage will be solemnized by a marriage celebrant or pursuant to section 32 of the Act.[168]

164. The new version of s 18 was inserted by the Minors (Court Consent to Relationships) Legislation Act 2018.
165. *Palamo v. Sale* [2020] NZFC 11107, [2020] NZFLR 866.
166. *See* Marriage (Forms) Regulations 1995, Form 1.
167. Section 23, Marriage Act 1955.
168. Section 32 relates to the marriage of members of the Society of Friends (Quakers).

117. Generally, a licence cannot be issued within three days of receiving notice, but the Registrar may shorten this if satisfied that the proposed marriage is not prohibited, that the requirements of the Act have been complied with and that the parties to the marriage would otherwise be inconvenienced. Section 28 of the Act allows the Registrar to issue a marriage licence or to solemnize a marriage, unless there is reasonable cause to believe that the marriage is prohibited, or any requirements of the Act have not been complied with.

118. Once a marriage licence has been obtained, a marriage celebrant may conduct the marriage, provided that the marriage licence has been delivered to the celebrant and provided that three months have not elapsed since the licence was issued. These provisions also apply to the solemnization of a marriage by a Registrar.[169] Section 29(1) states that a licence 'shall authorize but not oblige' a celebrant to solemnize the marriage, which implies that a celebrant can decline to go through with the ceremony. Under the Marriage (Definition of Marriage) Amendment Act 2013, which provided for same-sex marriages, the following subsection was added to recognize the objections of some religious bodies to same-sex marriages:[170]

> Without limiting the generality of subsection (1), no celebrant who is a minister of religion recognised by a religious body enumerated in Schedule 1, and no celebrant who is a person nominated to solemnise marriages by an approved organisation, is obliged to solemnise a marriage if solemnising that marriage would contravene the religious beliefs of the religious body or the religious beliefs or philosophical or humanitarian convictions of the approved organisation.

119. The religions listed in Schedule 1 are all mainline Christian denominations except for one that is Jewish. Other denominations and religions can apply under section 9, and over 1,000 have been approved (including some non-religious bodies).

120. Section 31 states that the marriage must be solemnized at the place specified in the marriage licence, between the persons named in the licence, in the presence of two witnesses as well as the celebrant. The rule that the ceremony had to take place 'with open doors' between the hours of 6 a.m. and 10 p.m. was abolished by the Marriage Amendment Act 1999, ostensibly to allow for marriages to take place with the dawning of the new millennium.

121. During the marriage solemnization each party must say to the other 'I AB, take you CD, to be my legal wife or husband' or 'words to similar effect'.[171] If a specified body requires other wording, that may be used so long as the Registrar is satisfied that the body's rules and procedures do require the alternative words and

169. Section 30, Marriage Act 1955.
170. Section 29, Marriage Act 1995.
171. Section 31(3) and (4).

that the parties are clearly identified and freely consent. Where one party to the marriage is outside New Zealand due to the existence of a state of war, armed conflict or by reason of conditions of their service in the armed forces of any British Commonwealth country, a Family Court judge may authorize that the marriage be solemnized in that person's absence and, if solemnized in accordance with this provision, the marriage shall be lawful.[172]

§4. Effects of Marriage

122. One effect of marriage is that it places the spouses under a duty to cohabit.[173] Although there is no effective means of enforcing this duty as restitution of conjugal rights decrees were abolished by section 189(3) of the Family Proceedings Act 1980, failure to cohabit for a period of two years will provide the ground for dissolution in New Zealand.[174] A separation order may be granted if there is a state of disharmony between the parties of such a nature that cohabitation is unreasonable.[175] Separation orders are now very rarely sought in New Zealand.[176]

123. Marriage makes the parties subject to the Property (Relationships) Act 1976. This Act operates most commonly where a marriage breaks down, at which point property is usually divided equally. However, these deferred entitlements may be claimed during the course of the marriage either by agreement between the parties[177] or by order of the court.[178]

124. Spouses, or two people in contemplation of marriage, may enter into an agreement contracting out of the provisions of the Property (Relationships) Act 1976 by virtue of Part 6 of that Act. In order for such an agreement to be valid, each party to the contract must have independent legal advice, and the agreement must be in writing and signed by both parties. If the agreement is signed within New Zealand, it must be witnessed by a barrister or solicitor of the High Court. If it is signed in any other British Commonwealth country, it must be witnessed by a solicitor of that country or a notary public. If the agreement is signed in a non-Commonwealth overseas country, it must be witnessed by a lawyer or a notary public. Spouses are free to enter into other agreements that certain items of property, such as gifts, are not subject to the Property (Relationships) Act 1976 (but they will not necessarily be enforceable), or that the law of some other country is to govern relationship property.[179]

172. Section 34.
173. *Excell v. Dept of Social Welfare* [1991] NZFLR 241 (HC).
174. Section 39, Family Proceedings Act 1980.
175. Section 22, Family Proceedings Act 1980.
176. A rare example is *Hanson v. Frank* [2021] NZFC 279, [2021] NZFLR 375, cited above in the context of domicile (para. 80).
177. *CIR v. Van Doorne* [1983] NZLR 495.
178. *Re Roberts* [1993] NZFLR 731.
179. Section 7A, Property (Relationships) Act 1976.

125. The common law presumption that a wife was the agent of her husband was abolished by section 49 of the Property (Relationships) Act 1976. As a result, a married woman has all the rights, powers, duties and obligations of a married man, and the ordinary rules of agency apply to both spouses.

126. The Property (Relationships) Act 1976 also abolished the presumptions of advancement, resulting trust and gift.[180] The Crimes Act 1961 abolished the presumption of compulsion when a married woman commits an offence in the presence of her husband,[181] and the rule that a husband and wife could not be guilty of conspiracy.[182]

127. Section 51(1) of the Property (Relationships) Act 1976 abrogates the common law rule that spouses could not sue each other in tort. Each spouse now has the same right of action against the other as if they were not married. If it appears that no substantial benefit would accrue, that the proceedings are vexatious or that the matter could be disposed of more conveniently under the Property (Relationships) Act 1976, the court may stay such an action.

128. A spouse or partner is competent and may be compelled to give evidence on behalf of either party to a civil or criminal proceeding. In the recent past, a spouse was not competent and compellable in criminal cases except as a witness for the defence.[183] A spouse could be a competent witness for the prosecution but was not compellable without the consent of the spouse charged with the offence, and any communication between spouses was privileged. The Evidence Act 2006 abolished the special rules relating to spouses giving evidence.

129. A wife is not compelled to adopt the surname of her husband, and where she does, it is by repute rather than the operation of law. Where one party does adopt the other's surname, that party may continue to use her married name notwithstanding the marriage being dissolved or may choose to revert to her name prior to the marriage or adopt another name by repute.[184] A party to a dissolved marriage who enters another marriage is free to retain the name from the previous marriage.[185]

130. Where either party to a marriage wishes to adopt the other spouse's surname, this is done by making a statutory declaration on the form provided by the Registrar-General.[186] Section 62 of the Births, Deaths, Marriages, and Relationships

180. Section 4(3), Property (Relationships) Act 1976.
181. Section 24(3), Crimes Act 1961.
182. Section 67, Crimes Act 1961.
183. Section 5(2), Evidence Act 1908 (now repealed).
184. *Fendall v. Goldsmid* (1877) 2 PD 263.
185. *Cowley v. Cowley* [1901] AC 450.
186. Sections 21–21B, Births, Deaths, Marriages, and Relationships Registration Act 1995 (Births, Deaths, Marriages, and Relationships Registration Act 2021, s 69 (when in force)).

Registration Act 1995[187] allows the party changing a name to request the Registrar-General to include the new name as part of the information on the marriage records.

131. The domicile of the parties is important in relation to determining the jurisdiction of the court. An example of this is section 37(2) of the Family Proceedings Act 1980, which provides that the parties cannot apply for dissolution in a New Zealand court unless at least one party is domiciled in New Zealand. The common law rule that a married woman automatically took up the domicile of her husband was abolished by section 5(1) of the Domicile Act 1976, so now each party to a marriage can have an independent domicile. Section 5(2) of the Domicile Act 1975 specifies that this rule applies regardless of in which country the marriage was solemnized, and irrespective of the domicile of the parties at the time of marriage.

132. The legal capacity of a married woman to own property is the same as that of a married man.[188] This means that the parties can own, possess and deal with property according to their individual beneficial and legal interests.[189]

133. Generally, a will is revoked when the person who made the will marries (or enters a civil union).[190] The primary exception to this rule is where the will is made in contemplation of marriage, in which case that marriage will not revoke the will. If a will is made in contemplation of a particular marriage and that marriage does not take place, whether the will has any effect depends upon the whole of the circumstances and the document.[191] If the marriage is dissolved, provisions of a will that benefit the other party to the marriage are null and void,[192] unless the will is designed to discharge any debt or liability between the parties, or where the will is expressly stated to apply despite the dissolution of the marriage. This second exception can apply either by the document itself or through a subsequent codicil. A trust which tends to restrain marriage, whether established by will or other means, is void.[193] However, restraints on widowed spouses from remarriage are not void,[194] nor are partial restraints on marriage.[195]

134. New Zealand replaced the common law duty of a husband to maintain his wife with the mutual liability of spouses to maintain each other.[196] This has the effect that where one party to a marriage cannot meet their own reasonable needs, the other party may be liable to pay such maintenance as is necessary to meet those needs. This obligation continues where the parties have ceased to live together and

187. See Births, Deaths, Marriages, and Relationships Registration Act 2021, ss 73 and 74 (when in force).
188. Section 49, Property (Relationships) Act 1976.
189. Section 19, Property (Relationships) Act 1976.
190. Section 18, Wills Act 2007. *See* below para. 423.
191. *Re Panapa* [1993] 1 NZLR 694.
192. Section 19, Wills Act 2007.
193. *Re McKay* (1914) 33 NZLR 811.
194. *Lichtenstein v. Lichtenstein* [1986] 2 NZLR 392 (1986) 4 NZFLR 25; 2 FRNZ 58. The point is not true of restraints on de facto relationships.
195. *Heathwaite v. New Zealand Insurance Co Ltd* [1951] NZLR 6.
196. Sections 63–70B, Family Proceedings Act 1980.

for a reasonable period after the marriage is dissolved. A claim can also be made against a person's estate, although the usual limitation period within which a claim must be made is twelve months from the grant of administration.[197]

135. In order to obtain maintenance, the applicant must show that the ground being relied upon is a real and substantial cause of the lack of ability to provide for the applicant's own reasonable needs. The applicant does not have a full onus of proof, although both parties have an evidential onus in respect of matters that they wish to establish.[198] Where the parties' marriage or civil union continues to exist (although they may have separated), the grounds are as follows:

- the ability/inability to be self-supporting, having regard to the division of functions during cohabitation, each party's likely earning capacity and 'any other relevant circumstances';
- responsibilities for daily care of any 'minor or dependent' children;
- the standard of living while living together;
- a physical or mental disability;
- an inability to obtain work; and
- the undertaking of training or education.

After the marriage or civil union has been dissolved or, in the case of de facto partners, the de facto relationship has ended, the fourth and fifth grounds, that is, a physical or mental disability or an inability to obtain work, cannot be relied upon for the purposes of justifying ongoing payments of maintenance.

136. The court may take into account the division of functions within the marriage to assess the loss of earning capacity.[199] The applicant must show an inability to obtain employment,[200] and the test will not normally be satisfied where the party seeking to be maintained worked and obtained a wide range of skills while the parties were living together. The fact that the recipient is retraining will not by itself justify maintenance liability. For example, where a woman was retraining to be a lawyer, the Court of Appeal held that she had a far greater capacity to support herself in her existing field of human resources and her ex-partner was not, therefore, required to support her while she was at law school.[201]

137. Where there has been a division of relationship property, the Court of Appeal suggested that two years after the division ought to be the usual maximum period of maintenance liability.[202] However, this is not a rule, and especially if there are dependent children, a longer duration may be justified.

197. Section 71, Family Proceedings Act 1980. For a rare case involving a claim against an estate, see *Guzman v. Estate of Osborne* [2020] NZFC 1983, [2020] NZFLR 142.
198. *McQueen v. Penn* [2016] NZCA 571, [2017] NZFLR 31 at [29].
199. *Mackie v. Mackie* [1993] NZFLR 213; (1992) 10 FRNZ 60 (HC).
200. *Appleton v. Appleton* (1993) 10 FRNZ 395.
201. *C v. G [Maintenance of former partner: period of liability]* [2010] NZFLR 497 (CA).
202. *Rainey v. Kwok* [2021] NZCA 199, [2021] NZFLR 406, at [34] and following, especially [37] and [38].

138. Under the original version of the current legislation, if the payment of maintenance would have the effect of depriving the paying spouse, or any dependant of that spouse, of a reasonable standard of living, liability may be negated or decreased.[203] This rule was abolished according to legislation that came into force in 2002. Section 66 of the Family Proceedings Act 1980 gives the court discretion to take an applicant's conduct into account where the conduct 'amounts to a device to prolong that party's inability to meet reasonable needs' or any other conduct of such nature and degree to make it repugnant to justice to make the other party liable to pay maintenance. The liability to meet the reasonable needs of a spouse is not negated by reason of the party needing to be maintained being on a state social security benefit.[204]

139. Section 65(1) of the Family Proceedings Act 1980 lists five matters to be taken into consideration by the court in determining any amount payable. These are:

(a) the means of each spouse, civil union partner, or de facto partner, including:
   (i) potential earning capacity;
   (ii) means derived from any division of property between the spouses, civil union partners, or de facto partners under the Property (Relationships) Act 1976;
(b) the reasonable needs of each spouse, civil union partner, or de facto partner;
(c) the fact that the spouse, civil union partner, or de facto partner by whom maintenance is payable is supporting any other person;
(d) the financial and other responsibilities of each spouse, civil union partner, or de facto partner; and
(e) any other circumstances that make one spouse, civil union partner, or de facto partner liable to maintain the other.

140. In considering the means of the parties, if the income of the liable party has fluctuated, the court must estimate future income, but there is no rule about averaging income over a given number of years where the liable party has had a drop in income.[205] Potential earning capacity includes the likelihood of the party working overtime,[206] while other relevant factors include the age, health, qualifications and further employment prospects of the parties.[207] Entitlements to superannuation funds are relevant in some situations only, whereas borrowed funds or gains from gambling are always relevant.

141. All earnings of an employed applicant will be taken into account unless it is reasonable for the applicant to give up employment for some reason (e.g., where

203. Section 65(3), Family Proceedings Act 1980.
204. *See* s. 62, Family Proceedings Act 1980, and *Richardson v. Richardson* [2012] 1 NZLR 796 (CA).
205. *Taylor v. Taylor* (1976) 11 ALR 123; 1 Fam LR 11404.
206. *Manhire v. Manhire* [1971] Recent Law 238.
207. *Williams v. Williams* [1974] Fam 55; [1974] 3 All ER 377.

he or she also has custody of children).[208] In the case of a person who would not have gone to work had the marriage continued, the court will take account of their potential earning capacity.

142. The next factor for the court to determine once liability to maintain has been shown is the reasonable needs of the parties. Reasonable needs are greater than those required to live at a subsistence level; however, they do not include luxuries or mere personal desires. They are assessed objectively, but the focus will always be on the parties' circumstances.[209] The needs of both parties to the application are relevant, and the standard of living of the parties while they were living together may be taken into account.[210]

143. The court must take into account the support given to another party in determining the level of maintenance. This support can be through a legal obligation or a voluntary assumption of responsibility. The person being supported could, for example, be a child, a relative of the liable person or a new partner, but it is a question of fact whether a stable de facto relationship exists.[211]

144. Sections 65(1)(d) and (e) (quoted above, paragraph 139) are self-explanatory.

145. Under section 82, interim maintenance can be ordered in advance of a final order. While there is a broad discretion to make an interim order, the courts have developed some principles. Collins J summarized the law as follows:[212]

(1) The provision exists 'to protect the position of an applicant who may have inadequate means to meet current needs pending determination of the proceedings, if and so far as it is reasonable in all the circumstances to do so'.
(2) The court has 'an unfettered discretion both as to whether an order should be made at all and as to the amount if an order is made'. The court must 'do what it thinks just', which will 'depend on all the circumstances of the particular case'.
(3) The court 'will necessarily pay particular regard to the reasonable needs of the applicant over the period for which an order will subsist and the means likely to be available to the applicant to meet those needs'.
(4) 'In assessing those needs the Court will take into account the standard of living the parties had adopted for themselves.'
(5) The term 'means' is used 'in the broadest sense to encompass any sums which the applicant could reasonably be expected to earn from his or her own efforts

208. *Attwood v. Attwood* [1968] P 591; [1968] 3 All ER 385.
209. *Smith v. Smith* (1985) 1 FRNZ 561 (HC).
210. Section 65(5), Family Proceedings Act 1980. Prior to an amendment in 2001, the previous standard of living was irrelevant unless there were special circumstances.
211. *Curline v. Curline* [1979] NZLJ 291.
212. *Dalrymple v Dalrymple* [2020] NZHC 637 at [24], drawing on quotes from the Court of Appeal in *Ropiha v Ropiha* [1979] 2 NZLR 245, at 247.

during the term of any interim order together with any other funds available to the applicant during that period'. Any 'moneys taken into account should be reasonably assured to the applicant'.

(6) Interim maintenance should not be ordered 'unless proper weight has been given to the applicant's capacity from all sources to meet her needs over that period. In principle, it is immaterial in that regard whether the source of funds is employment reasonably available to the applicant, private income, resources of capital, or welfare benefits provided by the State or some other body'.

§5. Void and Voidable Marriages

146. The concept of voidable marriages was abandoned in New Zealand when the Family Proceedings Act 1980 was passed. The court no longer has the power to declare a voidable marriage void on such grounds as non-consummation of the marriage. However, the concept of void marriages is recognized in the Family Proceedings Act 1980. In this case, the marriage is deemed not to have occurred at all either in law or fact due to some impediment. Theoretically, there is no need to obtain a decree that the marriage is void, but it is advisable for the parties to obtain a declaration to that effect, as this will allow the position to be regularized and the facts to be determined. It would also help the spouse obtain relief. Such a declaration made by a court of competent jurisdiction binds not only the parties and their privies but also the whole world.[213]

147. Section 27 of the Family Proceedings Act 1980 enables any person to apply to the Family Court for a declaration of whether a marriage is valid or has been validly dissolved, according to the law of New Zealand.

148. Orders dissolving a marriage, declaring a marriage *void ab initio*, or declaring that one party is presumed dead and the marriage is thereby dissolved must be recorded in accordance with section 59 of the Births, Deaths and Marriages Registration Act 1995 (see Births, Deaths and Marriages Registration Act 2021, sections 60 and 61, when in force). Additionally, it is unclear how far parties to a void marriage are estopped from asserting the invalidity of the marriage. In *Hodges v. Helleur*,[214] the petitioner was entitled to a nullity decree *ex debatio justitiae* in spite of relying on her own bigamy, and in *C v. C*, it was held the petitioner was entitled to the same decree in the case of a consanguineous marriage in spite of her full knowledge at the time the marriage took place.[215]

149. Under section 29 of the Family Proceedings Act 1980, the court has jurisdiction to declare a marriage void only if:

(1) the applicant was domiciled in New Zealand at the time of application; or

213. *De Reneville v. De Reneville* [1948] P 100, 111; [1948] 1 All ER 56, 60 per Lord Greene MR.
214. [1952] NZLR 652.
215. [1932] NZLR 1425.

(2) the applicant was a New Zealand resident at the time of application; or
(3) the respondent was domiciled in New Zealand at the time of application; or
(4) the respondent was a New Zealand resident at the time of application; or
(5) the marriage was solemnized in New Zealand.

150. Unlike valid marriages (i.e., a marriage that has been validly entered into and has not been dissolved), in the situation of a void marriage, a third party (or surviving spouse) may seek a decree that the marriage is void as the marriage is void *ipso jure* and *ab initio. In the matter of BEW,* [216] it illustrates that, in rare situations where it is appropriate, counsel may apply to the Family Court for a declaration that the marriage is void. In this case, Mrs W was severely mentally handicapped and had been made subject to the court's *parens patriae* jurisdiction shortly after giving birth. Counsel appointed to represent Mrs W applied to the High Court for direction, in the exercise of its *parens patriae* jurisdiction, that an application to the Family Court for an order declaring the marriage to be void be allowed to proceed. The husband opposed the application. The application itself was made on the basis of sections 29, 30 and 31 of the Family Proceedings Act 1980. Neazor J found that the court had jurisdiction based on section 17 of the Judicature Act 1908.[217] In determining whether to exercise the jurisdiction, Neazor J stated:[218]

> [T]he Court should consider whether the entry into marriage, the strength of doubts about the capacity of the person to consent, and the circumstances of that person after marriage, together convince the Court that the welfare and interests of the person concerned require that the validity of the marriage should be challenged.

151. The grounds upon which a marriage is to be regarded as *void ab initio* are listed in section 31(1) of the Family Proceedings Act 1980, and these grounds apply whether or not a declaration has been made by the court. Section 31(2) provides that nothing in section 31(1) affects the validity in New Zealand of a marriage that is not subject to New Zealand law or the jurisdiction of the Family Court to make an order declaring such a marriage to be *void ab initio*. Section 31(1) is, therefore, restrictive in that it relates only to marriages governed by New Zealand law. The grounds contained in section 31(1) are exclusive and are:

> (1) A marriage or civil union that is governed by New Zealand law shall be void ab initio (whether or not an order has been made declaring the marriage or civil union to be void) only where,—
> (a) in the case of a marriage or civil union that is governed by New Zealand law so far as it relates to capacity to marry,—
> (i) at the time of the solemnisation of the marriage or civil union, either party was already married or in a civil union; or

216. [1994] NZFLR 730.
217. Under which the inherent jurisdiction of England applied to New Zealand. The jurisdictional rule is now found in s 12 of the Senior Courts Act 2016.
218. [1994] NZFLR 730, 736–737.

(ia) at the time of the solemnisation of the marriage or civil union, 1 of the parties to the marriage or civil union was under the age of 16 years; or

(ib) at the time of the solemnisation of the marriage, 1 of the parties to the marriage was aged 16 or 17 years and the consent of a Family Court Judge required under section 18 of the Marriage Act 1955 had not been obtained; or

(ic) at the time of the solemnisation of the civil union, 1 of the parties to the civil union was aged 16 or 17 years and the consent of a Family Court Judge required under section 19 of the Civil Union Act 2004 had not been obtained; or

(ii) by reason of duress, mistake, or insanity, or for any other reason, there was at the time of the marriage or civil union an absence of consent by either party to marriage to or civil union with the other party; or

(iii) the parties to the marriage are within the prohibited degrees of relationship set out in Schedule 2 of the Marriage Act 1955, and no order is in force under section 15(2) of that Act dispensing with the prohibition; or

(iv) the parties to the civil union are within the prohibited degrees of civil union set out in Schedule 2 of the Civil Union Act 2004, and no order is in force under section 10 of that Act dispensing with the prohibition; or

(b) in the case of a marriage or civil union that is governed by New Zealand law so far as it relates to the formalities of marriage or civil union, the parties knowingly and wilfully married without a marriage or civil union licence, or in the absence of a marriage or civil union celebrant or Registrar of Marriages; or

(c) in the case of a civil union that is governed by New Zealand law so far as it relates to the formalities of civil union, the parties knowingly and wilfully entered into a civil union without a licence, or in the absence of a Registrar (as defined in section 3 of the Civil Union Act 2004) or civil union celebrant, or otherwise than in accordance with the rules and procedures of an exempt body (as also defined in section 3 of that Act).[219]

These rules have been discussed in the preceding paragraphs. Subparagraphs (ia)-(ic) were added by the Minors (Court Consent to Relationships) Legislation Act 2018.

219. 'Prohibited degrees' defined in sch 2, Marriage Act 1995 and sch 2, Civil Union Act 2004.

Chapter 2. Divorce

§1. Grounds

152. In New Zealand, the sole ground for marriage dissolution is if the marriage has broken down irreconcilably. This is evidenced only by the fact that the parties have been living apart for two years immediately preceding the application.[220] This led Judge Pethig, in a case where the husband was contesting the making of a dissolution order on the grounds that the marriage had not broken down irreconcilably, to state:[221]

> So what Parliament has said is that if people have lived apart for two years, then that is the sole ground which the Court must look to in order to dissolve a marriage. Once the evidence has been given of that, notwithstanding as we find from time to time that the parties for religious or emotional or other reasons would wish the marriage to continue and cohabitation to resume, we are powerless in this court to do anything further about that. Accordingly, the ground has been established.

This statement has been cited with approval in the High Court.[222]

153. The existence of a separation order is not essential for the purposes of the dissolution of marriage. However, such an order may be used as evidence that the parties have lived apart for the requisite period of time.

154. Since the passage of the Civil Union Act 2004, which applies to both opposite and same-sex couples, the rules under discussion also apply to the dissolution of a civil union. One exception is found in section 18 of the Civil Union Act: parties to a marriage can change their relationship to a civil union, and vice versa (prior to the extension of marriage to same-sex couples in 2013, only heterosexual parties to a civil union could change to a marriage). As pointed out in section 17, the parties need not dissolve their prior marriage or civil union (as the case may be); that is, the two-year waiting period does not apply. However, they still need to follow the usual procedures for the solemnization of the new form of relationship.

155. Living apart normally involves both a mental and a physical element. However, *Sullivan v. Sullivan* [223] recognized that the physical element is not always necessary. The fact that the parties are 'living apart under the one roof' must be demonstrated by the evidence viewed objectively. *Stoneham v. Stoneham* [224] identified the following factors to be considered in assessing whether parties are living apart under the same roof:

---

220. Section 39, Family Proceedings Act 1980.
221. *Marks v. Marks* 19 Aug. 1986 DC Blenheim FP 006/67/86.
222. *Bailey v. Bailey* [1992] NZFLR 702.
223. [1958] NZLR 912.
224. (1988) 4 FRNZ 487, 495; 5 NZFLR 140, 149.

(a) the cessation of sexual relations and personal contact;
(b) no companionship;
(c) little communication or confiding in each other;
(d) very little socializing apart from family occasions;
(e) no common shared interests;
(f) separate holidays;
(g) the division of assets and the fact that their incomes were kept separate;
(h) the division of household expenses; and
(i) the arrangements regarding expenses for the car.

156. Factors tending to negate living apart in the *Stoneham* case were:

(a) the purchase of a new home for the family to live in a year after the alleged living apart began;
(b) the fact that the parties were living in the same house for a number of years after the separation;
(c) the maintenance of the family unit to the extent of keeping a home for the children of the marriage (who in 1979 were aged 15, 12 and 9, respectively);
(d) Mrs Stoneham's pattern of doing most of the cooking for the family, whatever her reasons for that, and her reluctance to allow Mr Stoneham into the kitchen;
(e) the sharing of essential household expenses;
(f) the division of the household chores; and
(g) the shared family social functions and the entertainment of their overseas friends at their home.

The judge held that the parties were not living apart. It was not enough to find that neither party would move out of the home or that they had dependent children who needed a home.

157. In *Williams v. Williams*,[225] Judge Inglis QC considered it sufficient that a reasonable outsider fully informed of the facts and looking at the marriage two years prior to the application for the dissolution order would have considered the marriage to be irreconcilable, even where the parties were still living under the same roof.

158. The requisite mental element cannot be inferred from the mere fact that the couple is living apart. Rather, one party must have formed an attitude against continued cohabitation.[226] This may, in fact, be inferred from an objective test of the state of the parties' relationship if a reasonable outsider fully informed of the situation would conclude the marriage was at an end, and the failure of either spouse to acknowledge that fact could be seen as a failure to recognize the true state of affairs.[227] This mental element need not have been communicated to the other spouse. This can lead to the situation where the parties are living apart without the

225. (1998) 3 FRNZ 589.
226. *Sullivan v. Sullivan* [1958] NZLR 912.
227. *Williams v. Williams* (1988) 4 NZFLR 769, 781.

second spouse realizing it, as was the case in *McRostie v. McRostie*,[228] *Marriott v. Mariott*[229] and *Rumble v. Rumble*.[230] Judge Carruthers stated that this will not apply where one party has given rise to the belief that the marriage is still alive in the other party.[231] The mental element will be inferred where one spouse is 'brain dead',[232] but where the spouse is hospitalized, suffering irreparable physical and mental faculties, living apart will not commence until the other spouse accepts the relationship is at an end (either expressly or tacitly).[233]

159. If during the two years of living apart, the spouses resume cohabitation, unless the period of cohabitation exceeds three months for the purpose of a trial reconciliation, the spouses will be deemed to have been living apart.[234] There is also no presumption that resumption of sexual intercourse means the parties are not living apart.[235]

§2. Procedure

160. As stated above (paragraph 152), prior to an application for a dissolution order, the parties must have lived apart for at least two years. Once this requirement is satisfied, either party or both parties jointly can apply to the Family Court for an order dissolving the marriage, provided at least one spouse is domiciled in New Zealand.[236]

161. Most dissolution proceedings in New Zealand are undefended and proceed without controversy. In such circumstances, the order may be granted by a court Registrar and neither of the parties needs to appear.[237] An undefended order made by a judge takes effect immediately, while one made by a Registrar takes effect one month later. An order made by a judge in defended proceedings takes effect after one month, unless there is an appeal, in which case the order will not be effective until the appeal has been decided.[238]

162. In one case, the parties made a joint application falsely declaring that they had lived apart for two years. The dissolution was granted. The woman in due course remarried but this marriage did not last. The second husband opposed the dissolution on the grounds that the dissolution of the first marriage was invalid. It

228. [1955] NZLR 631.
229. [1956] NZLR 125.
230. [1990] NZFLR 311.
231. *Reeves v. Reeves* FC, Wellington FP 224/88, 10 Feb. 1989.
232. *Joe v. Joe* (1985) 3 NZFLR 675.
233. *Dorf v. Dorf* (1982) 1 NZFLR 331.
234. Section 40, Family Proceedings Act 1980.
235. Section 41, Family Proceedings Act 1980.
236. Section 37, Family Proceedings Act 1980.
237. Section 38, Family Proceedings Act 1980.
238. Section 42, Family Proceedings Act 1980.

was held, however, that the dissolution of the first marriage had taken effect notwithstanding the fraud.[239] Judge Murfitt considered that a dissolution order is absolutely final because of 'importance for parties and their children to know their status with certainty'; therefore, despite the order being made upon false evidence, a dissolution order must be considered conclusive evidence.[240]

163. As part of the procedure for applying for the dissolution order, the forms prescribed by the Family Proceedings Rules 1981 need to be filed. If the proceedings were commenced by a single applicant, notice needs to be served on the other party. Where the respondent is resident outside New Zealand, the manner of service differs in so far as the forms required to be served differ. A dissolution order cannot be granted unless the court is satisfied that appropriate arrangements have been made for the children.[241] Given that divorce is at least two years after the end of the relationship, matters relating to the children will usually have been settled.

§3. Effects

164. The first effect of dissolution is that there ceases to be an obligation on the part of the spouses to live together. Second, a dissolution order means that the parties are free to remarry.[242] Third, the liability to provide maintenance is affected. The grounds upon which maintenance can be awarded are reduced,[243] and the liability to maintain expires after a reasonable period of time.[244] In determining how long maintenance should last, the court can take account of the ages of the parties, the length of the marriage (which includes any period of living together unmarried) and the ability of the parties to be self-supporting (having regard to the division of functions while living together, likely earning capacity, responsibilities to children and 'any other relevant circumstances'). This means, for example, that an older woman who has fulfilled a more traditional wifely role with little or no prospect of employment may still receive maintenance for several years after the marriage has been dissolved.[245] Fourth, under the Family Protection Act 1955, a former spouse is not entitled to claim a share of the estate of a deceased former partner. Likewise, a former spouse has no right to share in the estate of a deceased partner upon an intestacy.[246]

239. *MAS v. SAE* [2007] NZFLR 467.
240. *Ibid.*, at [8].
241. Section 45, Family Proceedings Act 1980.
242. Section 43, Family Proceedings Act 1980.
243. Section 64, Family Proceedings Act 1980. *See* discussion of this above: Ch. 1, §4.
244. Section 64A, Family Proceedings Act 1980.
245. *Z v. Z (No. 2)* [1997] 2 NZLR 258 and *Slater v. Slater* [1983] NZLR 166.
246. Section 77, Administration Act 1969.

Chapter 3. Cohabitation Without Marriage

165. Until just after the turn of the century, New Zealand had no statutory control over the financial affairs of parties to a de facto relationship. This led the courts to develop the law on an ad hoc basis. The courts had become aware of the injustice that may have resulted from having no statutory control. Based on the equitable view that a person should not be able to stand on strict legal rights in a situation where this would amount to an injustice, the courts developed concepts such as the constructive trust to give the other party a suitable remedy.

166. On a piecemeal basis, the law recognized de facto relationships for certain purposes, particularly with respect to welfare and taxation laws. The Domestic Violence Act 1995 applied the law to both heterosexuals and same-sex couples (as well as various other categories such as 'close personal relationships').[247] However, it was not until a package of reforms in 2001, effective February 2002, that de facto relationships were placed on a firm statutory basis for most purposes, in particular for those concerning property division and inheritance. In broad terms, the rules relating to de facto relationships are the same as those for marriages. Following the passage of the Civil Union Act 2004, in force since 26 April 2005, civil unions were created and, with very few exceptions, the law for civil union partners is the same as that for married couples.

167. It should be noted that under New Zealand law, the statutory terms 'de facto partner' and 'de facto relationship' are used for the situation where two people live together without marriage or civil union. Other expressions such as cohabitation or domestic partnership have been avoided.

168. It should also be noted that, while there is no general procedure for people to follow when entering a de facto relationship, where a person is aged 16 or 17, the consent of the Family Court is needed.[248] This is similar to the rule for marriages between minors, discussed above (paragraph 114), introduced in response to concern about coerced or forced marriages. Consent was granted in a case that appears to have been brought to ensure that the two 17-year-olds received the right social security benefit.[249] There was no undue influence or coercion, and the application was supported by family and others.

169. Because in some residual cases, the pre-2001 law will still apply, this chapter will first discuss the relevant rules of common law and equity. It will then consider the new law on de facto relationships, followed by the law on civil unions.

170. As long as the parties do not come under one of the relevant statutes, it is possible to commence proceedings in either the District Court or the High Court for

247. The Family Violence Act 2018 replaced the Domestic Violence Act 1995.
248. Care of Children Act 2004, s 46A, substituted by the Minors (Court Consent to Relationships) Legislation Act 2018, s 20.
249. *Re Hopkins* [2020] NZFC 8575, [2020] NZFLR 749.

a de facto property claim, with the District Court having the same equitable jurisdiction as the High Court, subject to a financial limit of NZD 350,000.[250] Factors that may be considered in the decision of forum include the additional cost of a claim in the High Court and that a claim commenced in the High Court potentially decreases the appeal process if there are new or complex issues to be addressed.

171. One of the first New Zealand cases that recognized the full extent of the potential injustice resulting from the termination of a de facto relationship and used a constructive trust analysis was *Hayward v. Giordani*.[251] The Court of Appeal based its finding on the reasonable expectations of the parties. Previously, New Zealand had largely followed the English approach to the need to find an implied trust (often referred to as the common intention test) before allowing a de facto property claim to succeed. The inherent problems with this approach were recognized in *Hayward* and are the reason for the movement away from the common intention test. These problems were alluded to in *Pasi v. Kamana*,[252] with Cooke P refining the *Hayward* test stating:

> I respectfully doubt whether there is any significant difference between the deemed, imputed or inferred common intention spoken of by Lord Reid and Lord Diplock … and the unjust enrichment concept used by the Supreme Court of Canada. Unconscionability, constructive or equitable fraud, Lord Denning's 'justice and good conscience' and 'in all fairness': at bottom in this context these are probably different formulae for the same idea. As indicated in *Hayward v. Giordani*, I think that we are all driving in the same direction. One way of putting the test is to ask whether a reasonable person in the shoes of the claimant would have understood that his or her efforts would naturally result in an interest in property.

172. Subsequently, in analysing the reasonable expectation test, the Court of Appeal in *Lankow v. Rose* further refined the test, indicating that the following four factors must be present to find an equitable remedy:[253]

(1) contributions, direct or indirect, to the property in question;
(2) the expectation on the part of the claimant of an interest therein;
(3) such expectation is a reasonable one; and
(4) the defendant should reasonably expect to yield the claimant an interest.

The scope of the first point above has yet to be decided finally, as there is some judicial comment that the contribution need not be to the property in question. However, all judges agree the claim needs to be attached to a particular piece of property, and there needs to be a causal connection between the contributions and the claim to property. The contributions need not be solely financial, and there is an

250. Section 76, District Court Act 2016.
251. [1983] NZLR 140; (1983) 2 NZFLR 129.
252. [1986] 1 NZLR 603, 605; (1986) 2 FRNZ 120, 122; 4 NZFLR 417, 419.
253. [1995] 1 NZLR 277 (per Tipping J at 294); (1994) 12 FRNZ 682; [1995] NZFLR 1.

increasing tendency to see a wide range of actions in the relationships and the home as being relevant.[254] These contributions must be weighed against benefits received and must manifestly exceed those benefits.[255] An example of this is contained in *Lanyon v. Fuller*,[256] where it was held that the claimant's contributions to household expenses might amount to payment for boarding or lodging, not entitling the claimant to a share in the property.

173. In making this type of assessment, the court will look at the sacrifices that have been made as well as contributions. In *Fleming v. Beevers*,[257] Fraser J held that the plaintiff, through entering a de facto relationship with someone seventeen years her senior, had sacrificed the possibility of marriage to someone else with the resultant building up and sharing of matrimonial assets. Likewise, she had sacrificed the opportunity of living alone as a professionally qualified woman and building up her own separate assets.

174. In *Lankow v. Rose,* Mr Lankow's counsel argued that Ms Rose had not specifically made contributions expecting an interest in property. However, the court disagreed, with Hardie Boys J stating:[258]

> There is an essential difference between motive and expectation. The constructive trust is not a reward only for the calculating. Ms Rose's answer is not at all surprising. Indeed it would have been surprising had she said anything else. The answer says nothing as to any expectation she might have had as to the eventual outcome of her efforts. Moreover it must be put in the context of the whole of the evidence. ... I therefore have no hesitation in rejecting the submission that Ms. Rose by her own evidence demonstrated that she had no expectations.

175. An example of a situation where the expectation of an interest was not reasonable is *Gillies v. Keogh* (discussed in the next paragraph).[259] Throughout the relationship, the woman constantly said the house belonged to her. The typical case where a de facto partner seeks redress is where the property in question is in the name of the other partner. If, however, the property is held in both parties' names as joint tenants or tenants in equal shares, there is a presumption of equal division.[260] This presumption is rebuttable, with the onus being on the claimant to show why such sharing does not reflect the true situation.[261]

---

254. For example, *Nash v. Nash* [1994] NZFLR 921 (CA).
255. *Lankow v. Rose* [1995] 1 NZLR 277; [1995] NZLR 1; (1994) 12 FRNZ 682.
256. (1988) 4 FRNZ 134.
257. [1993] NZFLR 13.
258. *Lankow v. Rose* [1995] 1 NZLR 277, 283.
259. [1989] 2 NZLR 327; (1989) 5 FRNZ 490; 5 NZFLR 549.
260. Sections 340–343, Property Law Act 2007. Hinde McMorland and Sim *Land Law in New Zealand* (online, LexisNexis, Wellington) at para. [13.006] 'Unity of interest'.
261. *L v. P* 29 Nov. 1995 unreported, HC Auckland, HC 243/94. See, however, *Hau v. Hau* [2018] NZHC 881, [2018] NZFLR 464, e.g., at [34] on the equitable presumption of tenancy in common.

176. It can be seen that the intention of the parties still plays a substantial role in these cases, even where this intention is unilateral, as was the case in *Gillies v. Keogh.*[262] In this situation, the claimant was found not to have an expectation in the home, as Ms Keogh had, throughout the relationship, expressed the intention that the house was to belong solely to her. In appropriate cases, this assertion will not defeat the claim to an interest in property, as other remedies may still be available for a claimant if they have contributed in more than a minor way to the property in question. An example of this is a case where the male partner used his skill and expertise to renovate his partner's home, as well as supplying the necessary materials. He was a carpenter by trade, and although the circumstances were such that he could not hold a reasonable expectation to the property, he was still entitled to be rewarded for the expenditure incurred on a quasi-contract basis.[263]

177. If the expectation of an interest is reasonable, there is no presumption of equal division, although this was the outcome in *Lankow v. Rose*. Usually, the contributions of each party will be assessed and distributions made accordingly. Cooke P has indicated that the longer the relationship lasts, the more reasonable an expectation of an interest may be.[264] The amount of an award in a de facto property claim is generally less than in a statutory relationship property claim. The Court of Appeal justified this in *Lankow v. Rose*, stating:[265]

> In the case of a de facto union, the claimant does not start from a presumptive half share but rather from nothing. A de facto claimant must demonstrate first a case for an interest and then what that interest should be. The interest must broadly reflect the contributions. Arithmetical precision will generally be unattainable and is in any event not necessary. The Court must, however, do its best to reflect in the assessed shares the value of the claimant's contributions. That value will represent, if uncompensated, the amount of the unjust enrichment accruing to the defendant which in turn is the amount of the claimant's sacrifice.

178. The rules of common law and equity just outlined also applied where one of the parties died, and they may still do so in residual situations not covered by the statutory schemes. Prior to the 2001 legislation, unless named in a will as a beneficiary, the surviving partner needed to make a claim against the deceased's estate under the Law Reform (Testamentary Promises) Act 1949,[266] breach of contract, or claim under the same constructive trust analysis that applies *inter vivos*. Under the Law Reform (Testamentary Promises) Act 1949, there is a heavy burden on the

262. [1989] 2 NZLR 327; (1989) 5 FRNZ 490; 5 NZFLR 549.
263. *Daly v. Gilbert* [1993] NZFLR 513.
264. *Cormack v. Scott* [1995] NZFLR 289; (1995) 13 FRNZ 45. *See also Harvey v. Binder* [1992] NZFLR 506; (1991) 8 FRNZ 560.
265. *Lankow v. Rose* [1995] 1 NZLR 277, 295; (1994) 12 FRNZ 682, 699; [1995] NZFLR 1, 20 (CA).
266. This is discussed in Part IV, Ch. 2, s. 6, II.

plaintiff to prove the claim.[267] The breach of contract claim appears to have succeeded in *Fleming v. Beevers*,[268] due to the fact that when the male partner died intestate, all property passed to his ex-wife under the Administration Act 1969. The Court of Appeal found that the deceased had entered into a contract with the claimant to leave her property in his will, a contract which the woman could now enforce. Even if covered by the statutory schemes, testamentary promises and contractual claims are still possible.

179. There is no impediment to undertaking a constructive trust analysis of same-sex relationships. One example of this is *Julian v. McWatt*,[269] where the court was prepared to use the constructive trust analysis in a case that involved two men.

180. The 2001 reforms extended the following major areas of the law to de facto relationships:

(1) Property division. The Matrimonial Property Act 1976 was renamed the Property (Relationships) Act 1976. It was also extended to widowed parties, allowing a survivor of a de facto relationship to claim under the Act (the details of the 1976 Act are discussed in Part III).
(2) Maintenance. The rules governing the award of maintenance on dissolution of a marriage found in the Family Proceedings Act 1980 now apply to de facto relationships (this is discussed above in Part II, Chapter 1, §4).
(3) Succession. Apart from the ability of a survivor to claim under the Property (Relationships) Act 1976, claims for a greater share of the deceased's estate can be made under the Family Protection Act 1955 by close family members, now including surviving de facto partners (this is discussed below in Part IV, Chapter 2, §6). Where the deceased dies intestate, family members can succeed according to statutory rules found in the Administration Act 1969, now including surviving de facto partners (the law on intestate succession is discussed in Part IV, Chapter 1).

181. In order to come within the jurisdiction of these pieces of legislation, two conditions must be fulfilled. First, the couple must be a party to a 'de facto relationship' as defined in the legislation. Second, the de facto relationship must, subject to specified exceptions, have lasted three years. It follows that some de facto relationships that have not lasted three years and associations that do not satisfy the test for a de facto relationship will have to rely on the rules of common law and equity discussed above (paragraphs 169 and following).

182. One of the difficulties in any consideration of the definition of 'de facto relationship' is that there is more than one definition. The 'default' definition, that is, the one that applies where the relevant statute does not have a definition of its own, is found in section 14 of the Legislation Act 2019. It reads:

267. *Chambers v. Weston* (1982) 1 NZFLR 377, per Cooke P.
268. [1994] NZFLR 108 (CA).
269. [1998] NZFLR 257.

> Meaning of de facto relationship:
>
> (1) In any legislation, *de facto relationship* means a relationship between 2 people (regardless of their sex, sexual orientation, or gender identity) who—
>   (a) live together as a couple in a relationship in the nature of marriage or civil union; and
>   (b) are not married to, or in a civil union with, each other; and
>   (c) are both aged 16 years or older.
>
> (2) However, a relationship involving a person aged 16 or 17 years is not a de facto relationship unless that person has obtained consent for the relationship in accordance with section 46A of the Care of Children Act 2004.
>
> (3) In determining whether 2 people live together as a couple in a relationship in the nature of marriage or civil union, the court or person required to determine the question must have regard to—
>   (a) the context, and the purpose of the law, in or for which the question is to be determined; and
>   (b) all the circumstances of the relationship.
>
> (4) A de facto relationship ends if—
>   (a) the de facto partners cease living together as a couple in a relationship in the nature of marriage or civil union; or
>   (b) one of the de facto partners dies.

However, for the purposes of the main pieces of legislation that were amended in 2001, the definition in Section 2D of the Property (Relationships) Act 1976 Act applies:

> Meaning of de facto relationship
>
> (1) For the purposes of this Act, a de facto relationship is a relationship between 2 persons (whether a man and a woman, or a man and a man, or a woman and a woman) –
>   (a) who are both aged 18 years or older; and
>   (b) who live together as a couple; and
>   (c) who are not married to, or in a civil union with, one another.
>
> (2) In determining whether 2 persons live together as a couple, all the circumstances of the relationship are to be taken into account, including any of the following matters that are relevant in a particular case:
>   (a) the duration of the relationship;
>   (b) the nature and extent of common residence;
>   (c) whether or not a sexual relationship exists;
>   (d) the degree of financial dependence or interdependence, and any arrangements for financial support, between the parties;
>   (e) the ownership, use, and acquisition of property;
>   (f) the degree of mutual commitment to a shared life;
>   (g) the care and support of children;
>   (h) the performance of household duties;
>   (i) the reputation and public aspects of the relationship.

(3) In determining whether 2 persons live together as a couple, –
  (a) no finding in respect of any of the matters stated in subsection (2), or in respect of any combination of them, is to be regarded as necessary; and
  (b) a Court is entitled to have regard to such matters, and to attach such weight to any matter, as may seem appropriate to the Court in the circumstances of the case.

183. It will be seen that there are several crucial differences between these definitions. One result of this is that two people may legally be in a de facto relationship for certain purposes and not for others. Indeed, this possibility was accepted in an earlier Court of Appeal decision in *Ruka v. Department of Social Welfare*,[270] where the court was dealing with a woman who had received a state social security benefit despite a long-term relationship with a man and who was charged with benefit fraud. The majority of the Court of Appeal held that financial interdependence was a necessary condition before it could be said that, under the Social Security Act 1964 (now Social Security Act 2018), two people were in a relationship in the nature of marriage. As a result, the woman was acquitted. The majority accepted that this necessary condition might not apply in other contexts. Subsection (3)(a) of section 29A of the Interpretation Act 1999 envisages that different contexts and purposes may throw up different results. On the other hand, subsection (3)(a) of section 2D of the Property (Relationships) Act 1976 rejects the notion that there can be any necessary condition such as financial interdependence. There are two other differences between the two definitions above (paragraph 182). First, section 2D requires the parties to be aged 18 or over, while section 29A contemplates people aged as young as 16 as being in a de facto relationship. Second, section 29A contains a list of factors that are relevant to the question of whether two people are living together as a couple. Section 29A avoids any such list.

184. The court, in making a determination under section 2D, may be faced with two questions:

(1) Were the parties in a de facto relationship? and
(2) When did it begin?

The latter question may be important in deciding whether the relationship has lasted long enough to come under the legislation. In one of the leading cases, *Scragg v. Scott*, two High Court judges gave the following guidance:[271]

> The incidents and attributes of marriage, or for that matter de facto relationships, are not the same for all people and the ultimate question is to be answered in a broad practical way weighing up all the circumstances. … The test must inevitably be evaluative, with the Judge having to weigh up as best

270. [1997] 1 NZLR 154; [1996] NZFLR 913.
271. *Scragg v. Scott* [2006] NZFLR 1076, paras 25 and 37.

> he or she can all of the factors – not only those contained in Section 2D, but also any others there may be – and applying a common sense objective judgment to the particular case.

185. In one case, the court had to determine whether two adulterous adults were in a de facto relationship.[272] Mr and Mrs Hutchison were married for forty-seven years with three children and a business. For twenty-seven years of that marriage, Mr Hutchison was engaged in an adulterous affair with Ms Greig. The court was asked to consider whether the two were in a de facto relationship during the marriage. Gendall J, in the High Court, determined that there was no de facto relationship on the basis of three factors: whether the two 'lived together as a couple', whether there was a 'mutual commitment to a shared life', and 'the degree of financial interdependence between the parties'.[273] These factors were not satisfied as the relationship was more like a business one with intimacy. However, the marriage was the centre of the husband's primary commitment.

186. The situation just discussed involved the potential clashing interests of three people who did not all live together. What about a polyamorous relationship, where three people live together as a threesome? This issue came before the Court of Appeal in *Paul v. Mead*.[274] The High Court had held that there was no jurisdiction because section 2D refers to living as a 'couple', which is two people, not three.[275] The Court of Appeal reversed the decision, ruling that 'the Family Court has jurisdiction under the Property (Relationships) Act 1976 to determine claims to property as between two persons who were married, in a civil union, or in a de facto relationship, and also in a polyamorous relationship. That jurisdiction extends to determining claims among three people in a polyamorous relationship, where each partner in that polyamorous relationship is either married to, in a civil union with, or in a de facto relationship with, each of the other partners in that polyamorous relationship'. In other words, a multi-partner relationship of three people can in law be regarded as a combination of three separate de facto relationships.

187. In some cases, the parties may live in a common residence, but this will not necessarily be so if other factors point to the conclusion that the two people have been living together as a couple. The existence of a sexual relationship is relevant but not always decisive, and the same is true where the parties have other sexual parties:[276]

> [T]here may be many relationships where one or both parties do not limit their sexual behaviour to activity with the other yet they remain married or in a civil union or a de facto relationship. There may be instances where couples in a relationship operate on an understanding that each might have, from time to

---

272. *Greig v. Hutchison* [2015] NZHC, [2015] NZFLR 587. The Court of Appeal refused leave to appeal: *Greig v. Hutchison* [2016] NZCA 479, [2016] NZFLR 905.
273. *Greig v. Hutchison* [2015] NZHC 1309, [2015] NZFLR 587 at para. [57].
274. *Paul v. Mead* [2021] NZCA 649 at para. [106].
275. *Paul v. Mead* [2020] NZHC 666, [2020] NZFLR 1042.
276. *Scragg v. Scott* [2006] NZFLR 1076, para. [44].

time, other sexual partners. There may be instances where intermittent sexual behaviour occurs but is kept secret from a partner for many years. Sexual fidelity may be a factor which, depending on the circumstances, may indicate a lack of commitment but it depends on all the circumstances.

188. A further issue is how to consider parties whose relationship runs hot and cold and who may appear to part company but then resume their relationship. In some instances, where the parties drew a clear line, for example, by entering into a separation agreement, then any resumption of cohabitation means that a new de facto relationship has begun. However, some interruptions may not be enough to break the old de facto relationship:[277]

> [I]t seems quite possible that where the 'interruption' sits between two periods of living under the same roof, the circumstances prevailing during the interruption, although not sufficient to amount to a de facto relationship if they were considered in isolation, may take colour from the periods of living together, and thus constitute a continuous de facto relationship.

189. The Court of Appeal stated that there could be no 'blanket rule that treats parties involved with each other on an "on again, off again" basis as being involved in a single, continuous relationship'.[278] However, the judges also cautioned against analysing the end of a de facto relationship differently from the ending of a marriage. In other words, periods of separation by de facto couples should be seen similarly to periods of separation by married couples.

190. As already mentioned, for the purposes of property division, maintenance and inheritance, a de facto relationship must, in general, have lasted three years.[279] However, there are exceptions to this, with the result that some shorter de facto relationships will come under the respective statutory regimes. As a typical example, section 14A(2) of the Property (Relationships) Act 1976 reads as follows:[280]

> (2) If this section applies, an order cannot be made under this Act for the division of relationship property unless –
> (a) the Court is satisfied –
> (i) that there is a child of the de facto relationship; or
> (ii) that the applicant has made a substantial contribution to the de facto relationship; and
> (b) the Court is satisfied that failure to make the order would result in serious injustice.

---

277. *LS v. ZJ* [2005] NZFLR 932, para. [29]. Compare *O v. K* [2004] NZFLR 507, and *I v. L* [2004] NZFLR 714.
278. *Bourneville v. Bourneville* [2009] NZFLR 69 (CA).
279. The court can extend the period beyond three years, but this rarely happens. A de facto relationship lasting less than three years is technically known as one of short duration: *see* s. 2E of the Property (Relationships) Act 1976.
280. *See also* s. 70B(2), Family Proceedings Act 1980, s. 4A(2), Family Protection Act 1955 and s. 77B(2), Administration Act 1969.

191. The child referred to in (a)(i) need not be the child of both parties but may instead be a child from a previous relationship. With respect to 'substantial contribution', there are differing judicial viewpoints. While in one case the judge looked for a contribution 'far beyond' 'the norm',[281] another judge thought that the contribution need not be far beyond the norm at all.[282] The phrase 'serious injustice' was one that a High Court judge refused to further define, but accepted based on the fact that the woman had contributed more than she had received, thus satisfying the test.[283] Another High Court judge thought that there was 'a relatively high threshold' but on the facts saw little point in the parties' relitigating the issues if forced back on ordinary common law and equitable remedies.[284]

192. As earlier indicated, for most important purposes, de facto relationships are now treated much the same as marriages and civil unions. In some instances, there may be disputes over jurisdiction, but once that hurdle has been crossed, the substantive rules are the same for all three categories of association. These rules are discussed elsewhere in this monograph (e.g., *see* Part III for relationship property rules).

281. *Schmidt v. Jawad* [2003] NZFLR 1050, para. 15.
282. *LS v. ZJ* [2005] NZFLR 932, para. 66.
283. *Schmidt v. Jawad* [2006] NZFLR 410, Ronald Young J.
284. *S v. W* [2006] NZFLR 669, paras 133–136, Chisholm J.

Chapter 4. Filiation

193. There are two main ways of establishing paternity under New Zealand law. A declaration may be sought from the Family Court or the High Court under the Status of Children Act 1969, or a paternity order from the Family Court under the Family Proceedings Act 1980. The latter is used quite commonly for the purposes of obtaining child support, but in a number of situations, a paternity order is only prima facie evidence of paternity.

194. If, for example, there is a question relating to the succession to property and there is uncertainty about the relationship between the testator and the alleged beneficiary, a declaration under the 1969 Act may be necessary. Another situation is where a declaration is desired for immigration purposes, such as assisting a person to obtain New Zealand residency.[285] There are several other means of prima facie proof of paternity. They are an entry on the birth register, an acknowledgement of paternity and paternity orders granted by courts in certain overseas countries.[286]

195. Originally, only the High Court could grant paternity declarations under the Status of Children Act 1969. Concurrent jurisdiction was extended to the Family Court by an amendment passed in 2005. The amendment also gave the court power to make a declaration of non-paternity, that is, a declaration that the relationship of parent and child does not exist.[287] A similar power to grant an order of non-paternity was added to the Family Proceedings Act 1980.[288]

196. Paternity orders and declarations will often relate to the court's assessment of who is a biological parent. However, the Supreme Court has held that what is at stake is legal parenthood. Thus, where a man had been adopted as a child, he could not later obtain a paternity declaration against another man whom he claimed to be his biological father.[289] The adoption took precedence and determined that the adoptive father was the man's legal parent. Similarly, another case, which concerned the unsupported child's benefit, held that the term 'natural parent' in section 29 of the Social Security Act 1964[290] does not include the birth parent of a child who has been adopted.[291]

197. The Status of Children Act 1969 removed almost all distinctions between children born in or out of wedlock:[292]

---

285. *Re an application by Tamasese* [1999] NZFLR 43.
286. Section 8, Status of Children Act 1969. *See also* s. 7, Child Support Act 1991, which sets out a similar list of persons who may be liable parents under that Act.
287. Section 10(3), Status of Children Act 1969.
288. Section 51(1)(b), Family Proceedings Act 1980.
289. *Hemmes v. Young* [2006] 2 NZLR 1; [2005] NZFLR 887.
290. Now ss 46 and 47, Social Security Act 2018.
291. *R v. Chief Executive of the Ministry of Social Development* [2012] NZFLR 337 (per Courtney J).
292. Section 3(1), Status of Children Act 1969.

> For all the purposes of the law of New Zealand the relationship between every person and his father and mother shall be determined irrespective of whether the father and mother are or have been married to each other, and all other relationships shall be determined accordingly.

198. One exception is the presumption of parenthood, which applies only to married couples and not to civil unions or those living in de facto relationships. A man is presumed to be a child's father if the child was born to his wife or was born within ten months after the marriage had been dissolved.[293] The presumption can be rebutted by evidence to the contrary, and the standard of proof is the civil one, that is, the balance of probabilities. No change was made to this section when the Marriage (Definition of Marriage) Amendment Act 2013 extended marriage to same-sex couples. It follows that the presumption applies only to heterosexual married couples.

199. Section 10 of the Status of Children Act 1969 allows the court to make declarations as to paternity even where the putative father or the child has died. Applications may be made by the mother, the putative father or any other person 'having a proper interest in the result'. A paternity declaration is conclusive proof of paternity for all purposes.[294]

200. An application for a paternity order under the Family Proceedings Act 1980 may be made by the mother, by the mother's custodial parent if she is under 16, by a government social worker with the mother's consent, or by various people if the mother is dead, has abandoned the child or is unable to make the application herself, including the maternal grandparents, a guardian of the child, a social worker or anyone else with the leave of the court.[295] Either the mother or the putative father must reside or be domiciled in New Zealand, or alternatively, if the mother is dead, jurisdiction is conferred if the child resides in New Zealand.[296] The respondent must not be or ever have been in a marriage or civil union with the mother.[297] It follows that an order may be made against a current or former de facto partner.

201. An application must usually be brought within six years of the child's birth. One of the most important exceptions is where the mother and putative father lived together in a de facto relationship during the two-year period prior to the making of an application.[298]

202. In paternity proceedings, the onus is on the applicant to establish the claim on the balance of probabilities, giving due weight to the seriousness of the allegation.[299] The mother is not required to give evidence, and the former rule that

293. Section 5, Status of Children Act 1969.
294. Section 8(4), Status of Children Act 1969.
295. Section 47, Family Proceedings Act 1980.
296. Section 48, Family Proceedings Act 1980.
297. Section 47(2), Family Proceedings Act 1980.
298. Section 49, Family Proceedings Act 1980.
299. *Hall v. Vall* [1972] NZLR 95.

required her evidence to be corroborated has been abolished.[300] The most common forms of proof today are blood and DNA tests, which have been referred to as 'parentage tests' since 2005.[301] The court can recommend that the parties undergo parentage tests, but cannot force them to do so. Nevertheless, the Court of Appeal has held that a child may be placed under the guardianship of the court in order that consent can be given for tests on the child, despite the mother's objections.[302] A person refusing a parentage test has the right to explain the refusal, but the court can draw such inferences from the refusal as appear proper. This does not mean that a putative father who refuses a parentage test will automatically have an order made against him. It is a matter for the court to decide after weighing all the evidence.[303]

203. Special statutory rules apply where a child has been born as a result of an assisted reproduction procedure. In general, where gametes or an embryo have been donated, then the birth mother and her partner (married, in a civil union or de facto, so long as the partner consented) are the legal parents of the child.[304] This applies whether the partner is the opposite or same-sex as the birth mother, with the result that a person may have two women as legal parents.[305] Further, the birth mother is the legal mother even if she is not the genetic mother, for example, because she had another couple's embryo implanted and carried the child as a surrogate. The donor has no legal relationship with the child.[306] This rule is appropriate where the child is to be brought up by the birth mother and her partner, but it also applies where it is planned that the child be brought up by the 'donor' and his partner, that is, where the birth mother is a surrogate mother. In this situation, it is usually necessary for the child to be adopted, although in some instances the parties may instead seek to have the surrogate mother removed as a guardian.[307] The position of male same-sex couples is more complicated. It has been common for them to use a surrogate in, for example, California where the law treats the two men as the legal parents. The Californian law is not however recognized in New Zealand. A New Zealand adoption order may be necessary, but prior to the Marriage (Definition of Marriage) Amendment Act 2013, which extended marriage to same-sex couples, only one of the parties could adopt.[308] Since 2013, married same-sex couples can adopt.[309]

300. Section 52, Family Proceedings Act 1980.
301. Sections 54–59, Family Proceedings Act 1980.
302. *T v. S* [2005] 2 NZLR 696; [2005] NZFLR 433. In *Fletcher v. Blackburn [Guardianship]* [2009] NZFLR 354, Heath J reversed an order relating to DNA testing on the ground that the mother ought to be given one last chance to arrange for a test.
303. *Liggins v. Telfer* (1985) 3 NZFLR 592.
304. Sections 17 and 18, Status of Children Act 1969 (as amended in 2004).
305. *See KL L-A v. EA [Care of children]* [2008] NZFLR 536, where it was held that the female partner of the birth mother was a legal parent, there being sufficient evidence that they were living together in a de facto relationship at the time the child was conceived.
306. Sections 19–22, Status of Children Act 1969 (as amended in 2004).
307. For example, *Minkov v. Caldwell* [2014] NZFLR 922, where the social parents planned to leave New Zealand for jobs in Australia. It appears that the husband, whose sperm had been used, was wrongly registered on the child's birth certificate.
308. For example, *see Re An Application by BWS to Adopt a Child* [2011] NZFLR 621. *See* below Ch. 5.
309. *See Re an appln Reynard (to adopt a child)* [2014] NZFC 7652, [2015] NZFLR 87, discussed in the next chapter in the context of adoption.

204. The Law Commission has produced an Issues Paper on surrogacy.[310] Submissions from the public are being assessed and a final report will be produced. Ultimately, this may lead to discrete legislation on the subject.

310. Law Commission *Te Kōpū Whāngai: He Arotake - Review of Surrogacy* (Issues Paper 47, Wellington, 2021).

Chapter 5. Adoption

205. Adoption is governed by the Adoption Act 1955, the Adoption Regulations 1959, and the Adoption (Intercountry) Act 1997. The ability of adult adopted persons or their parents to access information is governed by the Adult Adoption Information Act 1985. Secondary legislation includes Adult Adoption Information (Fees) Regulations 1991 and the Adoption (Intercountry) Regulations 1998.

206. Currently, there is no express statutory provision for open adoption in New Zealand (apart from the Adult Adoption Information Act 1985, which is effective once the adopted person is an adult). Section 16 of the Adoption Act 1955 creates the legal fiction that an adoptive child is the child of its adoptive parents as if they gave birth to the child in lawful wedlock. Nevertheless, open adoption has been followed in practice for many years.

207. Section 3 of the 1955 Act provides:

(1) Subject to the provisions of this Act, a court may, upon an application made by any person whether domiciled in New Zealand or not, make an adoption order in respect of any child, whether domiciled in New Zealand or not.
(2) An adoption order may be made on the application of two spouses jointly in respect of a child.
(3) An adoption order may be made in respect of the adoption of a child by the mother or father of the child, either alone or jointly with his or her spouse.

208. An issue of some controversy is whether the parties to a de facto relationship can adopt or whether they must be married. The High Court in *Re Application by AMM and KJO to adopt a child*[311] applied the New Zealand Bill of Rights Act 1990 to hold first that the law was discriminatory on the grounds of marital status, and second to construe the word 'spouse' to include a de facto partner. Previous Family Court judgments had been split on this question.[312] However, in the course of the judgment, doubts were raised as to whether the ruling could extend to de facto same-sex couples and civil union couples (whether opposite or same-sex).

209. Subsequently, the Marriage (Definition of Marriage) Amendment Act 2013 extended marriage to same-sex couples and amended the definition of 'adoptive parent' in section 2 of the Adoption Act 1955 by replacing the words 'a husband and

311. [2010] NZFLR 629, per Wild and Simon France JJ. The case was a step-parent adoption in circumstances where the child was conceived by donor insemination and the donor's identity was unknown.

312. *Re Adoption by Paul and Hauraki* [1993] NZFLR 266 (where the judge was influenced by the fact that the couple regarded themselves as married by Māori custom, which is not recognized as a legal marriage), *In the matter of J (adoption)* [1998] NZFLR 961 (Māori and non-Māori) and *In the matter of C [Adoption]* [2008] NZFLR 141 took a broad view. A narrow view was taken in *In the matter of R* [1999] NZFLR 145 and *Re D (adoption)* [2000] NZFLR 529.

wife' with 'a married couple'.[313] As a consequence, the Family Court was able to allow a de facto, same-sex couple to jointly adopt the biological daughters of one of the applicants in *Re Pierney*.[314] Judge McHardy was convinced that such orders would be in the welfare and best interests of the children as it would provide security of relationship with their parents.[315] The judge also commented on the fact that if the ruling was not in favour of the applicants, then this would result in discrimination that is inconsistent with Parliament's efforts in widening the meaning of spouse in the Marriage Amendment Act as well as changing views of society on the topic.[316]

210. Before *Re Pierney*, the Human Rights Tribunal heard arguments from Adoption Action Incorporated who argued that Adoption Act 1955 was discriminatory in eight different ways.[317] The Tribunal agreed that the Act was discriminatory in seven out of the eight ways and issued a declaration of inconsistency accordingly.[318] The government of the day responded by saying that it was 'satisfied that, in practice, the provisions of the Adoption Act are interpreted in a rights consistent manner', and therefore they declined to engage in any large-scale reform of the Act.[319] As noted above (paragraph 13), adoption law reform has been advanced with the publication of the Ministry of Justice discussion paper.[320]

211. Another groundbreaking adoption decision was made in the case of *Re Gordon* where two divorced applicants successfully adopted their 18-year-old foster child.[321] It was the wish of the teenage daughter that the reality of the relationship be recognized, despite the divorce of the applicants. In considering the situation, Courtney J said:[322]

> [F]or some children adoption carries the incalculable social and emotional benefit of truly belonging to the family in which they have grown up. This means that, as young adults in finding their place in the world and later as parents themselves, adoptees continue to reap the benefit of being permanently connected to parents and wider family in a way that is only possible through legal status.
>
> Viewed against current social norms, I consider that discriminating against a couple on the ground that their marriage has been dissolved cannot be justified.

---

313. An example is *Re an appln Reynard (to adopt a child)* [2014] NZFC 7652, [2015] NZFLR 87, where an adoption was granted to two men who had two children by way of surrogacy in the United States and who had married after returning to New Zealand with the two children.
314. *Re Pierney* [2015] NZFC 9404, [2016] NZFLR 53.
315. *Ibid.*, at [6].
316. *Ibid* at [12]-[16].
317. *Adoption Action Incorporated v. Attorney-General* [2016] NZHRRT 9, [2016] NZFLR 113.
318. *See* above for declaration of inconsistency: para. 56.
319. Amy Adams, Minister of Justice, 'Government Response to declarations of inconsistency by the Human Rights Review Tribunal in *Adoption Action Incorporated v. Attorney-General*'.
320. Ministry of Justice *Adoption in Aotearoa New Zealand Discussion document* (Wellington, 2021).
321. *Re Gordon* [2019] NZHC 184, [2020] 2 NZLR 436.
322. *Ibid.*, at [29] and [30].

212. If an application by a couple is declined, then one partner can still apply under section 3(1) as an individual. The court may be reluctant to grant an adoption in favour of a lesbian mother's unmarried partner as a sole applicant.[323] However, a same-sex unmarried partner may adopt as an individual.[324]

213. Section 3(3) provides for step-parent adoptions, that is, where a natural parent and new spouse adopt a child. Because the effect of such an adoption is to exclude the other natural parent from having a legal place in the child's life, the courts are somewhat reluctant to grant such adoptions.[325] The position is different if the other parent is dead or has had nothing to do with the child for a long period. Despite this, step-parent adoptions still figure quite significantly in the statistics for adoptions.

214. Another area of particular concern in New Zealand is the treatment of the Māori customary practice of whāngai. Whāngai is a practice whereby a child is raised by members of the child's whānau other than the birth parents. This will often be an aunt and uncle or grandparents. Most whāngai arrangements are informal and do not involve the legal adoption of the child. This is because whāngai is fundamentally an open adoption where a relationship is fostered between both the birth parents and the whāngai parents in a different way from what European law is able to contemplate. Whāngai is not officially recognized in a general sense in any law of New Zealand,[326] which means that the legal position of whāngai parents is uncertain. This can lead to issues where there are disputes between whāngai parents and biological parents. This was the case in *Nikau v. Nikau* where the Court of Appeal identified that the law needs clarification in this area, but it declined to do so in this instance, preferring instead to determine the case on different grounds.[327] The Court of Appeal was satisfied that, in deciding against the whāngai parents, the trial judge had properly taken cultural factors into account, along with the Treaty of Waitangi (discussed above paragraph 2).

323. *Re T* [1998] NZFLR 769.
324. *See Adoption Application by T* [2008] NZFLR 185. In that case, the applicant was not in a relationship and was adopting his nephew, whom he had cared for since birth. In *Re An Application by BWS to adopt a child* [2011] NZFLR 621, two adoptions were granted individually to two American men who were a couple and who had moved to New Zealand. They each adopted their own genetic child, born in each case as a result of surrogacy. *Re Kennedy* [2014] NZFLR 797 involved a man whose heterosexual relationship broke down but who subsequently had a child through a Californian surrogate. The court approved the adoption by him, holding that payments made by him to the surrogate were compensatory and not in breach of New Zealand legislation against commercial surrogacy (*see* s. 14, Human Assisted Reproductive Technology Act 2004).
325. For example, *WVT v. RDC [Adoption]* [2008] NZFLR 843 (FC).
326. For certain specific purposes, it is recognized in Te Ture Whenua Maori Act 1993 (Maori Land Act 1993) where in s 4 it is defined as 'a person adopted in accordance with tikanga Maori' (Māori custom).
327. *Nikau v. Nikau* [2018] NZCA 566, [2018] NZFLR 826, at [29].

215. Section 4 sets out the main restrictions upon adoption:

(1) Except in special circumstances, an adoption order shall not be made in respect of a child unless the applicant or, in the case of a joint application, one of the applicants:
   (a) has attained the age of 25 years and is at least 20 years older than the child; or
   (b) has attained the age of 20 years and is a relative of the child; or
   (c) is the mother or father of the child.
(2) An adoption order shall not be made in respect of a child who is a female in favour of a sole applicant who is male unless the court is satisfied that the applicant is the father of the child or that there are special circumstances which justify the making of an adoption order.
(3) Except as provided in subsection (2) of section 3 of this Act, an adoption order shall not be made providing for the adoption of a child by more than one person.

The definition of 'child' limits the meaning to a person who has not attained the age of 20 years, unless there was an interim order for adoption in place when the person turned 20.

216. Section 7 of the Adoption Act provides that before an adoption order is made, the consent of certain persons is necessary. Section 8, however, provides for consent to be dispensed with in certain circumstances. The persons from whom consent is required include guardians of the child (whether by birth, court order, or any other means), the spouse of any applicant where the application is made in one spouse's name only, or in appropriate cases, the Chief Executive of Oranga Tamariki. The consent of a father who is not a guardian[328] is required only if the court thinks it is 'expedient' to obtain such consent. Section 7(7) provides that consent cannot be given until the child is at least ten days old. Section 7(6) allows the person placing the child up for adoption to make consent to the adoption conditional upon the child being brought up in a particular religion.

217. Consent to adoption can be dispensed with by the court under section 8 in the following situations:

(a) where the parent or guardian has abandoned, neglected, persistently failed to maintain, or persistently ill-treated the child, or has failed to exercise the normal duty and care of parenthood;
(b) the child's parent or guardian is unfit to have care and control of the child;
(c) consent has already been given or dispensed with in another British Commonwealth jurisdiction.

328. *See* Part II, Ch. 7.

In considering the first of these situations, a broad assessment over the whole of the child's life is necessary. Isolated acts of misconduct or neglect will not be sufficient to satisfy the exception.[329] Once it is determined that there are grounds for dispensing with consent, the sole factor in finally deciding to dispense with consent is the welfare and interests of the child. There is no place to consider the interests of the mother or person whose consent is being dispensed with.

218. Once consent has been given, interim orders may be made under section 5, unless special circumstances exist to justify an immediate final order. An interim order gives the applicant(s) lawful custody of the child, without amounting to a final adoption. Once made, an interim order remains in force for a year unless revoked or unless a final order is made within that time. An application for a final order may be made after the interim order has been in force for six months (or, rarely, if the court has specified a shorter period).[330] Section 15(1)(c) allows a further interim order to be made, but this action is unusual. An interim order places four restrictions on the applicants as follows:[331]

(1) The applicants must comply with any terms the order imposes.
(2) The applicants must allow reasonable visits by official social workers.
(3) The applicants must not take the child out of New Zealand without first having obtained the leave of the court.
(4) Applicants must notify their social worker of a change in residence at least seven days prior to moving.

Breach of either of the last two restrictions is an offence under section 27(1), the offender being liable to a term of imprisonment for three months, an NZD 15,000 fine, or both. In addition, the court may order the removal of the child to a place of safety.

219. The court retains the discretion to revoke interim orders under section 12, on the application of any person. While there is no statutory limitation on the meaning of that phrase, the Family Court in *T v. S (No. 1)* limited those who can apply to people with an 'immediate interest in the adoption proceedings'.[332] Judge Inglis has, however, noted that:[333]

> it cannot be permissible to use the discretionary power in section 12 as a back-door method of circumventing the clear statutory intention that a birth parent's consent to adoption, once given, cannot be withdrawn once the adoption application to which it relates is before the court.

329. *D-GSW v. L* [1989] 2 NZLR 314 (CA).
330. Section 13, Adoption Act 1955.
331. Section 15(2).
332. [1990] NZFLR 411.
333. *B v. H* Unreported, 25 Jan. 1996 Family Court Wanganui Registry Adoption 4/94.

220. If an application for adoption is refused, the applicants may appeal to the High Court within one month of the refusal.[334]

221. Once an interim order has been made, the person who gave consent cannot usually withdraw that consent.[335] The exception to this is where consent was not freely given. The burden of proving that the consent was not freely given is high, with the person alleging that fact having to show that freedom of choice was effectively destroyed.

222. Prior to making an interim or final order, the court must be satisfied that the applicants are fit and proper persons, the welfare and interests of the child will be promoted by the adoption, and any condition imposed by the birth parent(s) relating to religion will be abided by.[336] In addition to these requirements, a social worker must have prepared a report on the proposed adoption under section 10 of the Act unless the applicant is an existing parent.

223. As noted above (paragraph 206), there is no statutory procedure to enforce an open adoption. Welfare officials responsible for adoption have been following an open rather than a secret approach to adoption for the past thirty years. The success of this approach depends largely on the cooperation of the parties concerned. Where such cooperation breaks down, there is no straightforward legal mechanism for enforcing the agreed means of contact. Any agreement between the parties does not have the legal force of a contract.[337]

224. These issues arose in *Adoption of PAT* where the judge held that there was no jurisdiction to award a birth parent access to the adopted child.[338] The judge was concerned that such an order would be contrary to the legal fiction that is the foundation of the Adoption Act.[339] It might, however, be possible to make such a child a ward of court[340] and impose access (now called 'contact') rights in that way. Such an application was allowed in favour of the natural father in a case where the mother's second marriage to a man who became the adoptive father broke down.[341] Likewise, in another case, three sisters originally from Hong Kong were going to be adopted together. However, for one sister, the relationship with the adopting family did not work and the adoption, therefore, proceeded for the other two girls only.

334. Section 13A, Adoption Act 1955.
335. Section 9, Adoption Act 1955.
336. Section 11, Adoption Act 1955. In practice, it is usually hard to enforce the religious condition, especially if it relates to a religion which is not widely practised in New Zealand.
337. *Hamlin v. Rutherford* (1989) 5 NZFLR 426.
338. [1995] NZFLR 817.
339. *Ibid.*, at 376. Endorsed in *R v. Chief Executive of the Ministry of Social Development* [2012] NZFLR 377 (HC).
340. *See* Part II, Ch. 7.
341. *In the Guardianship of P* (1983) 2 NZFLR 289.

Despite the adoption and the decision in *PAT*, it was held that a parenting order under the Care of Children Act 2004 could be made seeking ongoing contact between the sisters.[342]

225. The law was simplified somewhat by the case of *Gordon v. Campbell*.[343] In this case, the judge held that a biological parent could apply for contact as 'any other person' under section 47(1)(e) of the Care of Children Act 2004. In this case, the child had been adopted by his maternal grandparents who initially agreed to provide contact between the child and his mother but subsequently resisted it as they believed it potentially to have a detrimental effect upon the child. The judge found that because the biological mother was a stranger in both fact and law, she must apply as 'any other person' and therefore must demonstrate that an order for contract is in the welfare and best interests of the child. The judge said that the mere fact that she is the child's mother and wishes to have contact with him is not enough: she must also provide evidence that she has a 'sustainable interest in promoting [the child's] welfare and best interest'.[344] The evidence was insufficient to do so in that specific case.

226. The Adult Adoption Information Act 1985 allows adopted persons (or their adopted parents in limited circumstances) to gather information about their birth parents. Similarly, it allows birth parents to obtain information about their children, as well as providing for a limited class of other people, such as doctors, to obtain information.

227. Section 4 of the 1985 Act allows an adopted person to apply for an original birth certificate on reaching 20 years of age. This will have the names of the birth parents. There are provisions under section 3 of the Act for the birth parents to 'endorse' a birth certificate, essentially imposing a veto on information. This applies only where the child was adopted prior to the Act's coming into force (i.e., 1 March 1986). The endorsement expires after ten years, but may be renewed under section 3(3).

228. Where a birth certificate is so endorsed, and a request is received under section 4, the birth certificate will be sent to the child with the names of the parents removed and the Registrar-General (of Births, Deaths, Marriages, and Relationships) is required to notify the applicant of the existence, effect and date of expiry of the endorsements.

342. *Re Adoption Application by PLL* [2009] NZFLR 1081 (FC). This case was distinguished in *EMO v. BSD [Jurisdiction]* [2011] NZFLR 947. There, a parenting order in favour of the applicant, a woman who had been in a relationship with the child's late grandmother, was in existence when an adoption order was made in favour of a great uncle and great aunt. The applicant sought contact and appointment as an additional guardian but it was held that the adoption meant that the parenting order ceased to be of any effect.

343. [2015] NZHC 1264; [2015] NZFLR 841.

344. *Ibid.*, at [96].

229. Where the person was adopted before 1 March 1986, the Registrar-General is required under section 5 to advise the child of the counselling services available and the fact that counselling is necessary before the original birth certificate can be obtained. The child is then required to notify the Registrar-General from whom they wish to receive counselling. The only exception is where the child is permanently resident outside New Zealand, in which case the Registrar-General is required to send a copy of the original birth certificate together with the address of Oranga Tamariki.

230. If the child was adopted after 1 March 1986, there is no compulsion to undergo counselling, but an applicant who desires counselling must notify the Registrar-General within twenty-eight days of receiving notification of the counselling services available.

231. Once the original birth certificate has been obtained, the adopted person may make a request under section 9 to the Chief Executive of Oranga Tamariki for identifying information about the birth parents. This request must be accompanied by an original birth certificate, and the Chief Executive must furnish the applicant with identifying information, where this is known. If the Chief Executive does not have details, but it appears information may be obtained without undue effort, a social worker is required to investigate the matter. There is no requirement that consent of the parents be obtained.

232. Any birth parent of an adult adopted person may request access to information about the person from the Chief Executive of Oranga Tamariki. There is provision for the adopted person to endorse the birth certificate under section 7, and this has the same effect as a birth parent endorsement; that is, there is no access to identifying information. Once Oranga Tamariki receives the request, if the adopted person is dead, it may disclose such information concerning the child as it thinks fit, including the child's circumstances at the time of death and the circumstances of the death.

233. If the Chief Executive is not satisfied that the adopted person is dead, the Registrar-General is asked whether or not there is an unexpired endorsement on the original birth certificate. If an endorsement is present, the Registrar-General so informs the Chief Executive, who, in turn, notifies the applicant. If there is no endorsement on the birth certificate, the Chief Executive can advise the applicant of the child's name and address, if it is known, as long as the consent of the child has been obtained. If the name and address of the child are not known, a social worker may attempt to locate the child so long as this would not require undue effort.[345]

234. Wherever a request for information is made, whether by the child or the birth parent(s), the applicant may request a social worker to approach the other party on the applicant's behalf.[346]

---

345. Section 8(2)(d), Adult Adoption Information Act 1985.
346. Section 10, Adult Adoption Information Act 1985.

235. While the number of adoptions of children within New Zealand has been dropping over the last few years, the number of overseas adoptions by New Zealanders has been increasing. The longstanding requirements for an overseas adoption to be recognized in New Zealand are:[347]

(1) The adoption must be valid in the place where it occurred.
(2) The adoptive parents must, as a result of the adoption, have a right to custody of the child superior to any birth parent.
(3) The adoption order must have been made by a court or judicial/public authority in a British Commonwealth jurisdiction, the USA, or a designated country. Alternatively, the adoption must have given the adoptive parents equal or superior rights to the natural parents in respect of the adopted child's property rights if the child dies intestate.

If these criteria are met, the adoption has the same effect as if it were an adoption order made in New Zealand.[348] *IS v. Attorney-General [Adoption: Shariah law]*[349] was a case seeking recognition of a Pakistani adoption effected according to custom and according to Muslim practice. The legal difficulty was that the adoption was not a full adoption in the New Zealand sense because, for example, the child did not lose inheritance rights from the birth parents. Nevertheless, the judge held that it fell within section 17.

236. New Zealand has ratified the Hague Convention on Protection of Children and Co-operation in Respect of Intercountry Adoption. By the Adoption (Intercountry) Act 1997, the Convention has the force of law in New Zealand. Broadly speaking, the Convention is designed to ensure that an adoption in an overseas country is in the child's best interests, appropriate consents have been obtained, counselling has been provided and the adoptive parents are suitable. Authorities in the state of origin and the receiving state have the responsibility for carrying out the necessary assessments.

237. In New Zealand, the Central Authority is the Chief Executive of Oranga Tamariki. There is, however, provision for the Chief Executive to delegate the functions to accredited non-profit organizations.[350] An adoption made in accordance with the Convention has the same legal effect as an adoption made in the usual way within New Zealand, although the Family Court, in accordance with Article 24 of the Convention, may refuse to recognize an adoption if it is manifestly contrary to public policy.

238. The New Zealand Family Court has had to deal with the question of whether the Convention applies in cases of surrogacy, most notably where the child was born in neighbouring Australia for the benefit of New Zealand genetic parents

347. Section 17, Adoption Act 1955.
348. Section 17, Adoption Act 1955.
349. [2011] NZFLR 145 (HC).
350. Sections 15–23, Adoption (Intercountry) Act 1997.

(i.e., with the help of in vitro fertilization), or in New Zealand for the benefit of Australian genetic parents. Unless the child's 'habitual residence' is in the country from which the child is to be removed, the Convention is irrelevant. It has been held that in the surrogacy cases just described, the child was not habitually resident in the country of birth but in the country where the commissioning couple intended to bring the child up. Thus, the Convention did not apply.[351]

239. Not all countries are signed up to the Convention, including many in the nearby Pacific area. Cases can arise with family and humanitarian aspects, plus an overlay of immigration considerations. In a case involving four children in dire circumstances in Ethiopia, the Court of Appeal allowed an aunt who was a New Zealand citizen to adopt three of them but not the eldest who having turned 20 was too old.[352] The parents had not been heard of for several years and were probably dead. The court asked whether the proposed adoption was capable of providing the children with a permanent family life. If so, then immigration concerns did not arise. Writing for the court, Goddard J said:

> Immigration legislation gives way where an adoption order is made precisely because our statute book proceeds on the basis that if the purposes of the Act are engaged, they prevail over the purposes of the Immigration Act. The private and public interests in protection of the family life of the New Zealand resident who adopts the child, and protection of the family life of the child who is adopted, override the immigration restrictions that would otherwise apply to a person who is not a New Zealand citizen and who wishes to come to New Zealand on a permanent basis.

240. In another case, an uncle was allowed to adopt two orphaned sisters in Sudan.[353] The main problem was proving the children's age in the absence of birth certificates. Despite inconsistent evidence, Edwards J accepted that the children were under 20 and considered that the adoption was not a means of bypassing immigration criteria. Cultural issues arose when an unmarried Nepalese woman, in New Zealand as a student, sought to have her baby adopted in New Zealand. In her home country, the extramarital birth would have brought shame. The adoption was allowed, and thus the international angle was avoided.

351. *In re application by L* [2003] NZFLR 529 (FC). *See also Re KJB and LRB [Adoption]* [2010] NZFLR 97 (FC), *Re An Application by BSW to adopt a child* [2011] NZFLR 621, and *Re Kennedy* [2014] NZFLR 797.

352. *Norman v. Attorney-General* [2021] NZCA 78, [2021] NZFLR 234 at [136].

353. *Solomon v. Attorney-General* [2020] NZHC 2521, [2021] NZFLR 113. The Family Court had denied the adoption: *Re Afewerek* [2020] NZFC 5878, [2021] NZFLR 100.

Chapter 6. Parental Authority

241. As a general rule, parents have limited authority, unless they are also guardians of a child.[354] Parental consent used to be required where a minor wished to marry or enter a civil union, but that changed so that consent from the Family Court is now required. Depending on the circumstances, the consent of the mother and less often the father is necessary for a child to be adopted.[355]

242. Parents (and other caregivers) are subject to the Oranga Tamariki 1989. This Act deals with children in need of care and protection, as well as youth justice, where a juvenile breaches the criminal law. The most common situations where a child is legally 'in need of care or protection' are where the child has been abused or neglected. Reports of ill treatment or neglect may be made to a government social worker or the police. Persons making such reports are immune from civil, criminal or disciplinary proceedings.[356] If upon investigation, it is reasonably believed that the child is in need of care or protection, the matter is referred to a Care and Protection Coordinator whose main task is to call a 'family group conference'. Such conferences are designed to enable the wider family to find a solution to the problems facing the child. This is especially important for Māori, who place great weight on belonging to the wider family and tribe ('*whānau*, *hapū* and *iwi*').

243. Parents and guardians are entitled to attend family group conferences along with other members of the family group and the child (depending on the child's age and maturity).[357] 'Family group' is defined widely to include not only blood relatives but also people with whom the child has 'a significant psychological attachment'.[358] Foster parents may, therefore, be part of the family group conference.[359] The Coordinator can exclude a person if that person's attendance would not be in the child's interests or would be undesirable for any other reason. This means, for example, that a child would not necessarily have to confront an alleged abuser.

244. The social worker responsible for the particular case has a residual power to reject a plan that the family group conference came up with, but, in practice, only a small number of plans are turned down. In cases where the family group conference is unable to agree on a resolution, the matter can be taken to the Family Court, which has power to make various orders for the well-being and support of the child. What is said in a family group conference is privileged, but this does not extend to violent actions and threats.[360]

245. As a general rule, a court cannot make care or protection orders unless a family group conference has been held (*see* section 72). The legislation does not say

354. *See* Part II, Ch. 7.
355. *See* Part II, Ch. 6.
356. Sections 15–16, Oranga Tamariki Act 1989.
357. Section 22, Oranga Tamariki Act 1989.
358. Section 2(1), Oranga Tamariki Act 1989.
359. This is confirmed by the leading case, *CMP v. D-GSW* [1997] NZFLR 1.
360. *H v. H [Family Group Conference; Privilege]* [2010] NZFLR 821 (FC).

how recently the conference has to have been held, and in theory it could have been held a long time ago. However, the conference must have related to the issues that are the subject of the application for a declaration and so, if circumstances have changed since the conference was held, then it will be stale and a fresh conference will have to be called.[361]

246. In all situations, the well-being and best interests of the child are the first and paramount consideration.[362] The processes set out in the Oranga Tamariki Act 1989 may lead to the removal of the child from the child's parents, which can, in effect, mean a reallocation of parental authority. A variety of orders can be made, including those relating to day-to-day care and guardianship.

247. Another important aspect of parenthood in New Zealand is liability for the financial support of the child. The area is governed by the Child Support Act 1991. This Act replaces court ordered child maintenance and operates on the basis of a standard formula rather than a discretionary judicial assessment. It is most commonly relevant to the situation where the child's parents are living apart, and the caregiving parent seeks financial assistance from the other parent. Other caregivers may, however, apply, and in rare circumstances, if the court makes a step-parent declaration, a step-parent may be liable.[363]

248. The formula starts with the liable parent's taxable income, which is reduced to take into account the liable parent's own living expenses and the number of the liable parent's dependants (usually from a new family). The original version of the formula then obtained a percentage according to the number of children being supported. Modifications to the formula occurred where care of the children was split or shared between the parents.

249. In 2015 the formula was significantly changed. In summary, the changes are as follows: the formula: (1) takes account of the recipient's income; (2) extends shared caring arrangements to include those where a party has 28% of the nights, i.e., the equivalent of two nights; and (3) takes into account the costs of bringing up a child, allowing for a higher amount where the child is over 12.

250. The rigidity of the formula means that it may work unfairly in some situations, either for the liable parent or for the recipient. The only way in which the formula can be challenged is by seeking a 'departure'. There is a long list of grounds for a departure, including the effect of duties to maintain other people, high costs of

361. *H v. The Chief Executive Officer of The Department of Child, Youth and Family Services* [2007] NZFLR 802 (HC).
362. Section 4A, Oranga Tamariki Act 1989.
363. Section 99, Child Support Act 1991. One of the few cases where a step-parent declaration was granted was where a mother sought support from her lesbian ex-partner: *A v. R* [1999] NZFLR 249. In *DS v. GW [Child support]*[2006] NZFLR 925, a step-parent declaration was denied even though the ex-husband had been heavily involved in the child's life and had for a period been the child's primary carer. Twelve years after the child's birth, DNA results proved that the husband was not the father.

contact with the child, educational expenses, the parties' respective financial positions, payments already made for child support and the receiving carer's occupation of the liable parent's property (or vice versa).[364] However, the person seeking a departure must show that there are 'special circumstances' and that an order is just and equitable and is 'otherwise proper'. The courts have interpreted these conditions narrowly, with the result that departures are not in practice granted liberally.[365]

251. Misconduct is not as such a ground for departure. Thus, a departure will not be granted where the recipient is guilty of unlawful child abduction.[366] However, the same is not necessarily true where there is an application for discharge, suspension or variation of a departure order because the statutory test is different and allows other matters to be taken into account. So, it was held that evidence that the mother had prevented the liable parent father from having any meaningful contact with the child could be relevant.[367]

252. A feature of many New Zealand families is the widespread use of family trusts. In one case, a court had by consent ordered the creation of two trusts for the children, out of which would come the children's reasonable expenses. It was held that this justified a departure in the liable parent's favour.[368] On the other hand, if the liable parent deliberately avoided child support by diverting income to a trust, a departure could be made in the recipient's favour. Even where there are legitimate business reasons for diverting such income, it may nevertheless be brought into account in determining whether a departure ought to be made.[369]

253. Child support is usually paid on a periodic basis, but the court has the power to order payment by way of lump sum where appropriate. Where the recipient is receiving a social security benefit, child support payments will be retained by the government to offset the cost of the benefit. Where the recipient is not receiving a benefit, the money is collected by the child support section of the Inland Revenue Department and then paid to the recipient.

---

364. Section 105, Child Support Act 1991.
365. The leading case is *Lyon v. Wilcox* [1994] 3 NZLR 422 (CA).
366. *C v. L [Child abduction]* [2008] NZFLR 960 (HC).
367. *AB v. CD [Child support]* [2011] NZFLR 529 (HC).
368. *MJA v. FJB [Child support]* [2011] NZFLR 849 (FC).
369. *B v. X [Child support]* [2011] NZFLR 481 (HC). The Court of Appeal allowed an appeal in this case, restoring the Family Court orders that favoured the mother: *EJD v. AJCB* [2013] NZCA 100, [2013] NZFLR 325. The court accepted that it could look through trust, company, and other structures, but the outcome in the case turned on other issues.

Chapter 7. Guardianship

254. One of the primary pieces of legislation concerning children is the Care of Children Act 2004. This Act sets out the basic lines of authority over the upbringing of children, including rights to day-to-day care and contact. Guardianship is defined as follows:[370]

> For the purposes of this Act, **guardianship** of a child means having (and therefore a **guardian** of the child has), in relation to the child, –
>
> (a) all duties, powers, rights, and responsibilities that a parent of the child has in relation to the upbringing of the child;
> (b) every duty, power, right, and responsibility that is vested in the guardian of a child by any enactment;
> (c) every duty, power, right, and responsibility that, immediately before the commencement, on 1 January 1970, of the Guardianship Act 1968, was vested in a sole guardian of a child by an enactment or rule of law.

255. The concept of guardianship is further elaborated in section 16:

> (1) The duties, powers, rights, and responsibilities of a guardian of a child include (without limitation) the guardian's
> (a) having the role of providing day-to-day care for the child (excluding testamentary guardianship); and
> (b) contributing to the child's intellectual, emotional, physical, social, cultural, and other personal development; and
> (c) determining for or with the child, or helping the child to determine, questions about important matters affecting the child.
>
> (2) Important matters affecting the child include (without limitation) –
> (a) the child's name (and any changes to it); and
> (b) changes to the child's place of residence (including, without limitation, changes of that kind arising from travel by the child) that may affect the child's relationship with his or her parents and guardians; and
> (c) medical treatment for the child (if that treatment is not routine in nature); and
> (d) where, and how, the child is to be educated; and
> (e) the child's culture, language, and religious denomination and practice.

256. While a guardian has the role of providing day-to-day care, this is subject to any parenting order that determines how day-to-day care is to be provided. As indicated in the previous paragraph, guardians must contribute to the child's development and determine questions about important matters. However, it must be noted that the wording of the section demands a less authoritarian and more supportive role than in some traditional statements of the law. This role can be read in tandem

370. Section 15, Care of Children Act 2004.

with the principles arising out of the landmark House of Lords' case of *Gillick v. West Norfolk and Wisbech Area Health Authority*.[371] These principles are distilled and applied in the New Zealand case of *Hawthorne v. Cox* and summarized as:[372]

> In my view, the principles underlying s 16(1) can be expressed as:
>
> (a) The younger the child, the more likely it is that decisions about important matters will need to be made by his or her guardian.
> (b) As the child gets older and becomes more mature, the guardianship role changes to that of an advisor or a counsellor, endeavouring to assist the child to make good decisions.

Put in these terms, the [Care of Children] Act is consistent with the philosophy underpinning *Gillick,* namely that a parent's interest in the development of his or her child does not amount to a 'right' but is more accurately described as a 'responsibility or duty'. The terms of section 16 itself reflect that proposition.

257. Consequently, in New Zealand, the traditional authoritarian role of parenthood or guardianship is tempered somewhat by the considerations just mentioned. The above dictum from *Hawthorn* is continued in the case of *Moore v. Moore* where separated parents disagreed over the faith that the children were to be raised in.[373] The mother wished they be raised as Jehovah's Witnesses pursuant to her own fervent beliefs. The father disputed this. The judge took particular care with the fact that it was children's own wish that they continue within the faith. The children were aged 6 and 4 years at the time of separation and 10 and 8 by the time of the judgment. The judge ruled that the children were not yet *Gillick* competent. Consequently, it was ruled that the children should not attend Jehovah's Witness meetings or church activities such as seminars or witnessing.[374] The judge believed that it was in the best interests of the children that there be a 'dilution in the intensity of their exposure to their mother's faith'.[375] However, the judge would not go so far as to restrict the mother from engaging with her children about the faith, the children having the right to be exposed to her religious beliefs and participate and engage with them with their mother in their own home. Had the children been *Gillick* competent, their rights under the New Zealand Bill of Rights Act 1990 would have prevailed unless this would likely have resulted 'in physical or emotional harm to the child'.[376]

258. It has also become clear in the context of 'relocation cases' that it is the welfare and best interests of the child that are paramount when considering any

371. [1986] AC 112.
372. [2008] 1 NZLR 409 (HC), at [60]-[61].
373. [2014] NZHC 3213, [2015] NZFLR 457.
374. *Ibid.*, at para. [164].
375. *Ibid.*
376. *Ibid.*, at para. [136].

decision by a guardian that affects the child. Cases about residence and, in particular, relocation to a different part of New Zealand or to an overseas country frequently come before the courts. The Court of Appeal has maintained that, in deciding relocation cases, no gloss should put on the fundamental test of the welfare and best interests of the child. So, on the one hand, no special weight should be given to the wishes of the person with primary care, nor on the other hand, should the concept of joint guardianship be treated as the starting point.[377] Despite changes made by the Care of Children Act 2004, it has been judicially stated that these earlier Court of Appeal authorities remain the law.[378] Furthermore, the Supreme Court in *Kacem v. Bashir* [379] stated that 'it is difficult to see how any presumptive weight can properly be given to either side of [the] competing but necessarily abstract contentions. To do so would risk begging the very question involved in what is necessarily a fact-specific inquiry' and '... if there were to be any presumptive approach to relocation cases, it is contestable what that approach should be, This is very much a policy issue for Parliament, not judges'. This case overrides an earlier judgment that stated that 'custody' [now outdated terminology] prima facie carries with it the right to determine where a child will live.[380]

259. In all decisions made under the Act, whether affecting guardianship or day-to-day care or contact, the welfare and best interests of the child are the first and paramount consideration.[381] The conduct of the parents is irrelevant unless it affects the welfare of the child. The views of the child must be taken into account, irrespective of the child's age and maturity.[382] Reasonable opportunities must be given for the child to express those views.[383] The sex of any of the parties is not, as such, to play a part in any decision-making, thus ruling out old notions that favoured mothers. The child's sense of time must be taken into account. In considering welfare and best interests, it is the particular child in the child's particular circumstances that must govern; that is, an individualized decision relating to the child must be made, not one based on generalizations.

377. *Stadniczenko v. Stadniczenko* [1995] NZFLR 493, *D v. S* [2002] NZFLR 116 and *D v. S* [2003] NZFLR 81 (No. 2).
378. *Brown v. Argyll* [2006] NZFLR 705, Priestley J.
379. [2011] 2 NZLR 1; [2010] NZFLR 884 (SC) at paras [23] and [36]. *See* further discussion of this case in para. 261 below.
380. *Wright v. Wright* [1984] 1 NZLR 366 (CA).
381. Section 4, Care of Children Act 2004.
382. When the Family Court (Supporting Children in Court) Legislation Act 2021 comes into force, a further subsection will be added: '(1AAA) The purpose of this section is to implement in New Zealand Article 12 of the United Nations Convention on the Rights of the Child.'
383. Section 6, Care of Children Act 2004. Failure to follow this procedure means that the law has been breached but does not necessarily mean that any order made is null and void: *C v. S [Parenting orders]*[2006] NZFLR 745 (Randerson J) and *HC v. PS* (CA 115/06, 18 Oct. 2006) (CA).

260. In a break from the previous law, section 5 of the Care of Children Act 2004 (rewritten by the Care of Children Amendment Act (No 2) 2013) sets out six principles that are relevant to the assessment of welfare and best interests:[384]

(a) a child's safety must be protected and, in particular, a child must be protected from all forms of violence (as defined in sections 39(2), 10, and 11 of the Family Violence Act 2018) from all persons, including members of the child's family, family group, whānau, hapū, and iwi;
(b) a child's care, development, and upbringing should be primarily the responsibility of his or her parents and guardians;
(c) a child's care, development, and upbringing should be facilitated by ongoing consultation and co-operation between his or her parents, guardians, and any other person having a role in his or her care under a parenting or guardianship order;
(d) a child should have continuity in his or her care, development, and upbringing;
(e) a child should continue to have a relationship with both of his or her parents, and that a child's relationship with his or her family group, whānau, hapū, or iwi should be preserved and strengthened;
(f) a child's identity (including, without limitation, his or her culture, language, and religious denomination and practice) should be preserved and strengthened.

261. Thus, the court must take account, *inter alia*, the desire for continuity, parental and guardian cooperation, links with the wider family group, safety and identity. The majority of the Supreme Court in *Kacem v. Bashir* [385] criticized the Court of Appeal for saying that principle (b) [since the 2013 amendment now found in (d) and (c)] gives particular emphasis to continuing relationships with both parents, meaning that 'there is some priority or weighting as between the various principles'. The majority considered that this was erroneous and [former] principle (b) does not have any presumptive emphasis. This decision was in the context of relocation (*see* paragraph 258 above) where there is no presumption against relocation as a result of [former] principle (b). However, the majority did accept that 'intrinsically principle (b) is likely to be of particular factual significance in relocation cases'. The lines, therefore, become rather thin, illustrated by the Supreme Court's conclusion that the Court of Appeal had not actually determined the facts of the particular case on the basis of its erroneous proposition.

384. When the Family Court (Supporting Children in Court) Legislation Act 2021 comes into force, a further principle will be added: '(g) a child must be given reasonable opportunities to participate in any decision affecting them'.
385. [2011] 2 NZLR 1; [2010] NZFLR 884 (SC) at paras [28] and [29].

262. The mother and father of a child are automatically guardians of the child if they are married, in a civil union or lived together at any time during the pregnancy.[386] The father who claims to be a guardian under this rule can seek a declaration to that effect from the Family Court.[387] A father whose name is, with the mother's agreement, mentioned in the child's birth certificate will also automatically be a guardian.

263. Changes made by the Care of Children Act 2004 mean that most unmarried fathers will be guardians of their children. The residual category where this is not so is made up of fathers who did not cohabit with the mother and whose names are not mentioned in the birth certificate. Such a father can seek appointment as a guardian.[388] In this situation, the court will look to a number of factors before making an appointment. These include the involvement of the applicant in the child's life, but the most important consideration is to ascertain the best interests of the child. The balancing exercise undertaken by the court also takes into account the relationship between the applicant and the mother in determining the best interests of the child. Under a rule introduced by the Care of Children Act 2004, the court must make an appointment 'unless to do so would be contrary to the child's welfare and best interests'. There is in effect a presumption in favour of appointment.[389]

264. 'Day-to-day care' includes care that is provided for one or more specified days or parts of days. The 'role of providing day-to-day care' includes 'exclusive responsibility for the child's day-to-day living arrangements'.[390] 'Contact' is defined to include 'all forms of direct and indirect interaction with the child', which could, for example, mean in some instances face-to-face contact and in others communication by electronic means.

265. The Family Court may appoint another person to be a guardian under section 27 of the Care of Children Act 2004. In this situation, the court may appoint a person as either a sole or an additional guardian, either generally or for a particular purpose. The power to appoint an additional guardian may be useful where a step-parent is taking a full part in the child's life (and a step-parent adoption is thought undesirable), or where a child is being brought up by another member of the family (as can happen especially in Māori and Pacific Island families). In relation to step-parents, the Care of Children Act 2004 introduced a new procedure in sections 21–25. This enables the child's guardians to appoint a step-parent as a guardian

386. Section 17, Care of Children Act 2004. In relation to children born before the commencement of the 2004 Act (1 Jul. 2005), a de facto partner must have been living with the mother, when the child was born, to be an automatic guardian (subs (3)).
387. Section 20, Care of Children Act 2004.
388. Section 19, Care of Children Act 2004.
389. Appointment was refused in *L v. R [Guardianship]* [2009] NZFLR 573 (HC) because of the uncertain effect it might have on the mother's new family and the fact that the boy, now aged 15, was opposed to it.
390. Section 8, Care of Children Act 2004.

without the need for a court order. A court Registrar simply checks that the documents for the appointment are in order. There are some restrictions on the appointment. The step-parent must have shared the care of the child for at least one year and must not have been involved in civil or criminal proceedings involving harm to a child, including child pornography.

266. The Family Court can also appoint additional guardians under section 110(1)(a)–(e) of the Oranga Tamariki Act 1989. For this to happen, the court must be satisfied that the child or young person is in need of care or protection.[391] The court has jurisdiction to appoint the Chief Executive of Oranga Tamariki, an *iwi* social service,[392] a cultural social service, a child and family support service, or any other person. Both this provision and the power in the Care of Children Act 2004 enable foster parents to be appointed guardians, thus gaining greater legal standing in relation to the child in their care. Where a child is in the custody or guardianship of the Chief Executive or similar agency, the latter has control over where the child is to live.[393] However, where the child has been placed in the custody of the Chief Executive under section 78 of the 1989 Act, the court may impose a condition about the residential placement of the child if necessary in the best interests of the child.[394]

267. The Children, Young Persons, and Their Families (Vulnerable Children) Amendment Act 2014 created the category of 'special guardianship' for children removed from their parent and in permanent care.[395] The object is to give the foster parents more security in bringing up their foster child and to limit the extent to which the birth parents can intervene. A special guardianship will provide the guardian with the day-to-day care of the child until he or she reaches 18 years of age, and it is the job of the guardian to specify the kind of ongoing role that he or she will take on in respect of what is best for the child. The legal link between the birth parents and the child is preserved. The court also has a role in specifying how guardianship rights will be shared between the special and existing guardians and which rights (if any) will be held exclusively by the special guardians.

268. Some legislative ambiguity gave rise to the litigation in *Chief Executive of the Ministry for Vulnerable Children v. Grant-Shepherd*.[396] The question was whether a person appointed as an additional guardian under section 110 could also be appointed as a special guardian under section 113A. The High Court overruled the judgment of the Family Court and said that if a person is appointed a guardian

---

391. *See* Part II, Ch. 6. Interim guardianship orders can be made under s 110A.
392. *Iwi* social service refers to an approved Māori tribal social service organization: s. 396, Oranga Tamariki Act 1989.
393. Section 362, Oranga Tamariki Act 1989.
394. *LC v. Ministry of Social Development* [2008] NZFLR 828 (CA). In *Chief Executive of Child, Youth and Family Services v. TK* [2007] NZFLR 12, Simon France J said that the parents, despite remaining guardians, have no right of veto. The Court of Appeal did not address this point in *LC*.
395. The Amendment Act inserted various sections into the 1989 Act, in particular ss 110A, 113A and 113B.
396. [2018] NZHC 1260, [2018] NZFLR 718.

or additional guardian, the court may also appoint them as a special guardian, provided that it is for the purposes specified within the legislation.[397]

269. Cultural issues have proven to be controversial. In *Chief Executive of Oranga Tamariki – Ministry for Children v. BH*,[398] Judge Otene concluded that 'for Māori children at the least, special guardianship is fundamentally irreconcilable with principles of well-being that speak to mana, whakapapa and whanaungatanga [dignity, kinship and family values]'. She refused to grant the orders that had been sought. On the other hand, in a decision a few months later, *Re WH*,[399] Judge Southwick QC expressly disagreed with Judge Otene, one reason being that the principles referred to cannot demote the paramountcy of the well-being and best interests of the child, which requires consideration of all factors affecting a particular child. A special guardianship order was granted in that case. The tensions apparent in these two judgments reflect wider tensions and an ongoing debate about the place of culture and indigenous world views in the family law context.

270. The parents may by deed or will appoint another person to be a guardian upon their death.[400] Such an appointment makes the person a testamentary guardian. If the person making the appointment was a guardian at the time of death, the appointee is automatically a guardian. Where the person was not a guardian at the time of death, the appointee may apply to the Family Court to be made a guardian, and if the Family Court sees fit, it may appoint that person as a guardian. A testamentary guardian does not have an automatic right to have a role in providing the child with day-to-day care but will have the other rights and responsibilities of a guardian.

271. The Care of Children Act states expressly that guardians must act jointly, although this is somewhat confused by the phrase 'in particular, by consulting wherever practicable with the aim of securing agreement'.[401] This rule of joint action does not apply to day-to-day care if one person has the exclusive role of providing such care. Where more than one person is a guardian of a child and they cannot agree on a course of action, any of them may apply to the Family Court for its direction regardless of whether or not the guardians share day-to-day care of the child.[402] A child aged 16 or over who disputes a guardianship decision can also take the matter to the court, where a judge can review the decision and make an appropriate order.[403]

272. One of the most common sources of litigation between guardians arises from disputes over day-to-day care when the child's parents have separated. Most

---

397. *Ibid.*, at [20].
398. *Chief Executive of Oranga Tamariki - Ministry for Children v. BH* [2021] NZFC 210, [2021] NZFLR 201 at para. [39].
399. *Re WH* [2021] NZFC 4090, [2021] NZFLR 216, especially at para. [70].
400. Section 26, Care of Children Act 2004.
401. Section 16(5), Care of Children Act 2004.
402. Section 46R, Care of Children Act 2004.
403. Section 46, Care of Children Act 2004.

disputes are resolved before they get to a full court hearing, formerly either through the help of Family Court approved counsellors, or after a mediation conference chaired by a Family Court judge.[404] Legislation passed in 2013 and in force from March 2014 replaced both of these mechanisms with 'parenting information programmes' and 'FDR',[405] the latter being a form of mandatory mediation. Once a matter reaches the Family Court, the judge can try to avoid a full hearing, for instance, by means of a settlement conference or occasionally counselling.[406] See the discussion above in the General Introduction §4 'The Courts Administering Family and Succession Law'. Where the dispute goes to trial, the child will often be separately represented by a lawyer known as 'lawyer for the child'. Prior to the 2013 legislation, such representation was mandatory, but that was changed so that two conditions have to be satisfied. Section 7 of the Care of Children Act 2004 reads as follows:

> A court may appoint, or direct the Registrar of the court to appoint, a lawyer to represent a child who is the subject of, or who is a party to, proceedings (other than criminal proceedings) under this Act if the court –
>
> (a) has concerns for the safety or well-being of the child; and
> (b) considers an appointment necessary.

273. An allied change is that the court must order that the parties contribute to the cost of the child's lawyer unless the court considers that the order would cause serious hardship to the relevant party or a child.[407] The contribution is one-third of the costs to be paid by each party, with the state paying the remaining third. The same costs recovery rule applies to reports ordered by the court, such as a psychologist's report. In determining which parent should have day-to-day care, there is no presumption that one parent will be better because of that parent's gender.[408] The court resolves questions of day-to-day care by granting a parenting order. Section 48 of the Care of Children Act 2004 expressly envisages that both parties may, in appropriate cases, be granted day-to-day care, that is, with different times specified. There has been a trend, predating the 2004 Act, for the court to grant a shared

404. Sections 7A–19A, Family Proceedings Act 1980.
405. *See* especially the Family Disputes Resolution Act 2013 and ss 46D–46F and 47B, Care of Children Act 2004. The 2014 changes have been the subject of a critical ministerial report: The Final Report of the Independent Panel Examining the 2014 Family Justice Reforms *Te Korowai Ture ā-Whānau* (Ministry of Justice, Wellington 2019). As a result, the Family Court (Supporting Children in Court) Legislation Act 2021 (when in force) amends s 11(2) of the Family Dispute Resolution Act 2014 by adding '(ba) ensure that the children who are the subject of the dispute are given any reasonable opportunities to participate in the decisions affecting them that the FDR provider considers appropriate'.
406. Sections 46P and 46Q, Care of Children Act 2004.
407. Sections 131 and 135A, Care of Children Act 2004.
408. Section 4(2), Care of Children Act 2004.

parenting order, instead of 'custody' to one party and 'access' to the other. The 2004 Act reinforces the trend, as well as refashioning the terminology.[409]

274. To assist it to decide what is best for the welfare and best interests of the child, the court will have the benefit of a social worker's report and may also seek reports from specialists such as child psychologists and psychiatrists. The court will consider the overall physical, mental, emotional, cultural and religious well-being of the child. The court will be mindful of other factors such as the degree of bonding with the respective parents, the desire for stability in the child's life and the undesirability of splitting up siblings.

275. Applications for a parenting order can be made by the parents, a step-parent or a guardian, and by other persons only with the leave of the court.[410] There is no presumption that in a dispute between parents and non-parents, the parents should be favoured.[411] In all such cases, the welfare and best interests of the child are the paramount consideration.

276. Where the role of providing day-to-day care is granted to one parent, it is usual for the other parent to have contact with the child.[412] Two provisions in the Care of Children Act 2004 reinforce the desirability of ensuring that both parents maintain links with the child. First, section 47A requires that an application for a parenting order be accompanied by a statement of whether and how the other parent (or other persons where the dispute involves a non-parent) is to play a role with the child. Second, section 52 obliges a court that proposes to grant one person exclusive day-to-day care to consider what contact the other parent should have.

277. Special rules used to apply where there has been violence.[413] Broadly speaking, the court could grant unsupervised contact (or, far less likely, day-to-day care) to the violent party only if it was satisfied that the child would be safe. A 'violent party' was one: (i) who had a protection order under the Family Violence Act 2018 against him or her in favour of the other party or a child or (ii) who had an allegation of physical or sexual violence towards the other party or a child proven against them. The significance was in part that a protection order could be made on

409. However, other statutes such as the Oranga Tamariki Act 1989 still retain 'custody' language. The usage in the Child Support Act changed from April 2015 when amendments came into force replacing, for example, the word 'custodian' with 'receiving carer'.
410. Section 47, Care of Children Act 2004.
411. *H v. D* [1974] 2 NZLR481, following the House of Lords in *J v. C* [1970] AC 668. The point is reinforced by the High Court decision in *K v. G* [2004] NZFLR 1105 (Gendall and Ellen France JJ). In *FES v. SAKS [Parenting orders]* [2011] NZFLR 320, the Family Court gave day-to-day care to a 15-year-old's aunt because of hostility to the mother. In *KMT v. RAB [Parenting order]* [2011] NZFLR 170, a Māori mother handed her baby over to friends, who were given day-to-day care, partly because there was conflict between the birth mother and father.
412. Section 48(3), Care of Children Act 2004.
413. Sections 58–62, Care of Children Act 2004. The rules were changed by amending legislation passed in 2011 and then, as explained in the text, repealed by the Care of Children Amendment Act (No. 2) Act 2013, in force from 31 Mar. 2014.

the basis of psychological abuse, not merely physical or sexual abuse. Under section 59 of the Care of Children Act 2004, as redrafted in 2013, if the court is not satisfied that the child will be safe with the relevant person, it can order that contact be 'supervised'. Supervision may be done by an approved provider or a particular person, such as a family member or friend, whom the court has approved. Section 5A has a more general rule requiring the court, when determining parenting and guardianship proceedings under the 2004 Act, to take into account the existence of a protection order under the Family Violence Act 2018, the circumstances in which the order was made, and the written reasons for it. Also to be taken into account are any family violence offences, and any relevant safety concerns notified under the 2018 Act by an assessor or service provider. The Family Court (Supporting Children in Court) Legislation Act 2021 adds a new subsection to section 5A:

> (1A) In taking into account the principle in section 5(a), the court must have regard to—
> (a) the purpose of the Family Violence Act 2018, under which an order specified in subsection (1)(b) was made; and
> (b) the principles set out in section 4 of that Act guiding the achievement of that purpose.

278. Common disputes arising between guardians involve the important matters described in section 16 above (paragraph 255). The biggest cases are often relocation cases of which *Kacem v. Bashir* is an example.[414] Another example is education. *Cavanagh v. Cavanagh* was a case where the separated parents could not agree over which school to send their daughter to.[415] The Pākehā (non-Māori) father applied to the Family Court for directions about which school the child should attend. He argued that if his daughter attended a Māori-immersion school his relationship would be harmed as he would not be able to connect culturally or talk about things that his daughter had done at school. The father would therefore prefer a Catholic school of his choice. In the alternative, the mother argued that their daughter should go to a Māori-immersion school in order to connect her with her culture and assist in forming a strong cultural identity. The judge engaged in an analysis of the law regarding the balancing of the factors contained in section 5 of the Care of Children Act. She noted that every principle aside from (a), relating to a child's safety, is engaged in this case, and each must be considered in turn, it being possible that one or more be given greater or lesser weight depending upon the circumstances. The judge thus ordered a compromise of a third, bilingual school. In making this decision, she acknowledged that the continuity factor contained in section 5(d) would be defeated by changing school, but all other factors would be served by this compromise.

---

414. [2011] 2 NZLR 1, [2010] NZFLR 884 (SC). *See* above para. 261.
415. [2017] NZHC 1546, [2017] NZFLR 701. In *JAPM v. MEF [Guardianship]* [2008] NZFLR 816, the mother wanted a 13-year-old daughter to attend a Presbyterian school, whereas the father wanted her to attend a Catholic school. The court found in favour of the mother because this accorded with the girl's views and it represented more of an extension of the education she had had previously. Similarly, in *Keen v. Bradford* [2020] NZHC 2213, [2020] NZFLR 638, on appeal the High Court ordered that the child shift from a Catholic school to a state one.

279. Vaccination has been a source of dispute, exacerbated by the Covid-19 pandemic. In one case, which fell under the Oranga Tamariki Act 1989, the court emphasized that the question was fact specific to the particular child, but ordinary child vaccinations in accordance with Ministry of Health guidelines were ordered as there were no personal reasons why the child in question should not be vaccinated.[416] On the other hand, in another case, Covid vaccination was not mandated largely based on the 12-year-old boy's opposition to being vaccinated.[417]

280. Guardians can consent on behalf of a child to medical, surgical and dental procedures.[418] However, the consent of a married child, one in a civil union, or one aged 16 or over will be as valid as if the child were an adult. Following the House of Lords decision in *Gillick v. West Norfolk and Wisbech Area Health Authority*,[419] it is commonly understood that the consent of younger children will be valid, depending on their level of maturity and understanding.

281. Guardianship terminates automatically upon the child's marriage, civil union, entry into a de facto relationship, reaching the age of 18, or adoption.[420] A court can remove a guardian from office but, if the guardian is a parent, only on very narrow grounds. In the latter situation, the court must be satisfied that 'the parent is unwilling to perform or exercise the duties, powers, rights, and responsibilities of a guardian, or that the parent is for some grave reason unfit to be a guardian of the child'.[421]

282. A child may be placed under the guardianship of the court, commonly known as a 'wardship'.[422] The wardship power was inherited from the British common law, under which the High Court is *parens patriae*, with special responsibility for minors and people with disabilities. For a long time in New Zealand, wardship was solely within the jurisdiction of the High Court. However, amendments passed in 1998 extended the jurisdiction to the Family Court. The jurisdiction may be invoked by a wide range of persons, including the child and any other person with leave of the court. Where a child is made a ward of court, someone else, for example, the Chief Executive Oranga Tamariki, will be appointed to act as the court's agent. Wardship may be used in many situations, but one of the controversial areas is where guardians object to medical treatment which doctors consider

---

416. *GF v. Chief Executive of Oranga Tamariki – Ministry for Children* [2020] NZFC 8449, [2020] NZFLR 860.
417. *Long v. Steine* [2022] NZFC 251 at para. [50] (boy was held to be *Gillick* competent).
418. Section 36, Care of Children Act 2004.
419. [1986] 1 AC 112. *See* further discussion above at para. [236] and following. In *Hawthorne v. Cox* [2008] 1 NZLR 409; [2008] NZFLR 1, Heath J accepted that *Gillick* applied in New Zealand and was reflected in the Care of Children Act 2004. In *ARB v. KLB [Guardianship dispute]* [2011] NZFLR 290 followed *Gillick* in a case about the choice of a doctor and dentist for a 14-year-old girl.
420. Section 28, Care of Children Act 2004.
421. Section 29, Care of Children Act 2004.
422. Sections 30–35, Care of Children Act 2004.

necessary in the child's interests.[423] In one case, wardship was used to prevent the televising of an interview with a child who had been declared to be in need of care and protection under the Oranga Tamariki 1989.[424] The extent of wardship powers is also illustrated by a case where an order was made restricting the involvement of a pregnant mother in the filming of her labour and giving birth. Controversially, the High Court judge held that the order could relate to an unborn child.[425]

283. New Zealand has ratified the Hague Convention on the Civil Aspects of International Child Abduction.[426] The Convention applies where a child has been abducted from one Convention country to another and provides for the return of the child to the child's country of habitual residence. The abduction must be in breach of the other parent's 'rights of custody' which include rights of access.[427] A New Zealand court may refuse to order the return of a child if a year has elapsed and the child is settled, the applicant was not actually exercising rights of custody,[428] the applicant had consented to or acquiesced in the removal of the child, there was a grave risk of physical or psychological harm or of the child's being placed in an intolerable situation,[429] the child objects, or human rights and fundamental freedoms are at stake.[430] The Supreme Court had to deal with a case where a year had elapsed and the child had become settled in New Zealand.[431] The question was how the residual discretion to order return was to be exercised. The majority held that it was necessary to balance the welfare and best interests of the child with the deterrence policy of the Convention. Where, for instance, the abducting party had engaged in misconduct such as concealment, return was more likely to be ordered. These rules were applied in the case of *Simpson v. Hamilton* where, although the girl's mother had engaged in misconduct, a significant amount of time had elapsed (five years) and the girl strongly objected to being returned to Germany. Further, the

423. *Re J (an infant) B and B v. Director-General of Social Welfare* [1996] 2 NZLR 134 (CA) (Jehovah's Witness parents objecting to blood transfusions), *Re Norma* [1992] NZFLR 445 (Samoan family wishing to use traditional medicine) and a series of widely publicized cases involving a boy whose parents objected to chemotherapy treatment to deal with cancer: *Healthcare Otago Ltd v. Williams-Holloway* [1999] NZFLR 792, 794, 798, 804, 812 and *Newspapers Publishers Association of New Zealand Inc. v. Family Court* [1999] 2 NZLR 344. In *Re C; Hutt District Health Board v. B [Guardianship: life support]*[2011] NZFLR 873, Mallon J used the wardship powers to make a declaration that a nutrition tube did not need to be reinserted into a 7-year-old child who had a terminal genetic condition and who was expected to die within a matter of days or weeks. Given the child's condition and the evidence that the procedure carried risks in itself, it was held that it was not in the child's best interests to have the operation.

424. *Child, Youth and Family Services v. TVNZ* [2006] NZFLR 241, Winkelmann J.

425. *Re an Unborn Child* [2003] 1 NZLR 115 (Heath J).

426. Part 2, Subpart 4, Care of Children Act 2004. The Convention is set out in Schedule 1 of the Act.

427. *Gross v. Boda* [1995] 1 NZLR 569.

428. The Court of Appeal in *Ryan v. Phelps* [1999] NZFLR 865 took a very broad approach to this phrase in a situation where the mother who had gone to the United States wanted the children returned to Australia. It was held that she was continuously exercising her right to determine the children's place of residence, which was a right of custody under Australian law.

429. The courts take the view that there is a heavy onus on the party seeking to raise this ground: for example, *see Smith v. Adam* [2007] NZFLR 447 (CA).

430. Section 13, Care of Children Act 2004.

431. *Secretary for Justice v. HJ* [2007] NZFLR 309 (Elias CJ in the minority, favouring the view that the sole test should be the welfare and best interests of the child).

child's lawyer for a child reported that Anna was very happy at her school and had made good friendships but remained in a fragile and vulnerable state. Consequently, it was concluded that 'the custody rights that the Hague Convention was designed to protect could not currently be exercised'.[432] The Supreme Court refused leave for a further appeal, in effect upholding the Court of Appeal's conclusions.[433]

284. As noted, a grave risk to the child may be a reason for not ordering return. In general, this is a very hard reason to satisfy, especially where the evidence is mainly about the potential harm to the parent. However, the Court of Appeal eased the test slightly in *LRR v COL*,[434] where Goddard J said 'the impact of return on the abducting parent may be relevant to an assessment of the impact of return on the child'. The party opposing return needs to provide the factual foundation for this.

285. Under Article 15 of the Convention, the country to which a child has been abducted can seek an advisory opinion from a court in the country from which the child was abducted. In *Fairfax v. Ireton*, [435] the Court of Appeal held that a New Zealand court, faced with such a request, should provide answers only on domestic law and not on the application of the Convention itself.

432. *Simpson v. Hamilton* [2019] NZCA 579, at [84].
433. *Simpson v. Hamilton* [2020] NZSC 42, [2020] NZFLR 37.
434. *LRR v. COL* [2020] NZCA 209, [2020] 2 NZLR 610, [2020] NZFLR 98 at para. [93] and following.
435. [2009] 3 NZLR 289; [2009] NZFLR 433 (CA).

Chapter 8. Kinship and Relationships of Affinity

286. On the whole, New Zealand law gives priority to parents as guardians. The opportunities for other kin to obtain guardianship, day-to-day care and contact rights are limited.[436] Step-parents have better rights than kin to apply for such orders, but, in many other respects, step-parents have few rights and responsibilities unless they adopt the child or are appointed an additional guardian.

287. However, the Oranga Tamariki Act 1989 gives much greater recognition to the wider kin, including the Māori *whānau*.[437] Where a child is abused or neglected or has engaged in juvenile crime, the family group conference has a central role in deciding what should happen to the child.

288. Kin has no rights to property *inter vivos*. Certain relatives are, however, entitled to a share of an estate on an intestacy and have rights to claim under the Family Protection Act 1955.[438]

---

436. *See* Part II, Ch. 7.
437. *See* Part II, Ch. 6.
438. Part IV.

Part III. Matrimonial Property Law

Chapter 1. Rights and Obligations of Spouses

§1. General Principles

289. The principal legislation governing matrimonial property law in New Zealand is the Property (Relationships) Act 1976. The Act is by and large a deferred community property regime and, therefore, will generally not affect property ownership until an application to the court under the Act is made.[439] Usually, such an application will be made after the parties have separated. However, it is possible for the parties to a happy marriage or relationship to seek an order dividing their property.[440] This may occur for several reasons, one of which is possible taxation advantages in shifting title to property from one party to another. The provisions in the Act for relationship property agreements, used most commonly to settle cases after separation, may also be used during the course of a happy marriage or relationship.[441]

290. The Act takes its objectives from the purposes section, section 1M. In summary, this is to reform the law; to recognize the equal contribution of parties to a marriage partnership, civil union or de facto relationship; to provide for a just division of the parties' relationship property when the marriage, union or relationship ends by separation or death and in certain other circumstances, while taking account of the interests of any children. Section 1N also sets out four principles:

(a) the equal status of men and women;
(b) that all forms of contribution are treated as equal;
(c) the need to have regard to the economic advantages and disadvantages that arise from separation; and
(d) the desire to resolve questions 'as inexpensively, simply, and speedily as is consistent with justice'.

439. Section 19, Property (Relationships) Act 1976.
440. Section 23, Property (Relationships) Act 1976.
441. For example, *An application by Roberts* [1993] NZFLR 731 and *CIR v. Van Doorne* [1983] NZLR 495.

291. Overall, this means that the Act is heavily biased in favour of an equal division of relationship property. In certain circumstances, it also looks at the contributions as a whole, not contributions to particular items of property as was the position previously.[442] However, very significant amendments were made to the law by legislation passed in 2001 and in force from 1 February 2002. The new legislation, while maintaining and in some ways reinforcing the emphasis on equal sharing, also reintroduced an element of greater judicial discretion where the income and living standards of the separating parties are significantly different, as will be discussed later.

292. The original Act (called the Matrimonial Property Act 1976) applied to legal marriages only and also did not apply where one of the spouses died. As part of the reforms passed in 2001, the regime was extended to the parties to a 'de facto relationship' (including a same-sex one)[443] and also, with some small modifications, to the situation where a partner dies. Following the creation of civil unions by the Civil Union Act 2004, the 1976 Act was further applied to these unions. In general, the same rules apply to all three forms of domestic partnership: marriage, civil union and de facto relationship. Obviously, the definition of 'de facto relationship' is unique to such relationships, and there are differences between marriages and civil unions on the one hand and de facto relationships on the other, where the partnership is one of short duration.

293. On 23 July 2019, the Law Commission presented a three-year review of the law relating to the division of relationship property on separation.[444] The Commission concluded that the law in the Property (Relationships) Act 1976 is outdated and no longer fit for purpose. As part of its final report, the Commission recommended:

- that if a family home was owned by one partner prior to the relationship, then only the change in the value of the home during the relationship should be shared;
- that the courts be given greater powers to divide trust property. This would apply when the trust holds property produced, preserved or enhanced by the relationship;
- introducing Family Income Sharing Arrangements (FISAs) which would require some partners to share income for a limited period following separation. The purpose being to alleviate any economic disparities between separated partners;
- placing the children's best interests at the forefront of relationship property matters, specifically when considering occupation of the family home;
- improving the way relationship property matters are resolved in practice to address behaviour that causes delays and increases costs.

442. *See* generally the Matrimonial Property Act 1963.
443. The definition of the phrase 'de facto relationship' is discussed above: Part II, Ch. 3.
444. Law Commission ***Review of the Property (Relationships) Act 1976 – Te Arotake i te Property (Relationships) Act 1976*** **(R143, Wellington 2019).**

In response, the government put the recommendations on hold until a further review of the laws related to succession had been completed, as recommended by the Commission. As that review has now been completed,[445] the government is in a position to revisit the whole system, relationship property and succession concurrently.

§2. The Household Expenses

294. By common law, a married woman could act as an agent for her husband for the purpose of household management to keep it adequately supplied with the necessities of their standard of living. This presumption arose largely from cohabitation of the spouses and has now been removed by section 49 of the Property (Relationships) Act 1976. A husband or wife may still act as an agent for their spouse, but this will arise through the ordinary rules of agency.

295. Generally speaking, responsibility for household expenses rests with the individual partner. However, the question of household debts may become important when relationship property is being divided. Unless a debt is a 'relationship debt', liability for it rests with the debtor. Relationship debts are, however, taken into account in the division of property, so that effectively they are shared. Section 20(1) of the Property (Relationships) Act 1976 defines a relationship debt to be the one incurred:

(a) by the spouses or partners jointly; or
(b) in the course of a common enterprise carried on by the spouses or partners, whether alone or together with another person; or
(c) for the purpose of acquiring, improving, or maintaining relationship property; or
(d) for the benefit of both spouses or partners in the course of managing the affairs of the household; or
(e) the purpose of bringing up any child of the marriage, civil union, or de facto relationship.

Household debts are most likely to fall within (d) and will, therefore, usually be shared. Debts which do not fall within the above definition are 'personal debts' and remain the entire responsibility of the party who owes the debt.

§3. The Matrimonial Home

296. The matrimonial home, known as 'the family home' since the 2001 amendments, may be owned in several different ways. Title may be in the name of only one of the partners. The partners may own the home jointly, either as joint tenants or as tenants in common. In the absence of words creating a tenancy in common, a

445. Law Commission ***He arotake i te āheinga ki ngā rawa a te tangata ka mate ana | Review of succession law: rights to a person's property on death*** **(R145, Wellington, 2021).**

joint tenancy is presumed.[446] A joint tenancy means that the property is owned equally, although it is possible for a co-owner to apply to the court claiming that the beneficial ownership is other than equal. Another important feature of a joint tenancy is the right of survivorship, that is, where one party dies, the other automatically becomes the sole owner. Where a home is co-owned, either party can apply to the court for an order that the home be sold.[447] If the applicant owns half or more of the home, the court is bound to make the order unless there is some good reason for not doing so.

297. An alternative form of ownership is to register the house under the Joint Family Homes Act 1964. This procedure is available only to married couples. To do this, the following circumstances must be present:[448]

(1) Settlement is made by the registered proprietor(s).
(2) The settlor/settlors must be able to repay all debts other than those charged on the property without the aid of that property.
(3) Neither spouse is the owner of another joint family home.
(4) The spouses reside, or will reside within six months, in a dwelling house on the land.

Additional requirements for registration as a joint family home include a notice published in newspapers. If this is not done, creditors have the same recompense against parties for a period of two years as if the home was held only in one party's name. The rationale underlying this is that registration cannot occur to defeat potential creditors' claims. The notice allows creditors to lodge objections.

298. At one time, registering a home as a joint family home was very popular. It provided tax breaks, assisted people in getting cheap mortgages from the state and offered protection against creditors. While such protection is still available, the other advantages have largely disappeared, with the result that few registrations now take place. A move to repeal the Joint Family Homes Act 1964 was promoted by a Member of Parliament but was not passed.

299. The law which impacts on the family home most significantly is that which operates when the parties separate. Orders for the division of the home (and family chattels) can be made irrespective of strict legal and beneficial ownership. The definition of family home contained in the Property (Relationships) Act[449] is as follows:

Family home –

446. Section 47, Land Transfer Act 1917.
447. Section 339, Property Law Act 2007.
448. Section 3, Joint Family Homes Act 1964.
449. Section 2, Property (Relationships) Act 1976.

(a) means the dwellinghouse that either or both of the spouses or partners use habitually or from time to time as the only or principal family residence, together with any land, buildings, or improvements appurtenant to that dwellinghouse and used wholly or principally for the purposes of the household; and
(b) includes a joint family home.

300. In some cases, the family home may be a homestead. This is especially likely to arise when the home is on a farm. A homestead is where the home is on an un-subdivided piece of land not used wholly or principally for the purposes of the household.[450] Whether or not there is a homestead is a factual assessment. Sometimes, if the land is not being run as a serious business and is used for various family purposes, the whole may amount to the family home. Otherwise, it will be a household. The significance of this is that the house will have to be notionally detached from the rest of the land, and the house and land will be divided according to different rules. The Court of Appeal in *Hyde v. Hyde*,[451] in considering whether there is a homestead or a family home with large surroundings, has re-emphasized a common-sense approach. A court should first consider whether the family home definition is satisfied and, only if it is not, should it go on to consider the definition of homestead. The Court of Appeal rejected a so-called global approach where a much broader assessment is made of the land.

301. Section 8 of the Property (Relationships) Act 1976 provides that the family home, whenever acquired, is relationship property and thus is subject to the division rules of the Act. One qualification on this is that one of the parties must own the home at least partially. If a family trust or family company owns the home, then it is prima facie beyond the jurisdiction of the court.[452] However, where there is no home or it is not owned by one of the parties, the court can make up for this by ordering that the parties share equally in some other part of the relationship property.[453] For a home to qualify as the family home, it must have been used as such during the marriage, a subsequent period of combined occupation following dissolution not qualifying.[454] This rule presumably also applies to civil unions.

302. The home (and family chattels)[455] are to be divided equally under section 11. This rule of equal division is subject to two exceptions: (i) marriages, civil

450. *See* definition of 'homestead' in s. 2, Property (Relationships) Act 1976. *See also* s. 12.
451. [2010] 1 NZLR 224; [2009] NZFLR 594. *See also* the follow-up High Court decision in *Hyde v. Hyde* [2011] NZFLR 35 where the land in question was finally divided.
452. *See* the discussion below (para. 329) of *Clayton v. Clayton [Vaughan Road Property Trust]* [2016] NZSC 29, [2016] 1 NZLR 551, [2016] NZFLR 230, under which in some circumstances a party's bundle of rights in a trust may count as property that is potentially relationship property available for division under the 1976 Act.
453. Section 11(3), Property (Relationships) Act 1976.
454. *Cossey v. Bach* [1992] 3 NZLR 612; (1992) 9 FRNZ 300.
455. Family chattels are defined in s. 2 of the Property (Relationships) Act 1976, with the definition turning on whether the item was used for 'family purposes'. Furniture, household appliances, cars, even family pets are typical examples of family chattels.

unions and de facto relationships of short duration (covered by sections 14, 14AA and 14A; s 13 prior to the 2001 Amendment Act); and (ii) extraordinary circumstances (covered by section 13; s 14 prior to the 2001 Amendment Act).

303. A marriage, union or relationship of short duration is one that is less than three years, or if the court thinks it just, one that has lasted for a longer period.[456] Richardson J addressed the exercise of the discretion to extend the period in *Martin v. Martin* [457] stating:

> The first part of the subsection imposes a time test. The three-year period is calculated from the date of the marriage up to the date the parties ceased to live together as husband and wife ... Any periods of cohabitation with the motive of reconciliation which were not in excess of three months may be excluded from the computation.
>
> The second is directed at other cases where the Court 'having regard to all the circumstances of the marriage considers it just'. That phrase must refer to the justice of declaring the marriage to be a marriage of short duration: whether it is just to regard the marriage of short duration rather than whether it is just for the parties to share the property equally. So the consequence of finding the marriage was of short duration are not a relevant consideration.
>
> In the context of Section [2E] 'the circumstances of the marriage' must, I think, refer to factors affecting the quality of the marital relationship, the manner in which the parties lived together and the time they did so. On this approach it may be just to treat a marriage which lasted more than three years as a marriage of short duration if, while maintaining the marriage in outward appearances, the parties led essentially separate lives and departed from the mutual sharing and support implicit in the concept of marriage as a partnership.

In summary, the three-year period will be extended only in rare situations, that is, ones where the marriage, union or relationship continued but only as a shell. In computing the length of a marriage or civil union, a prior period of living together as de facto partners is taken into account (likewise, if the parties had preceded one form of registered association by the other form, for example, the parties converted their marriage into a civil union).[458]

304. If there is a marriage or civil union of short duration, the equal division of the home and chattels may be avoided if one of the following three conditions is satisfied:

(a) The asset was owned wholly or substantially by only one party at the time when cohabitation began.

---

456. Section 2E, Property (Relationships) Act 1976.
457. [1979] 1 NZLR 97, 109.
458. Section 2B, 2BAA, 2BA, Property (Relationships) Act 1976.

(b) It was acquired by succession, survivorship, gift or as a beneficiary under a trust.
(c) The contribution to the period of living together by one party clearly was disproportionately greater than that of the other party.

Where the requirements set out in either section 14 or section 14AA have been fulfilled, the equal division rule is replaced by division according to the contributions of the parties to the marriage or civil union. A de facto relationship of short duration is treated differently. In general, according to section 14A, such a relationship is entirely outside the jurisdiction of the Act, but there are exceptions.[459] Where an exception brings the relationship within the Act, division is according to contributions to the relationship.

305. The second exception to an equal division of the home and chattels is found in section 13 of the Property (Relationships) Act 1976. This allows for a departure from the equal division presumption in section 11 in 'extraordinary circumstances that, make equal sharing ... repugnant to justice'. The test for extraordinary circumstances is strict, with Woodhouse J explaining it as follows:[460]

> [T]he phrase 'extraordinary circumstances' refers, I think, to circumstances that must not only be remarkable in degree but also unusual in kind. It is vigorous and powerful language to find in any statute and I am satisfied that it has been chosen quite deliberately to limit the exception to those abnormal situations that will demonstrably seem truly exceptional and which by their nature are bound to be rare.

306. The Court of Appeal held on the facts of *Martin* that the test had not been satisfied. The marriage lasted only three and a half years, and the husband provided the home and the day-to-day finances for the family's living. However, the wife remained at home looking after their child and two children from her previous marriage. Woodhouse J's statement was later reaffirmed by the Court of Appeal in *Wilson v. Wilson* [461] where Richardson J stated:

> Section [13] allows departure from the equal sharing regime only where it is established that there are 'extraordinary circumstances that, in the opinion of the Court, render repugnant to justice' that equal sharing ... right down to the present time, we have emphasized that the just division of the matrimonial property to which the long title of the Act refers must reflect the proper recognition of the presumption of equal contributions of husband and wife to the marriage partnership. The matrimonial home and family chattels are accorded a particularly entrenched protection. It is difficult to envisage any stronger use of language than is reflected in 'extraordinary circumstances' and 'repugnant

459. *See* Part II, Ch. 3 above.
460. *Martin v. Martin* [1979] 1 NZLR 97, 102.
461. [1991] NZFLR 107, 116; (1990) 7 FRNZ 115, 125.

to justice' to emphasize the stringency of the test which has to be satisfied in order to justify departure from the equal sharing regime.

307. In *Joseph v. Johansen,* [462] the wife argued that section 13 applied and that, therefore, she should get a greater share of matrimonial property (as it was then called) than her spouse. The case concerned a situation where the husband was an alcoholic, and as a result, her contributions far outweighed his. In its analysis, the Court of Appeal considered section 13 in the light of section 18(3) (now section 18A), which excludes misconduct from a consideration of the parties' contributions unless it was 'gross and palpable' and has 'significantly affected the extent or value of the relationship property'. The court was careful to point out that section 18 (now section 18A) does not apply to section 13 directly, and alcoholism is not, therefore, in itself enough to satisfy section 13. It may, however, mean that the alcoholic person is able to contribute far less to the marriage, and, if the disparity in contributions between the parties is truly gross, equal division may be departed from.

308. On the facts of *Joseph v. Johansen*, the court awarded the wife 65% of the property. This can be contrasted with *McLaren v. McLaren* [463] where the alcoholism was known of before the marriage, and, therefore, the court declined to depart from the presumption of equal division. Another case involved a relationship where the husband was an abuser and contributed nothing to the relationship.[464] In fact, Judge Inglis believed that when contributions were balanced, the husband found himself decisively in debt to his ex-partner. In combination with the fact that the husband had used the marriage to escape criminal conviction in Zimbabwe, and had lived off of his wife's earnings in New Zealand, such a situation was accordingly judged to be extraordinary.

309. If the court decides that there are extraordinary circumstances within the meaning of section 13, then, as with section 14, 14AA and 14A, the equal division rule is replaced by division according to the contributions of the parties to the marriage, union or relationship.

310. Where there are two potential family homes, only one will be classified as the family home, with the other falling under another classification of property for purposes of division. In the event that two homes were in existence when the parties started living together, section 16 of the Act ameliorates potential unfairness. That section allows the court to make an adjustment to the shares in other relationship property, including the share in the family home, to compensate for the inclusion of only one home in the pool of relationship property.

311. When proceedings are brought under the Property (Relationships) Act 1976, a major question for the court is to decide how to give practical effect to the division of the property. Issues arise such as whether the court should make an order

---

462. [1993] 10 FRNZ 302.
463. [1982] 1 NZFLR 273.
464. *Banda v. Hart* (1998) 17 FRNZ 667, [1998] NZFLR 930.

for sale or occupation of the family home. An order for the sale of the home may leave the parent who is providing the principal care and the children in a poor position as far as accommodation is concerned. However, if the home is left in the possession of one of the parties for any length of time, then this may unfairly lock the other party's funds up so that they cannot be used (e.g., to buy another house). The court has broad discretion in deciding how to resolve this question,[465] but it must 'have particular regard to the need to provide a home for any minor or dependent child of the marriage, civil union, or de facto relationship, and may also have regard to all other relevant circumstances'.[466]

312. One potential problem facing couples is the possibility that the home will be attached by creditors. As a partial protection against this, each spouse or partner has a 'protected interest' in the home.[467] This amounts to half the equity in the home or the 'specified sum', whichever is smaller. The specified sum can be adjusted from time to time and currently is NZD 103,000.[468] The protected interest is not liable for the unsecured personal debts of the other spouse.

§4. Transactions Between Spouses

313. Section 4(3) of the Property (Relationships) Act 1976 removes the common law presumptions of advancement, resulting trust and gift. It is, however, still possible for one spouse (or civil union or de facto partner) to gift property to the other, and prima facie this will be separate property.[469] This will be rebutted where the gift was used for common use and benefit of both spouses or both partners.

314. Although at common law, spouses were denied the capacity to enter into contracts with each other, this rule no longer applies. Married women have full legal capacity,[470] and, as long as relationship property remains undivided under the Property (Relationships) Act 1976, each spouse or partner can deal with his or her property according to the law governing ordinary transactions between strangers.[471] In principle, therefore, there is nothing to prevent spouses or partners from entering into contracts with each other (e.g., for business purposes). The court must be sure, however, that they had the necessary intention under the law of contract to enter into legal relations.[472] Given that this will not always be clear, such contracts should be carefully drafted.

465. Section 27, Property (Relationships) Act 1976 and *Doak v. Turner* [1981] 1 NZLR 18 (CA).
466. Section 28A, Property (Relationships) Act 1976.
467. Section 20B, Property (Relationships) Act 1976.
468. Section 53A, Property (Relationships) Act 1976; Property (Relationships) Specified Sum Order 2002.
469. Section 10(3), Property (Relationships) Act 1976.
470. Section 49, Property (Relationships) Act 1976.
471. Section 19, Property (Relationships) Act 1976.
472. *Balfour v. Balfour* [1919] 2 KB 571.

315. Prior to entering a marriage, civil union or de facto relationship, the parties may make an agreement under Part 6 of the Property (Relationships) Act 1976 and thereby contract out of the statutory regime provided for in the Property (Relationships) Act. Such an agreement may also be entered during or after the marriage, union or relationship. In some instances, the agreement may be made during the course of a happy partnership, in effect implementing the equal division rules for taxation advantages.[473] More commonly, agreements are entered into by way of settling differences between the parties after their relationship has broken down. The agreement may specify that property which would otherwise be relationship property will be separate property, potentially including the family home.

316. The formal requirements of Part 6 need to be complied with strictly if an agreement is not to be set aside. The court does, however, have power to overlook non-compliance where this would not materially prejudice the interests of either party.[474] These requirements are that both parties receive independent legal advice. The agreement is witnessed by a lawyer of the High Court of New Zealand (or if overseas, by a notary public or a solicitor of a Commonwealth country), and both parties must have signed the agreement.[475] The lawyer must certify that the effect and implications of the agreement have been explained. Minors may enter into agreements under section 21I, but if they wish to do so in contemplation of marriage or civil union and have not reached the age of 18, the approval of the court is necessary.

317. An agreement under Part 6 may be challenged under the ordinary rules of law and equity. Much more common, however, is a challenge using the special powers provided for in the Act. Section 21J provides that the court may set aside an agreement where it would cause 'serious injustice' to give effect to the agreement. The factors the court may consider are contained in section 21J(4):

> [T]he Court must have regard to:
>
> (a) the provisions of the agreement;
> (b) the time since the agreement was made;
> (c) whether the agreement was unfair or unreasonable in the light of all the circumstances at the time it was made;
> (d) whether the agreement has become unfair or unreasonable in the light of any changes in circumstances since it was made (whether or not those changes were foreseen by the parties);
> (e) the fact that the parties wished to achieve certainty as to the status, ownership, and division of property by entering into the agreement;
> (f) any other matters that the Court considers relevant.

473. *CIR v. Van Doorne* [1983] NZLR 495.
474. Section 21H, Property (Relationships) Act 1976. The onus of proof lies with the party wishing the agreement to be upheld: *Fowler v. Leicester* [1994] NZFLR 241; (1993) 11 FRNZ 470.
475. Section 21F, Property (Relationships) Act 1976.

318. Many agreements have been set aside under these provisions. The court will not do so lightly, but one test which has frequently been used is to compare entitlements under the agreement with the foregone entitlements under the Act. If the difference between the two is sufficiently great, the court is likely to set the agreement aside on the basis that it is or has become unreasonable.[476] This broad discretion has led to the court's setting aside agreements due to the birth of a child[477] and inadequate information being provided to an instructing solicitor.[478]

319. A somewhat different attitude is apparent where the agreement is a prenuptial one rather than a later agreement settling issues on separation or divorce. Where the parties entered into a prenuptial agreement with their eyes open, the court is going to be reluctant to upset it in later years.[479] Likewise, where during cohabitation the parties entered an agreement for taxation advantages, the subsequent breakdown of the partnership will not justify setting aside the agreement.[480]

320. The 2001 amendments made changes designed to make it harder for agreements to be set aside. A test of 'unjust' was replaced with 'serious injustice', and paragraph (e) of section 21J(4) was added. The Court of Appeal in *Harrison v. Harrison* [481] held that in contracting out agreements (less so for settlement agreements), serious injustice was more likely to be shown 'by an unsatisfactory process resulting in inequality of outcome rather than mere inequality of outcome itself'. With respect to paragraph (e), the Court of Appeal rejected the argument that the court could enquire into the states of mind of the parties to see if they really did intend to achieve certainty. This is presupposed. On the facts, the Court of Appeal upheid an agreement that the wife did not greatly wish to make because she did so in order to achieve reconciliation (which did not in the event endure).

321. In giving advice to one party in relation to a Part 6 agreement, the lawyer owes a common law duty of care to the other party. If the advice is negligent, the other party may be able to sue the solicitor for damages.[482] However, it has been held that there is no duty of care to the other party for a failure to provide the lawyer's certificate, as mentioned above in paragraph 316.[483]

476. *Aldridge v. Aldridge* [1983] NZLR 576 and *Docherty v. Docherty* [1983] NZLR 586.
477. *McMahon v. McMahon* (1989) 5 FRNZ 51, [1990] NZFLR 37.
478. *Coxhead v. Coxhead* [1993] 2 NZLR 397; (1993) 10 FRNZ 46.
479. *Wood v. Wood* [1998] 3 NZLR 234 and *Place v. Pleat* [1997] 2 NZLR 354.
480. *Cox v. Cox* [1992] NZFLR 97 (CA).
481. [2005] 2 NZLR 349; [2005] NZFLR 252.
482. *Connell v. Odlum* [1993] 2 NZLR 257 (CA).
483. *Radisich v. Templeton* [2009] 3 NZLR 276; [2009] NZFLR 779 (HC).

Chapter 2. The Marriage Settlement

322. Pre-marriage settlements are not common in New Zealand. Usually, upon marriage, couples continue their financial and property arrangements much as before. Because of the rule that marriage automatically revokes existing wills (except ones made in contemplation of marriage), recently married couples may make out new wills.

323. In a relatively small proportion of cases, marrying couples may enter prenuptial agreements under Part 6 of the Property (Relationships) Act 1976, contracting out of the statutory regime otherwise imposed by that Act. The situations where this happens tend to be where one of the parties is getting married for a second time and wishes to keep existing property separate or where one of the parties has business or professional assets and likewise wishes to keep them separate. The requirements for prenuptial agreements have been discussed above (*see* Chapter 1, §4). As noted, such agreements can be challenged, although there is greater reluctance on the part of the courts to set aside a prenuptial agreement than one entered into at the end of the marriage. Civil union and de facto partners may also enter into Part 6 agreements.

324. Another way in which marriage settlements (or settlements by those involved in civil unions or de facto relationships) can occur is through the creation of a family trust. Property in the name of the trust is owned by the trust and not by the marrying parties, but the husband and wife may be beneficiaries under the trust and even trustees. They are often established for taxation and business reasons and are common in the farming and business sectors. They do not have to be established at the time of marriage but may already exist or be created at some later date. Payments to beneficiaries are usually at the discretion of the trustees. Family trusts are subject to the usual rules applying to trusts (including, for example, the court's power to remove trustees and appoint new ones).[484]

325. Following amendments in 2001, the court has a new power to compensate a disadvantaged party where property has been transferred to a trust.[485] Where relationship property has been transferred after the parties began living together and the effect has been to defeat one party's rights or claims under the Act, the court can compensate that party. The capital of the trust cannot be reached but, as a residual power, if no other remedy is possible, the court may make an order that the claimant be paid part or the whole of the trust's income. There are also powers where relationship property has been transferred to a company (although without even a residual power to reach the company's income).[486]

326. There is also a special power in section 182 of the Family Proceedings Act 1980 under which the court can enquire into the existence of settled property

484. Section 114, Trusts Act 2019.
485. Section 44A–44C, Property (Relationships) Act 1976.
486. Section 44D–44F, Property (Relationships) Act 1976.

(whether by way of an antenuptial or postnuptial settlement) and make orders as it thinks fit. One of the principal restrictions on this power is that it can be exercised only after the marriage or civil union between the parties has been dissolved (and thus does not apply to former de facto partners or separated persons). This provision has tended to be used where there is little relationship property and where the home is owned by the trust.[487] The Supreme Court in *Ward v. Ward* [488] held that, in considering a claim under section 182, the proper approach is to ask what the parties' expectations were at the time of the settlement and then to ask whether those expectations had been defeated by the changed circumstances such as a relationship breakdown. The test was not based on need, hardship or fairness, and there is no equal division rule under section 182 as there is under the Property (Relationships) Act 1976. This decision firmly establishes that section 182, although anomalous, can be used to reach property held by family trusts.

327. Examination of section 182 continued in *Clayton v. Clayton [Claymark Trust].*[489] The Supreme Court in this case took a broader approach than that found in *Ward v. Ward.* First, it held that section 182 involves a two-step process. First, it must be determined that the particular trust is a nuptial settlement. The second step is to assess how to exercise the court's discretion to make orders with respect to the trust. In the first step, the court determined that the correct analysis is to look at the proximity between the settlement on one hand and the marriage on the other. Second, the court pointed out that the rationale underlying section 182 is not the same as that of the Property (Relationships) Act. Therefore, it does not follow that once the first step is satisfied, a 50/50 division will be appropriate. The judge must make a decision on the merits of the particular case. Mr and Mrs Clayton settled out of court after submissions had been made to the Supreme Court, but the court believed the legal question to be important enough to issue a judgment. There was therefore no need for the court to make any orders as to the proper division of property, but it did indicate that in the case before it a 50/50 division may be fair.

328. Further development occurred in yet another Supreme Court decision, *Preston v Preston.*[490] The lower courts had made no award under s 182, mainly because the trust had been set up to protect the husband's children from an earlier marriage. Jurisdiction was accepted, so the issue turned was whether an order should be made. The Supreme Court rejected the zero award and opted for a 15% share for the ex-wife. This was modest given the following: the husband's children were the final beneficiaries, the source of the assets (essentially from the first marriage), and the short length of the marriage (five years). *Preston* is a further signal that the Supreme Court is continuing to interpret s 182 in a generous but flexible way. Yet, the provision is anomalous and, in the light of the Law Commission's report, wholesale revision of the law relating to trusts and relationship property is likely.

---

487. For example, *Kidd v. Kidd Re Polkinghorne Trust* (1988) 4 NZFLR 756, *Chrystall v. Chrystall* [1993] NZFLR 772 and *A v. A* [1999] 2 NZLR 199.
488. [2010] 2 NZLR 31.
489. [2016] NZSC 30, [2016] 1 NZLR 590, [2016] NZFLR 189.
490. *Preston v. Preston* [2021] NZSC 154, [2021] NZFLR 304.

329. The ability of the Property (Relationships) Act 1976 to reach property held in a trust was tested by a second decision involving the same parties, *Clayton v. Clayton [Vaughan Road Property Trust].*[491] In this second decision, the trust deed for the Vaughan Road Property Trust (VRPT) allowed Mr Clayton, as 'Principal Family Member', to appoint all of the assets of the trust to himself and remove all other beneficiaries, without being encumbered by any fiduciary duty to any of the beneficiaries. In the judgment of the Supreme Court concerning this trust, there were two primary questions. The first was whether the trust was a sham or an illusion because of the ability of Mr Clayton to assign all assets to himself. The Supreme Court answered this question in the negative for reasons unimportant to this text. The second was whether the assets amounted to relationship property were available for equal division. This second question was answered in two parts. First, the Supreme Court found that the broadly drafted definition of 'property' in section 2 of the Property (Relationships) Act, so far as it refers to 'any other right or interest', must be given an expansive definition in order to fit the aims, objectives and social context of the Act. Therefore, the power to appoint all of the assets of the trust to himself can be seen as 'property', which the court then classified as 'relationship property'. The second part of the question relates to the value of this power. The court found that there was no reason to differentiate the value of the power to appoint all the assets from the value of the assets that the power related to. Therefore, one hundred per cent of the assets could be divided in half and distributed equally. The takeaway from this case is that powers to control a trust may constitute 'property' under the Property (Relationships) Act. Cases following *Clayton v. Clayton [Vaughan Road Property Trust]* have suggested that this will only be the case where the powers are unfettered by any kind of fiduciary duty to beneficiaries or where the context of the case is commercial rather than relationship property.[492]

491. [2016] NZSC 29, [2016] 1 NZLR 551, [2016] NZFLR 230. Followed, among other cases by the Privy Council on appeal from the Cook Islands Court of Appeal in *Webb v. Webb* [2020] UKPC 22, [2021] 2 NZLR 376, and *Higgins v. Higgins* [2020] NZFC 9654, [2020] NZFLR 898.

492. *Da Silva v. Da Silva* [2016] NZHC 2064, *Brkic v. White* [2021] NZCA 670; [2021] NZFLR 344, and *Pisidia Holdings Ltd v. Darby* [2019] NZHC 1216, [2019] NZFLR 96 (among other cases).

Chapter 3. The Legal Matrimonial Regime

330. The Property (Relationships) Act 1976 is the principal source of law relating to the division of property on separation or divorce.[493] It contains rules determining which property is shared under the Act and further rules setting out how that property is to be divided. Broadly speaking, relationship property is shared equally, but there are several exceptions to this.

331. By legislation that came into force on 1 February 2002, the number of exceptions was reduced. At the same time, however, the court was given an important new power – to order a compensatory payment where the income and living standards of one spouse are likely to be significantly higher than the other because of the division of functions within the relationship. This new power has the potential to reverse the impact of equal sharing in a large proportion of cases.

332. As has been mentioned elsewhere, the new legislation made widespread changes, including the extension of the law to de facto partners and to the survivor following the death of the other party. By the Civil Union Act 2004, the regime was also extended to civil unions.

333. An application under the Act must initially be brought before the Family Court. Nevertheless, either on its own initiative or on the application of one of the parties, the Family Court may order that proceedings be removed to the High Court. This is at the particular judge's discretion and will only be done in circumstances where the judge considers that the High Court is the more appropriate venue. In determining this, the judge must have regard to the following:[494]

(a) the complexity of the proceedings or of any question in issue in the proceedings;
(b) any proceedings before the High Court that are between the same parties and that involve related issues;
(c) any other matter that the Judge considers relevant in the circumstances.

Section 39 of the Property (Relationships) Act 1976 gives parties to proceedings that have been determined an automatic right of appeal to the High Court as long as the application is made within twenty-eight days of the decision. If an appeal is to be heard, section 39(4) gives the court being appealed from the discretion to waive the requirement that the appellant provide security for costs. Section 39B provides a further appeal to the Court of Appeal.

334. The circumstances in which an order may be made under the Property (Relationships) Act are found in section 25(2) and are:

(a) in the case of a marriage or civil union:

---

493. *See* B Atkin *Relationship Property in New Zealand* (3rd ed, LexisNexis, Wellington, 2018)
494. Section 38A, Property (Relationships) Act 1976.

(i) that the husband and wife or civil union partners are living apart (whether or not they have continued to live in the same residence) or are separated; or
(ii) that the marriage or civil union has been dissolved; or

(b) in the case of a de facto relationship, that the de facto partners no longer have a de facto relationship with each other; or
(c) that one spouse or partner is endangering the relationship property or seriously diminishing its value by gross mismanagement, or by wilful or reckless dissipation of property or earnings; or
(d) that either spouse or partner is an undischarged bankrupt.

Upon dissolution of a marriage or civil union, either party may apply for orders under the Act as of right within twelve months and, where more than twelve months have elapsed since the dissolution, with the leave of the court.[495] Where a de facto relationship has ended, an application can be made within three years, again with a discretion vested in the court to extend the period.

335. Section 25(1) states that, where an application is made under the Act, the court may make such orders as it thinks just (subject to the provisions of the Act), in determining respective shares of relationship property, or any other order it is empowered to make under the Act. The court may also use the power contained in section 25(3) to make any order at any time relating to status, ownership, vesting, or possession of any specific property as it considers just. This power is, again, subject to the provisions of the Act.

336. The Act applies to movables and immovables within New Zealand, and movables outside New Zealand if either party was domiciled in New Zealand.[496] As a result, the New Zealand Court of Appeal has said:[497]

> Because the Act does not apply to immovables situate outside of New Zealand, we do not think such property can be said to fall within the classifications of matrimonial property and separate property in Sections 8 and 9, or within the provisions in respect of the matrimonial home in Sections 11 and 12. To so classify a foreign immovable is to apply the Act to it, which Section 7 does not authorise.

337. Where property is converted from immovable to movable between the date of separation and the date of hearing, it has been held that the latter date determines whether the property is to be treated as immovable or movable for the purposes of the Act.[498] In addition, section 7 leaves open the common law with regard as to categorization of property as movable or immovable. As a result, in

495. Section 24, Property (Relationships) Act 1976.
496. Section 7, Property (Relationships) Act 1976.
497. *Samarawickrema v. Samarawickrema* [1995] 1 NZLR 14, 18; (1994) 12 FRNZ 482, 486; [1994] NZFLR 913, 917.
498. *Shepherd v. Shepherd* [2009] NZFLR 226 (HC).

Smaal v. Boersma, [499] it was decided that the law of the country in which the property is situated also determines whether that property is movable or immovable.

338. Section 7A allows the spouses to agree that the Act will apply to foreign immovables, but such an agreement must be evidenced in writing. An agreement may state that the law of a foreign country will govern. This is subject to a number of restrictions including the following:[500]

(1) The agreement must have been made on or before marriage, civil union or de facto relationship. This may be hard to satisfy in some situations. For example, a South African agreement contracting out of that country's community property regime was held to fall outside section 7A(2) because it was made after the parties' de facto relationship began (even though it was before their marriage).[501]
(2) Merely specifying that New Zealand law is not to apply is insufficient. The other country must be specified.
(3) The agreement must either be in writing, or be otherwise valid in the country whose law applies.
(4) The court has an overriding duty to ensure justice is done, and, therefore, may set aside the agreement if it would be contrary to justice or public policy.

The court requires expert evidence of the effect of any agreement under the relevant foreign law. Without such evidence, the agreement will not override the New Zealand Act.[502]

339. Despite the rule that the Act does not apply to foreign immovables, the courts have nevertheless found ways of indirectly taking a foreign immovable into account. *Walker v. Walker*[503] was a case concerning the husband's purchase of foreign realty with proceeds of the sale of 'matrimonial' property after separation. The Court of Appeal held that, as the shares to which the parties were entitled were to be determined as at the date of separation,[504] the subsequent purchase could in effect be ignored, and the wife was, therefore, awarded a full half share of the property in New Zealand, calculated as of the separation date.

340. However, where the overseas immovable was acquired before or during the marriage, the court has no power to make compensatory adjustments in New Zealand to take account of the potential unfairness of significant items of property being outside the court's jurisdiction. Thus, in *Samarawickrema,* [505] the Court of

499. (1992) 9 FRNZ 187.
500. Section 7A(2) and (3), Property (Relationships) Act 1976.
501. *Herbst v. Herbst* [2013] NZHC 3535; [2014] NZFLR 460 per Brown J at [27]–[29].
502. *Koops v. Den Blanken* [1998] NZFLR 891 upheld by the Court of Appeal (unreported CA 262/98, 17 Aug. 1999).
503. [1983] NZLR 560; (1983) 2 NZFLR 240.
504. Section 2G, Property (Relationships) Act 1976.
505. *Samarawickrema v. Samarawickrema* [1995] 1 NZLR 14, (1994) 12 FRNZ 482; [1994] NZFLR 913.

Appeal rejected the trial court judge's order giving the wife a greater share of New Zealand property on condition that she agree not to apply for division of property in the overseas country (Sri Lanka). In *Samarawickrema*,[506] the Court of Appeal did not, however, overturn the decision in *Enright v. Fox*[507] where the judge said the existence of foreign realty might be taken into account to compensate one spouse under section 16 of the Property (Relationships) Act 1976. Hardie Boys J considered that the existence of foreign reality might, in fact, be allowed to be taken into account as an extraordinary circumstance as allowed for by section 13.[508]

341. Property is classified under the Act as either relationship property or separate property. Relationship property is defined quite specifically and is further divided between the home and chattels and the remaining relationship property. Each classification of relationship property carries with it a presumption of equal division. Prior to the 2001 amendments, this presumption was stronger with regard to the home and family chattels than other property, but that is no longer the case. Section 8(1) of the Property (Relationships) Act 1976 which defines relationship property reads:

> (1) Relationship Property shall consist of –
> (a) the family home whenever acquired; and
> (b) the family chattels whenever acquired; and
> (c) all property owned jointly or in common in equal shares by the married couple or by the partners; and
> (d) all property owned by either spouse or partner immediately before their marriage, civil union, or de facto relationship began; if
> (i) the property was acquired in contemplation of the marriage, civil union, or de facto relationship; and
> (ii) was intended for the common use or common benefit of both spouses or partners; and
> (e) subject to sections 9(2) to (6), 9A and 10, all property acquired by either spouse or partner after their marriage, civil union, or de facto relationship began; and
> (ee) subject to sections 9(3) to (6), 9A and 10, all property acquired after the marriage, civil union, or de facto relationship began, for the common use or common benefit of both spouses or partners, if –
> (i) the property was acquired out of property owned by either spouse or partner or both of them before the marriage, civil union, or de facto relationship began; or
> (ii) the property was acquired out of the proceeds of any disposition of any property owned by either spouse or partner or both of them before the marriage, civil union, or de facto relationship began; and
> (f) [repealed]

---

506. [1995] 1 NZLR 14; (1994) 12 FRNZ 482; [1994] NZFLR 913.
507. (1989) 5 NZFLR 455; 5 FRNZ 33.
508. *See* Part III, Ch. 1, s. 3.

(g) the proportion of the value of any life insurance policy ..., or of the proceeds of such a policy, that is attributable to the marriage, civil union, or de facto relationship; and
(h) any policy of insurance in respect of any property described in paragraphs (a) to (ee); and
(i) the proportion of the value of any superannuation scheme entitlements ... that is attributable to the marriage, civil union, or de facto relationship; and
(j) all other property that is relationship property under an agreement made under Part 6; and
(k) any other property that is relationship property by virtue of any other provision of this Act or by virtue of any other Act; and
(l) any income and gains derived from, the proceeds of any disposition of, and any increase in the value of, any property described in paragraphs (a) to (k).

Richardson J, speaking when the Act applied only to marriage, has said of this exhaustive definition:[509]

> Broadly speaking, an asset is matrimonial property if it is produced by the contributions of the parties to the marriage partnership, that is, if it is that sense a product of the marriage partnership, or it has a sufficient common association with both spouses.

Relationship property subject to division falls under section 11 with a strong presumption of equal division.

342. Section 8 must be read in conjunction with the definition of 'property' contained in section 2 of the Property (Relationships) Act 1976, which is very broad and includes real or personal property, any estate or interest in any real or personal property, any debt, anything in action and any other right or interest. 'Owner' has a similarly broad meaning. In *Z v. Z (No. 2),* the Court of Appeal held that enhanced earning capacity is not within the ambit of the Act[510] in spite of the broad definition of 'property'. Likewise, future earnings of a spouse may not be taken into account. However, as discussed above (paragraph 329), the bundle of rights in a trust may amount to a property interest capable of being classified under the Act,[511] and, in another expansive decision, copyright in a painting can be property as distinct from the painting itself.[512]

343. Some cases have considered whether university degrees can be regarded as relationship property. The first case to consider this issue was

509. *Sloss v. Sloss* [1989] 3 NZLR 31, 35; (1989) 5 FRNZ 148, 151; 5 NZFLR 497, 506.
510. *Z v. Z (No. 2)* [1997] 2 NZLR 258; [1997] NZFLR 241; (1996) 15 FRNZ 88.
511. *Clayton v. Clayton [Vaughan Road Property Trust]* [2016] NZSC 29, [2016] 1 NZLR 551, [2016] NZFLR 230.
512. *Palmer v. Alalaakkola* [2021] NZHC 2330, [2021] NZFLR 515.

Coombes v. Heycoop [513] where the court held that the degree itself was not relationship property. The husband was, however, awarded 65% of the home due to the finding that during her study, the wife's contributions to the marriage partnership had been less than would normally be expected, and, therefore, the situation was an extraordinary circumstance within section 13. In *I v. I,* [514] the husband was undertaking medical training and had to move to London, England. As a result of this, the wife could not further her career, and she used separate property to purchase the family home. The court said this was an extraordinary circumstance and divided the property 65/35. In both cases, the separation occurred shortly after the qualification was obtained, and therefore, in a marriage of a longer duration, a court may be unwilling to depart from the equal division provisions owing to lapse of time, evening out the contributions of both parties.

344. Section 8(1)(d) requires that property must be owned immediately before the marriage, union or relationship. A hire purchase agreement or a similar agreement will not negate this condition, but a considerable delay between the acquisition of the property and the marriage, union or relationship may cast doubt upon whether it was purchased 'in contemplation of the marriage, civil union, or de facto relationship'. If an item was bought for the 'common use or common benefit', it need not be exclusively for that purpose. It is sufficient if it was partially intended for that purpose.

345. The issue of whether the assets of a commercial partnership are relationship property has largely been resolved by *Maw v. Maw.*[515] This case concerned a farming partnership between two brothers established prior to the marriage in question. After the marriage took place, the partnership acquired two more farms. The issue before the court was what was relationship property and what was separate partnership property. Under partnership law, the farms were partnership property. However, the husband's beneficial interest in the partnership property, that is, his right to a proportion of the surplus after realization of assets and payment of debts and liabilities,[516] was classified as being relationship property under section 8(1)(e) of the Property (Relationships) Act 1976 (although the case was decided before the changes enacted in 2001, the result ought to be the same).

346. Another issue for consideration is the classification of superannuation schemes. Prior to the 2001 changes, if a superannuation scheme had been contributed to at all during the marriage, the pre-marriage contributions were included as part of the matrimonial property. Following 2001, only the proportion attributable to the period of living together is relationship property. It should also be noted that

513. (1992) 9 FRNZ 559.

514. (1994) 12 FRNZ 490; [1995] NZFLR 276.

515. [1981] 1 NZLR 25. This is supported by the Supreme Court decision in *Rose v. Rose* [2009] 3 NZLR 1; [2009] NZFLR 814.

516. *Brenssell v. Brenssell* [1998] NZFLR 28; (1997) 16 FRNZ 41.

the definition in section 2 of 'superannuation scheme entitlement' refers to a pension, benefit or right to which a person 'is entitled or may become entitled'. The courts have interpreted this to include future contingent benefits, not just the cash-in value of the policy.

347. The courts have recognized two types of schemes – defined benefit and defined contribution schemes. The type of scheme will determine the amount that is awarded to the other party. The benefits of the first of these depend largely on the length of service and salary level at retirement. Such a scheme came before the court in *Haldane v. Haldane*.[517] At the time of the hearing, the contributions amounted to NZD 9,737, and the husband argued that only this amount should be used in any award. His spouse argued that the value of the benefits upon retirement should be used to assess the present value of the policy as an item of matrimonial property, as the benefits were far more than the amount of contributions. The court preferred the wife's argument. It took as the starting point the likely prospective benefits which the policyholder would receive (excluding the amount attributable to contributions after the date of separation) and then discounted the amount to present-day value and further discounted for contingencies such as early retirement, death or sickness.

348. The benefits of the second type of scheme are related much more to the level of contribution plus interest. The scheme came before the Court of Appeal in *Callaghan v. Callaghan* [518] where there were equal contributions on the part of employer and employee. The court held that in this situation, the fairest approach to valuing the policy was to take the immediate surrender value as at the date of separation.

349. Under section 8(1)(e), property acquired after the date when cohabitation began will be relationship property, but this is subject to a number of exceptions. These include assets acquired by gift, inheritance or as a beneficiary under a trust settled by a third party (section 10) and property acquired out of the proceeds of separate property. Where, however, property acquired out of separate property was acquired for the parties' common use or benefit, it is relationship property. These somewhat complex rules, plus the rules discussed in the following paragraphs, call in some instances for a careful analysis of the source of property, the purpose of acquisition and the dates on which various transactions were made. While ordinary wages and salary (and purchases derived from them) will be relationship property, the classification of farms, businesses, investments and similar undertakings is harder to predict. Much will depend on the facts of each case.

350. Property that is not classified as relationship property is separate property and is in general outside the scope of the Act. The ownership of separate property is determined according to the usual rules governing legal and equitable interests.

517. [1981] 1 NZLR 554; (1981) 1 NZFLR 43 (CA).
518. [1987] 2 NZLR 374; (1987) 4 NZFLR 584; (1986) 2 FRNZ 106.

Sections 9 and 10 set out the rules for determining what is separate property. As with the definition of relationship property, the rules are not straightforward and are subject to several qualifications.

351. Section 9 of the Act defines separate property as follows:

(1) All property of either spouse or partner that is not relationship property is separate property.
(2) Subject to sections 8(1)(ee), 9A(3), and 10, all property acquired out of separate property, and the proceeds of any disposition of separate property, are separate property.
(3) Subject to section 9A, any increase in the value of separate property, and any income or gains derived from separate property, are separate property.
(4) The following property is separate property, unless the Court considers that it is just in the circumstances to treat the property or any part of the property as relationship property:
  (a) all property acquired by either spouse or partner while they are not living together as husband and wife or as civil union partners or as de facto partners;
  (b) all property acquired, after the death of 1 spouse or partner, by the surviving spouse or partner, as provided in section 84.
(5) Subject to subsection (6), all property acquired by either spouse or partner after an order of the Court (other than an order made under section 25(3)) has been made defining the respective interests of the spouses or partners in the relationship property, or dividing or providing for the division of that property, is separate property.
(6) However, where relationship property has been divided on the bankruptcy of a spouse or partner, –
  (a) the family home and any family chattels acquired after that division may be relationship property; and
  (b) any other property acquired by either spouse or partner after the discharge of that spouse or partner from bankruptcy may be relationship property.

352. These rules are subject to section 9A, which enables separate property to become relationship property in the circumstances mentioned below:

(1) If any increase in the value of separate property, or any income or gains derived from separate property, were attributable (wholly or in part) to the application of relationship property, then the increase in value or (as the case requires) the income or gains are relationship property.
(2) If any increase in the value of separate property, or any income or gains derived from separate property were attributable (wholly or in part, and whether directly or indirectly) to actions of the other spouse or partner, then:
  (a) the increase in value or (as the case requires) the income or gains are relationship property; but

(b) the share of each spouse or partner in that relationship property is to be determined in accordance with the contribution of each spouse or partner to the increase in value or (as the case requires) the income or gains.

(3) Any separate property, or any proceeds of the disposition of any separate property, or any increase in the value of, or any income or gains derived from, separate property, is relationship property if that separate property or (as the case requires) those proceeds or the increase in value or the income or gains are used:

(a) with the express or implied consent of the spouse or partner that owns, receives, or is entitled to them; and

(b) for the acquisition or improvement of, or to increase the value of, or the amount of any interest of either spouse or de facto partner in, any property referred to in section 8(1).

(4) Subsection (3) is subject to section 10.

Section 9A has given rise to more litigation than section 9. Where reliance is placed on section 9A, the actions of the other party must be shown to have increased the value of the property, and if there is no causal connection between the contributions and increase, the court will decline to make an award. A farmer's wife may, for example, have spent a lot of time assisting with the farming operation, but this may have helped to produce income without affecting the capital value of the farm. If, however, the causal connection is proven, the whole increase in value from the date of the spouse's actions is relationship property, even if some of the increase is attributable to external factors such as inflation.[519] However, by a change made by the 2001 amendments, this property is not divided equally but according to contributions to the increase in value. The 2001 amendments also added the words 'whether directly or indirectly' in subsection (2). The Court of Appeal in *Nation v. Nation*[520] has said that the changes are significant, so that 'the Court should look at matters in the round and not take an overly technical approach'. The causal connection must still be proven, but the Supreme Court decision in *Rose v. Rose*[521] has made this task easier. It held that 'an increase in value is divisible between the parties unless it can truly be shown that it has not derived from the conduct of the non-owning spouse in any material way', as, for instance, in the case of passive investments.[522] Despite this, it was also held that the non-owning party cannot share in any component of a relationship property increase that is due to inflation.

353. In *French v. French,*[523] the argument by a farmer's wife based on section 9A was unsuccessful, but the Court of Appeal turned to another provision to overcome the potential injustice to the wife. Section 17 enables the court to make a compensatory award where the actions of one party (or the application of relationship

519. *Hartley v. Hartley* [1986] 2 NZLR 64 (CA).
520. [2005] 3 NZLR 46, para. [69].
521. [2009] 3 NZLR 1; [2009] NZFLR 814.
522. *Ibid.*, at para. [44].
523. [1988] 1 NZLR 62; (1987) 4 NZFLR 553; 2 FRNZ 559.

property) have 'sustained' the other party's separate property. The court gave 'sustained' a broad meaning, that is, keeping the property going, not necessarily saving it from ruin. This meant that the court in *French* felt justified in making an award to the wife. Although it was found that the increase in value of the farm was attributable to inflation, she had helped sustain the property in question. An award under section 17 is discretionary, but the Court of Appeal in *French* indicated that the discretion should be exercised liberally. It is not easy, however, to work out in advance exactly what the amount of any award might be.

354. The exception in section 9(4) is normally used where the proceeds of the sale of relationship property are used to acquire other property after separation. Another example arises from *Batterham v. Batterham*[524] in relation to fishing quota allocation after separation. The court justified treating the fishing quota as relationship property under section 9(4), as the quota was allocated on the basis of past fishing history, including the period during the parties' marriage.

355. How redundancy pay received after the date of separation should be classified depends upon whether the payment was made in recognition of prior service or if it was due to the inconvenience of having to find alternative employment. If it is the former, it will be classed as relationship property using the discretion in section 9(4), while the latter will remain separate property. In each situation, it is a question of fact for the court to determine.[525]

356. Section 10 is directed to succession and gifts and states:

(1) Subsection (2) applies to the following property:
  (a) property that a spouse or partner acquires from a third person:
    (i) by succession; or
    (ii) by survivorship; or
    (iii) by gift; or
    (iv) because the spouse or partner is a beneficiary under a trust settled by a third person;
  (b) the proceeds of a disposition of property to which paragraph (a) applies.
  (c) property acquired out of property to which paragraph (a) applies.
(2) Property to which this subsection applies is not relationship property unless, with the express or implied consent of the spouse or partner who received it, the property or the proceeds of any disposition of it have been so intermingled with other relationship property that it is unreasonable or impracticable to regard that property or those proceeds as separate property.
(3) Property that 1 spouse or partner acquires by gift from the other spouse or partner is not relationship property unless the gift is used for the benefit of both spouses or partners.

524. [1993] 1 NZLR 742.
525. *Wharfe v. Wharfe* (1988) 4 NZFLR 634 and *Roberts v. Roberts* [1990] NZFLR 193.

(4) Regardless of subsections (2) and (3) and section 9(4), both the family home and the family chattels are relationship property, unless designated separate property by an agreement made in accordance with Part 6.

357. The main point of section 10 is to treat inheritances, gifts and benefits from trusts as separate property for the reason that these acquisitions owe nothing to the marriage, union or relationship. However, because of the centrality in any relationship of the home and chattels, these items are relationship property, even if acquired in the ways otherwise covered by section 10. The items may be converted into relationship property if they have been 'intermingled' with other relationship property with the consent of the spouse of the partner. Whether such intermingling has occurred is a question of fact depending on how practical it is to trace the inherited property. Where half a farm was acquired by bequest and the other half subsequently bought out of relationship property, it was held that there had been no intermingling as the inherited share was still identifiable.[526]

358. The courts have faced the question of whether an asset was acquired by gift or sale. For tax purposes, it has not been uncommon for a farmer to shift the title to the farm to a son or daughter. To avoid paying gift duties (taxes), this is done by 'selling' the farm to the child subject to a mortgage. Over a period of years, the farmer will then give the farm to the child by reducing the mortgage. In substance, this arrangement is a gift, but the Court of Appeal has held that the parties are bound by the form of the transaction and, therefore, it is to be treated as a sale, falling outside section 10.[527]

359. Once the classification of property as either relationship or separate has been made, the division rules can be considered. Separate property falls outside the scope of the Act. The division rules apply only to *relationship* property. However, there are some powers that enable the court to make orders that affect separate property, for example, where separate property has been sustained (section 17), where a personal debt has been paid out of relationship property (section 20E), orders that separate property be used to satisfy the other party's share of the relationship property (section 33(3)(n)) and compensation where relationship property has been transferred to a trust or company (section 44C and 44F). All relationship property is prima facie divided equally between the parties, but this is subject to two exceptions, marriages of short duration and extraordinary circumstances. These are discussed above.[528] Prior to the changes in 2001, property other than the home and chattels was subject to a less rigorous exception, viz., where it could be shown that one party had made a clearly greater contribution to the marriage partnership than the other. This exception no longer exists.

526. *Jackson v. Jackson* (1984) 2 NZFLR 374 (CA).
527. *Mills v. Dowdall* [1983] NZLR 154 (CA).
528. Part III, Ch. 1, s. 3.

360. Where one of the two exceptions arises, division will be according to contributions to the marriage, civil union or de facto relationship. Where this occurs, division will be according to such contributions. Section 18(1) defines these contributions very broadly as follows:

(a) the care of:
  (i) any child of the marriage, civil union, or de facto relationship;
  (ii) any aged or infirm relative or dependant of the husband or the wife;
(b) the management of the household and the performance of household duties;
(c) the provision of money, including the earning of income, for the purposes of the marriage civil union, or de facto relationship;
(d) the acquisition or creation of relationship property, including the payment of money for those purposes;
(e) the payment of money to maintain or increase the value of:
  (i) the relationship property or any part of that property; or
  (ii) The separate property of the other spouse or partner or any part of that property;
(f) the performance of work or services in respect of:
  (i) the relationship property or any part of that property; or
  (ii) the separate property of the other spouse or partner or any part of that property;
(g) the forgoing of a higher standard of living than would otherwise have been available;
(h) the giving of assistance or support to the other spouse or partner (whether or not of a material kind), including the giving of assistance or support that:
  (i) enables the other spouse or partner to acquire qualifications; or
  (ii) aids the other spouse or partner in the carrying on of his or her occupation or business.

Section 18(2) states that there is no presumption that monetary contributions are to be considered of greater value than those of a non-monetary nature.

361. Section 18A is the only provision allowing a negative contribution to be directly taken into account, and it will be rare in its application. Where it does apply, the result will be a reduction in that spouse's or partner's contribution, thereby potentially reducing the maximum share of property awarded to that party. This section allows misconduct to be taken into account, but only where the misconduct is 'gross and palpable' and has 'significantly affected the extent or value of the relationship property'.

362. One of the rare cases where conduct was gross and palpable involved a marriage which took place in Zimbabwe between a New Zealand woman and a Zimbabwe man, followed by a move to New Zealand.[529] The marriage enabled the man to escape possible extradition on hijacking charges. The man started drinking

529. *Banda v. Hart* [1998] NZFLR 930.

heavily and was violent towards his wife. All the financial contributions came from the wife. In an unusual result, the judge dismissed the husband's application, vesting all the property in the wife.

363. While section 18A is narrowly drafted, negative contributions may nevertheless indirectly affect the assessment of the parties' contributions. This happened in *MacKenzie v. MacKenzie*.[530] The case concerned a wife who, due to a mental illness, killed her three children. While this behaviour did not fall within section 18A, in making its assessment the court considered it could be taken into account either by discounting the wife's contribution or, alternatively, by recognizing the additional contributions of the husband.

364. As part of the 2001 amendments, two sections were added that markedly affect the otherwise strong equal sharing regime. These are found in section 15 and 15A. Section 15A relates to the situation where there is economic disparity between the parties and where one of them has diverted efforts to increasing the value of their own separate property. This section has hardly ever been mentioned in the case law and will not be further discussed.

365. Section 15, on the other hand, has led to a lot of litigation[531] Section 15 is designed to allow the court to remedy the financial disadvantage that flows from the fact that one party is in a much better income-earning position than the other. This means that the first party can adjust much more easily to the economic consequences of relationship breakdown. Jurisdiction to grant compensation depends on:

(a) there being a significant disparity between the parties' likely income;
(b) a similar disparity in their likely living standards; and
(c) a causal connection between these two disparities and the division of functions while the parties lived together.

A claim may be lost because of a failure to fulfil any one of these conditions. For example, an income disparity may be explained by the fact that one of the parties was already qualified and earning more before they started cohabiting. Alternatively, one party may be earning little because of their own career choices rather than anything to do with the relationship. The leading Court of Appeal decision is *X v. X [Economic disparity]*,[532] where it was held that the division of functions need not be the only or the substantial cause of the disparity. Further, the court held that, where one person had been working while the other had been out of the workforce, for example, to care for children, there is a presumption that the division of functions was an operative cause. Compelling evidence is needed to rebut the presumption. The Supreme Court built upon this presumption in *Scott v. Williams* where it

530. (1984) 3 NZFLR 79.
531. *See*, for example, among early cases, *de Malmanche v. de Malmanche* [2002] NZFLR 579, *P v. P* [2005] NZFLR 689, and *M v. B* [2006] 3 NZLR 660, [2006] NZFLR 641 (CA).
532. [2010] 1 NZLR 601; [2009] NZFLR 985 (CA).

held that the presumption will become more difficult to rebut the longer the relationship continues. The kind of evidence that a court will look for in determining that the disparity is not because of the division of roles is of things such as a debilitating illness or inheritance.[533]

366. Assuming that there is jurisdiction to grant compensation, the court still has general discretion to decide whether to do so and for this purpose may take into account likely earning capacity, child care responsibilities and 'any other relevant circumstances'. One thing that the court may consider is whether child support and an award of maintenance would adequately compensate for the disparity.

367. The final question is the amount of compensation to be awarded. Compensation is not at large. It must come out of relationship property (although under the underutilized section 15A, separate property can be resorted to). In theory, this means that one party may end up with 100% of the relationship property, but in some cases, judges have checked their awards against the respective shares that the parties will end up with. The statute gives no guidance on how to work out the level of compensation, and the calculation has proven to be difficult for both judges and actuarial experts alike. Sometimes the focus has been loss of career opportunities for the claimant rather than enhancement of the other person's earning capacity. However, the Supreme Court has criticized this approach:[534] the calculation may, instead, begin with the amount of the disparity in likely income earning and the number of years that this disparity is likely to continue. Because the compensation has a future element, some discounting for this is usually necessary. Other contingencies such as altered employment situations may also need to be accounted for.[535] Finally, the calculated sum will usually be halved to ensure that the disparity is shared equally.

368. The sharing of property under the Property (Relationships) Act 1976 may be affected by the value placed on the relevant property. The date when the value is to be ascertained is the date of hearing, but the court has discretion to choose another value.[536] The discretion has been used frequently where one party has made significant contributions after the parties' separation. By altering the value of an item of property such as the home, the court can in effect give that party a credit for those contributions.[537] Since the 2001 amendments, the courts have gained a more direct power under section 18B to compensate for contributions made after separation or death (for the latter, *see* section 86). There has been some controversy over whether section 18B should be used to compensate for childcare. The Court of Appeal in *X v. X [Economic disparity]*[538] determined that the section not be used as a form of retrospective maintenance, for instance, where one of the parties had

533. *Scott v. Williams* [2017] NZSC 185, [2018] 1 NZLR 507, [2017] NZFLR 1.
534. *Scott v. Williams* [2017] NZSC 185, [2018] 1 NZLR 507, [2017] NZFLR 1, especially at [326].
535. This is broadly in line with the Court of Appeal decision in *X v. X [Economic disparity]* [2010] 1 NZLR 601; [2009] NZFLR 985 (CA).
536. Section 2G, Property (Relationships) Act 1976.
537. *Meikle v. Meikle* [1979] 1 NZLR 137 and *Rush v. Rush* (1986) 4 NZFLR 236 (CA).
538. [2010] 1 NZLR 601; [2009] NZFLR 985 (CA).

failed to pay maintenance. There is also a power in section 18C under which compensation can be granted where, through deliberate action or inaction, one party has materially diminished the value of the relationship property. In *Hutt v. Hodge,* [539] the court emphasized that the action or inaction had to be deliberate, rather than the diminishing in the value of the property. Thus, indifference to the consequences of action or inaction will suffice. The Court of Appeal, however, declined to follow this and took the much narrower line that it had to be shown that the person had to intend to diminish the value of the property.[540]

369. The valuation of some items of property may be quite controversial, especially shares and goodwill of businesses and partnerships. The Court of Appeal in *Z v. Z (No. 2)* [541] was faced with a claim to a share in the husband's accountancy firm, but the partnership agreement specifically stated that there was no goodwill in the business. However, the Court of Appeal said that this did not mean that there was no goodwill for the purpose of relationship property law and, adopting the so-called super profits approach, held that the husband's access to clients and an income stream was the subject of valuation and division under the Act.

370. The division rules are also affected by debts. The question is whether debts are to be shared by both parties or whether the debtor has to bear the liability alone. Broadly speaking, 'personal debts' remain with the debtor, while 'relationship debts' are shared. The key definition is found in section 20(1):

> relationship debt means a debt that has been incurred, or to the extent that it has been incurred –
>
> (a) by the spouses or partners jointly; or
> (b) in the course of a common enterprise carried on by the spouses or partners, whether alone or together with another person; or
> (c) for the purpose of acquiring, improving, or maintaining relationship property; or
> (d) for the benefit of both spouses or partners in the course of managing the affairs of the household; or
> (e) for the purpose of bringing up any child of the marriage, civil union or de facto relationship.

371. Paragraph (b) is commonly argued, and the Court of Appeal developed the test for what is a common enterprise in *Wilson v. Wilson.* Richardson J stated:[542]

> It does not require that the husband and wife participate equally in the control or in the profits. Their respective roles in the enterprise will be a matter for agreement between them. But it must be an enterprise which is carried on by

539. [2007] NZFLR 438 (HC).
540. *GFM v. JAM* [2013] NZCA 660, [2013] NZFLR 418.
541. [1997] 2 NZLR 258; [1997] NZFLR 241; (1996) 15 FRNZ 88.
542. [1991] 1 NZLR 687, 693; [1991] NZFLR 107, 112; (1990) 7 FRNZ 115, 121.

them in common. They must be in it together. Whether a common enterprise is carried on by the husband and wife will necessarily depend on the particular circumstances and so will involve considerations of fact and degree.

372. The case concerned indebtedness incurred by the husband when purchasing shares in what was essentially a family restaurant and, as his spouse was treated largely as another employee without any control over the running of the business, the court found that there was no common enterprise. The debt was, therefore, the husband's personal one.

373. Following the 2001 amendments, the result could be different depending on whether or not the restaurant is classified as relationship property. The 2001 enactment extended paragraph (c) from acquisition of the home and chattels to all relationship property. Thus, the debt would be a relationship one and would, therefore, be deducted from the net value of the relationship property under section 20D. This effectively means that both parties would share the debt. If not, the debt would remain the husband's alone. Under section 20E, if a personal debt is paid out of relationship property, then the other party is to be compensated accordingly.

374. One issue that has arisen in relation to debts is whether the court can make any order at all where the debts outweigh the value of relationship property, in other words, where the parties have a negative equity in their property. While it may be odd to do so, courts have generally found a way of granting relief.[543]

375. Another change made by the 2001 amendments was to give the court power to grant compensation where relationship property was transferred to a trust or company (*see* above, paragraph 325). The effect of the transfer has to be to defeat the claims or rights of one of the parties, but it is not necessary to show that this was the intention. Bad faith or improper motive need not be shown.[544] In essence, these powers are designed to deal with a large number of family trusts and family companies in New Zealand. Without them, one of the parties could easily be prejudiced by the placement of property beyond the court's jurisdiction.

376. A further major reform in 2001 was the extension of the 1976 regime to survivors upon the death of their spouse or partner.[545] Where the survivor is adequately provided for, for example, under the deceased's will, there is no need to invoke the regime. However, there will be situations where this is not so and where the survivor's share in relationship property has not been recognized. If the survivor wishes to apply under the 1976 Act, early notice of this option must be given to the administrator of the estate.

---

543. For example, *C v. W [Relationship property]* [2008] NZFLR 865 (FC) and *Tapuae v. Mawson* (High Court, Napier, CIV-2009-441-0464, 10 Dec. 2009) (HC).

544. *Nation v. Nation* [2005] 3 NZLR 46 (CA). In *R v. G; G v. R [Lottery winnings]* [2011] NZFLR 1040, the winnings from a lottery ticket were transferred to a trust. The man's argument that he bought the ticket on behalf of the trust failed and, according to the Court of Appeal, the transfer fell within s. 44C.

545. *See* Part 8, Property (Relationships) Act 1976.

377. In general, the rules already discussed for *inter vivos* claims apply in death. Nevertheless, there are some modifications designed largely to assist the survivor. First, only the survivor can apply as of right, but the deceased's personal representative may do so if the court grants leave. Leave will be granted only if failure to do so would cause 'serious injustice', for example, to a beneficiary of the estate.[546] Second, there is a presumption that, in the absence of evidence to the contrary, property that was owned by the deceased is relationship property. This rule does not apply to gifts, inheritances or payments from a trust settled by a third party.[547] Third, the rule that equal sharing is set aside for marriages and civil unions of short duration does not apply unless equal sharing is shown to be 'unjust'.[548] However, de facto relationships of short duration are treated exactly the same on death as on separation; in other words, to come within the Act, they must have lasted three years (subject to the exceptions discussed above).[549] Finally, the rule of survivorship, that is, that a survivor of jointly owned property automatically succeeds to the whole of the property on the death of the other joint tenant, is set aside, so that the property in question comes under the jurisdiction of the Act.[550] This is likely to mean that it will be relationship property to be divided equally, and thus this rule will count against the survivor.

378. Once the shares in the relationship property have been determined, including any adjustments for such things as post-separation contributions, economic disparity, payment of personal debts and transfers to trusts and companies, the court has a wide range of orders it can make to give practical effect to the primary order determining the parties' shares in relationship property. These include ordering the sale of the property, the vesting of property in the name of one of the parties, ordering the transfer of property and ordering the payment of a sum of money.[551]

546. Section 88, Property (Relationships) Act 1976; *Public Trustee v. Whyman* [2005] NZFLR 433 (CA) and *Public Trust v. Relph* [2009] 2 NZLR 819 (HC).
547. Section 81, Property (Relationships) Act 1976.
548. Section 85, Property (Relationships) Act 1976.
549. Paragraphs 190 and following.
550. Section 83, Property (Relationships) Act 1976.
551. *See* especially s. 33, Property (Relationships) Act 1976.

Chapter 4. Conventional Matrimonial Regimes

379. The regime set out in the Property (Relationships) Act 1976 is the one that is most commonly used by people in New Zealand. There is no other regime that is set out as such in New Zealand legislation. As has been noted already, since the Property (Relationships) Amendment Act 2001, the regime also applies to de facto relationships and widowed parties and, following the passage of the Civil Union Act 2004, also to civil unions. The 1976 Act provides for 'contracting out' of the familiar scheme. Such agreements are often entered into prior to the commencement of a relationship or to record a settlement of differences between parties who have separated, but they may also settle differences between a survivor and the deceased's person's estate. The detailed rules relating to this type of agreement have been discussed above.[552]

552. Part III, Ch. 1, s. 4.

Part IV. Succession Law

Chapter 1. Intestate Succession

§1. The Opening of the Succession

I. Death

380. Any evidence which satisfies the court of the death of a person for whom a grant of administration is sought is acceptable.[553] An example is a certified copy of the death of the person in the Register of Deaths. An executor's oath will be sufficient proof of death and will be given where:

(1) the executor was present when the deceased died;
(2) the executor attended the funeral for the deceased;
(3) the executor saw the body; or
(4) the executor can prove death by reference to an annexed certified copy of the entry in the Register of Deaths.

Every administration as defined in section 2 of the Administration Act 1969 is sufficient evidence of death of the testator or intestate in the absence of evidence to the contrary.[554] Death does not include miscarriage or stillbirth.[555]

II. Missing Persons and Absentees

381. Rule 27.12 of the High Court Rules sets out the grounds upon which a person may apply for a grant of probate or administration in the absence of an identified body. This applies whether there is a will or an intestacy. Such application must be supported by affidavits detailing the circumstances under which the application is made, the facts from which the High Court is invited to infer death, and

553. Rule 27.12, High Court Rules 2016.
554. Section 17, Administration Act 1969. 'Administration' means probate of the will of a deceased person, and includes letters of administration of the estate of a deceased person, granted with or without a will annexed, for general, special, or limited purposes, and in the case of a trustee corporation includes an order to administer and an election to administer.
555. Section 2, Births Deaths, Marriages and Relationships Registration Act 1995 (section 4, Births Deaths, Marriages and Relationships Registration Act 2021, when in force).

whether or not the person alleged to be deceased had a life insurance policy.[556] As a general rule, affidavits should state the circumstances in which the person was last seen, the particulars of the estate, whether any advertisements have been placed in newspapers attempting to locate the missing person and the applicant's belief that the person is deceased. Before granting such an application, the court must be satisfied that death is a practical certainty in so far as no other reasonable possibility is open to explain the absence[557] and that all reasonable enquiries have been made. *Re Moss* [558] is precedent for the fact that, where nobody can be produced, a certificate of death following a coroner's inquest is not sufficient for the court to presume death.

382. If there is no evidence that a person was alive at some point during a period of seven years or more and it can be proved that:

(1) there are people who would have been likely to have heard from the person during that period;[559]
(2) these people have not heard from the person; and
(3) all appropriate enquiries have been made with no result,[560]

the presumption is that the person has died within that period. This seven-year period may be decreased by the court if sufficient enquiries have been made. The issue of whether a person is to be presumed dead is a question of fact for the court.[561]

383. If a court in a foreign jurisdiction where a person was resident has presumed death and made an order vesting the deceased's estate, a New Zealand court will presume death without further evidence. If, however, there was no vesting order, further evidence will be required.[562]

556. Rule 27.2(2)–(6). If the alleged deceased had a life insurance policy, the applicant must serve the application and affidavits on the insurer.
557. *Re Montgomery* [1940] NZLR 950 (SC and CA).
558. [1955] NZLR 110.
559. *Re Liebeskind* (1952) Times 11 Dec. 1952.
560. *Chard v. Chard* [1956] P 259, 272; [1955] 3 All ER 721, 728.
561. Rule 27.12(2), High Court Rules 2016 provides for an application to be made to the court that the person be presumed dead. Further, under ss 32–36, Family Proceedings Act 1980 the Family Court can grant an order that a person is presumed to be dead and that that person's marriage is dissolved.
562. *Re Spenceley* [1892] P 255, *Re Schulhof* [1948] P 66, [1947] 2 All ER 841; *Re Dowds* [1948] P 256.

§2. THE HEIR

I. Capacity to Succeed

384. The capacity to succeed on an intestacy depends largely on whether the person falls within one of the categories set out in the Administration Act 1969. Broadly, a surviving spouse or partner and the deceased's children will be entitled to succeed. In some cases, parents and other relatives such as grandparents and siblings may succeed. Since the passage of the Status of Children Act 1969, legitimate and illegitimate children are treated on the same basis. Adopted children are treated as the legal heirs of the adoptive parent.[563] Likewise, where a child is born as a result of a procedure such as donor insemination, the child will be treated as a child of the man married to the mother.[564]

385. Prior to the Administration Amendment Act 2001 (in force from 1 February 2002), a de facto partner had no right to succeed on an intestacy. This was changed. The de facto relationship must have lasted three years, subject to the same exceptions that apply under the Property (Relationships) Act 1976.[565] Following the passage of the Civil Union Act 2004, civil union partners have also been able to share on an intestacy. However, a divorced spouse or civil union partner has no right to succeed on an intestacy, nor does a former de facto partner who was no longer living with the deceased at the date of death. Where there is a separation order in force between the deceased and the surviving spouse, the latter loses the right to succeed to the intestate's estate.[566]

386. An important limitation on the principal rules governing intestacies is the ability of parties to challenge the distribution of the estate under the Family Protection Act 1955 and the Law Reform (Testamentary Promises) Act 1949 (discussed later).[567] These Acts are invoked most commonly to challenge a will, and, as the people entitled to claim under the Family Protection Act are similar to those entitled to succeed on an intestacy, it is not often that the distribution of an intestate's estate is in fact challenged.

---

563. Section 6, Adoption Act 1955. *See Grant v. McDermott* [2014] 2 NZLR 696 (HC) where the deceased had been adopted and died intestate as to the residue of his estate, leaving few relatives. It was held that the son of his adoptive sister (adopted by the same adoptive parents) was entitled to the residue and not the other children of the deceased's birth mother. In *Re Estate of Berghan* [2020] NZHC 1399, [2020] 2 NZLR 585, the intestate deceased man's biological daughter, who had been adopted by her mother and stepfather, was granted letters of administration partly in recognition of *tikanga* Māori (Māori practices) despite not being entitled to a share of the estate under the Administration Act 1969.

564. Part 2, Status of Children Act 1969.

565. Section 77B, Administration Act 1969. On the three-year rule, *see* Part III, Ch. 3, para. 130.

566. Section 26(1), Family Proceedings Act 1980.

567. Chapter 2, s. 6.

387. Persons may disclaim their interest in an estate under section 81 of the Administration Act 1969, provided they are of sound mind and of full age. Subsection (2) and (3) of that section set out the conditions attached to making a valid disclaimer:

(1) The disclaimer must be made during the successor's lifetime.
(2) The disclaimer must relate to the whole of the successor's interest in the estate.
(3) The disclaimer must be made within one year of the grant of administration, unless the court grants an extension of time.
(4) The successor must not have entered into enjoyment of the whole or any part of the interest, nor transferred, assigned, mortgaged, settled or otherwise disposed of the interest or any part of the interest.
(5) The successor must not provide for an assignment of the interest, or claim valuable consideration for making the disclaimer.

388. Any disclaimer must be irrevocable, and the court may disclaim on behalf of minors and persons of unsound minds. The requirements of section 81 became an issue in *Warrender v. Warrender*.[568] The deceased and his wife had separated fifteen years before his death and entered a matrimonial property agreement settling all their property claims. The husband died intestate without any children. After the death, the widow entered into a 'compromise' with the deceased's siblings about the administration of the estate, which included her agreeing to her share of the property being 10% of the estate and foregoing her right to seek letters of administration. She later changed her mind: she claimed the whole of the estate and the right to apply for letters of administration. Woodhouse J rejected her claims. He held that, although the Act does not provide for 'contracting out', there was no sound policy reason for not allowing it, which is what the wife had done. Furthermore, the compromise was not a waiver and did not therefore have to comply with the conditions in section 81 listed in the previous paragraph.

II. *Commorientes*

389. *Commorientes* are governed by the Simultaneous Deaths Act 1958. Section 3 provides that:

> (1) In any case where, after the commencement of this Act, 2 or more persons have died at the same time or in circumstances which give rise to reasonable doubt as to which of them survived the other or others –

568. *Warrender v. Warrender* [2013] NZFLR 565 (HC); [2013] NZAR 603. In *Re Estate of Berghan* [2020] NZHC 1399, [2020] 2 NZLR 585, mentioned above (para. 384), the biological daughter of the intestate deceased (adopted by the mother and stepfather) was given letters of administration, one reason being that the deceased's seven adult siblings recorded that they gave their beneficial interest in the estate to the daughter. This was in effect a disclaimer.

(a) The property of each person so dying shall devolve, and if he left a will it shall take effect unless a contrary intention is shown thereby, as if he had survived the other person or persons so dying and had died immediately afterwards.
(b) Every donatio mortis causa made by any other person so dying to any other person or persons so dying shall be void and of no effect.

The effect of this is to deem that each party survived the other so far as their own will or intestacy is concerned. It is still open to interested parties to challenge the distribution of the estate by proving one party survived the other, but the burden is on the party alleging the fact.[569]

III. Unworthiness to Succeed

390. The Succession (Homicide) Act 2007 revises the New Zealand law on homicidal heirs. The Act relates to persons who are guilty of killing another person or 'a child who has not become a person'.[570] It does not include someone acquitted of homicide on the grounds of insanity. Also excluded is killing by a negligent act or omission, infanticide, suicide pacts and assisted suicide. The usual proof will be a conviction in New Zealand. A conviction overseas is admissible evidence. Where a person has been acquitted or the prosecution has been stayed or withdrawn, a court can still determine on the civil standard of the balance of probabilities whether the person was guilty of culpable homicide.

391. If the Act applies, the killer is in general not entitled to inheritance rights (including on an intestacy) nor to a claim under the Property (Relationships) Act 1976. Where property was owned with the victim as joint tenants, it is converted into a tenancy in common in equal shares. The practical effect of this is that, assuming the killer and victim had been joint tenants, the killer will receive only a half share instead of the whole of the jointly owned property. Despite these rules, the killer may claim under the Property (Relationships) Act 1976 for a benefit for the services or other economic benefits provided to the victim. Likewise, a claim may be made under the Law Reform (Testamentary Promises) Act 1949 where services had been provided to the victim on the basis of a promise that they would be recognized in the deceased's will.[571]

569. *Re Pechar* [1969] NZLR 574. The Family Protection Act 1955 does not expressly rule out homicidal heir from making a claim but a court may refuse to make an order if there has been disentitling conduct: s. 5. *See* further Part IV, Ch. 2, s. 6, II.
570. Section 4(1), Succession (Homicide) Act 2007 (definition of 'killer').
571. Section 10, Succession (Homicide) Act 2007.

§3. The System of Descent

I. The Classes of Heirs

A. *Surviving Spouse*

392. The Administration Act 1969 is the primary legislation governing intestate succession. It classifies the heirs of the deceased in section 77. The surviving spouse (not including a divorced spouse or one where there is a separation order in force)[572] will usually take the greater share of the estate, but this depends on the other relatives who may be alive. Under the Administration Amendment Act 2001, a de facto partner is also entitled, so long as the de facto relationship has lasted three years.[573] Following the Civil Union Act 2004, civil union partners have also been included among the heirs entitled to succeed. The rights of the surviving spouse or (civil union or de facto) partner can be summarized as follows:

(a) If there are no children or parents, the surviving spouse or partner takes the estate absolutely.
(b) If there are children, the spouse or partner takes the personal chattels, a fixed sum of money (which is adjusted from time to time)[574] and one-third of the remainder.
(c) If the deceased leaves a surviving parent, the spouse or partner takes the personal chattels, a fixed sum of money (which is adjusted from time to time) and two-thirds of the remainder.

B. *Descendants*

393. 'Issue' is defined in section 2 of the Act as including unborn children at the time of death, provided they survive birth. If the issue survives the intestate, two-thirds of the residuary estate is held in statutory trusts for them (i.e., after taking account of the surviving spouse or partner's entitlements). The statutory trusts provide equally for all children who reach full age (20 years), marry or enter a civil union. Until the child reaches majority, there is a power of advancement for the maintenance, education and benefit of the child.[575]

572. *See* Ch. 1, s. 2, I.
573. Section 77B, Administration Act 1969. The three-year rule is subject to exceptions: *see* Part III, Ch. 3, para. 130.
574. From 1 Jun. 2009 the prescribed amount is NZD 155,000: Administration (Prescribed Amounts) Regulations 2009, reg 5.
575. Section 78, Administration Act 1969.

C. Ascendants

394. The deceased's parents have limited rights to succeed. If there is a surviving spouse or partner and no issue, the surviving parent is entitled to a third of the residuary estate (i.e., after the surviving spouse or partner's right to the chattels and the specified sum are satisfied). If there are two parents, their shares are equal. The parents are entitled to the whole estate if there is no surviving spouse, partner or issue.

D. Collaterals

395. If no spouse, partner, issue or parents of the intestate survive, the estate is held for the siblings of the intestate regardless of whether they are full or half-blood siblings. If none of the foregoing survive, the estate is divided equally among the maternal and paternal grandparents. If the grandparents do not survive, their place can be taken by maternal or paternal uncles and aunts, as the case may be.

II. Representation

396. Representation of an estate of a person who dies intestate is obtained by means of a grant of letters of administration. The court can make such a grant whether or not the deceased person left any estate in New Zealand or elsewhere and whether or not the person to whom the grant is made is in New Zealand.[576]

397. Where the deceased died wholly intestate, administration is granted to one or more persons beneficially interested in the estate of the deceased if they make an application for the purpose.[577] This means that, if there is a surviving spouse or partner, that person would prima facie be entitled to letters of administration.[578] Otherwise, preference is given, in order, to children, parents, siblings, grandparents and then uncles and aunts. Where there are 'special circumstances', the court can grant letters of administration to someone who has no beneficial interest in the estate. This happened in a case with an overlay of *tikanga* Māori (Māori practice).[579] The applicant had been adopted by her mother and stepfather. Her biological father died intestate. His siblings disclaimed their interest in the estate, leaving no other relatives. The applicant's *whakapapa* (Māori heritage) and connections to her biological family led to the conclusion that there were special circumstances.

398. Trustee companies may apply for administration of a deceased's estate. On intestacies, this work is often done by the Public Trustee. Where any person, whether domiciled in New Zealand or elsewhere, dies in New Zealand or elsewhere

576. Section 5, Administration Act 1969.
577. Section 6, Administration Act 1969.
578. Rule 27.35(1), High Court Rules 2016.
579. *Re Estate of Berghan* [2020] NZHC 1399, [2020] 2 NZLR 585.

intestate, leaving property situated in New Zealand, the Public Trustee may apply for a grant of administration of that person's estate.[580] Where such an application is made, the Public Trustee is entitled as of right to the grant of administration, provided that if some other person in New Zealand, being a person who would be entitled to the grant of administration, applies for a grant of administration, then the court may grant administration to that person. Where the intestate is a Māori, the role is carried out by the Māori Trustee.[581]

III. The Anomalous Succession

399. Special rules apply in respect of the distribution of estates which comprise wholly or partly Māori freehold land. Under Te Ture Whenua Māori Act 1993 (the Māori Land Act 1993), an owner of a beneficial interest in Māori freehold land has no capacity to dispose of the interest by will, other than to persons who fall within certain classes as listed in the Act.[582] Apart from children and remoter issue of the testator, the classes include blood relations of the testator and other owners of the land who are members of the *hapū* associated with the land and *whāngai* of the testator.

Similarly, in the case of the succession to Māori freehold land on intestacy, the Act provides special rules governing those entitled to succeed and the proportions to which they are entitled.[583] Essentially this is children in equal portions, and if no issue, brothers and sisters in equal portions. However, if the deceased leaves neither children nor brothers or sisters, the Act looks to the derivation of entitlement of the deceased and settles on the issue of the person nearest in the chain of title to the deceased.

IV. Adoption

400. Adopted children are treated as the legal heirs of the adoptive parent.[584] This is not true of children adopted by Māori custom (*whāngai*), unless the person falls within Te Ture Whenua Māori Act 1993 (*see* above, paragraph 214).

580. Section 77, Public Trust Act 2001.
581. Section 12C(1), Māori Trustee Act 1953.
582. Part IV of the Te Ture Whenua Māori Act 1993 (Māori Land Act 1993). *See* in particular s. 108. 'hapū' is generally accepted to mean subtribe. 'Whāngai' is defined in s. 5(1) of the Act and means a person adopted in accordance with Māori customs and practice.
583. Section 109, Māori Land Act 1993.
584. Section 16, Adoption Act 1955.

§4. THE RIGHTS OF THE STATE ON THE *BONA VACANTIA*

401. The rights of the state on the *bona vacantia* are governed by section 77 of the Administration Act 1969. Where no one takes an absolute interest under any of the earlier rules that relate to surviving spouses, partners, issue and other relatives, then the following applies:

> All of the estate belongs to the Crown as bona vacantia, and the Crown may (without prejudice to any other powers), out of all or any part of the estate, provide for –
>
> - dependants (whether kindred or not) of the intestate; and
> - other persons for whom the intestate might reasonably have been expected to make provision.

Chapter 2. Testamentary Succession

§1. The Capacity to Make a Will

402. The general rule is that anyone who has acquired the age of 18 years[585] and who possesses the requisite mental capacity may make, change, revoke or revive a will.[586] The main restriction on this is that the testator must comply with the formalities contained in the Wills Act 2007. These formalities are discussed in §2, Different Types of Wills (below).

403. There are several points to note about the age requirement, to which there are several exceptions. The first is that there is an exception where the testator is or has been married, in a civil union or a de facto relationship at an earlier age. Likewise, a will made by someone under 18 in contemplation of a marriage or civil union is valid so long as the marriage or civil union occurs. Other people under 18 may receive approval from the Family Court, as long as the court is satisfied that the person understands the effect of what they are doing.[587] The final exception enables members of the armed forces on operational service or at sea, seafarers at sea and people about to train for or join the armed forces or join a ship as a seafarer to make a will despite being under 18 years of age.

404. Banks v. Goodfellow[588] contains the classic statement of testamentary capacity:

> As to the testator's capacity, he must, in the language of the law, have a sound and disposing mind and memory. In other words, he ought to be capable of making his will with an understanding of the nature of the business in which he is engaged, a recollection of the property he means to dispose of, of the persons who are the objects of his bounty, and the manner in which it is to be distributed between them. It is not necessary that he should view his will with the eye of a lawyer, and comprehend its provisions in their legal form. It is sufficient if he has such a mind and memory as will enable him to understand the elements of which it is composed, and the disposition of his property in its simple forms.

This often requires medical evidence, the value and function of which may be difficult to assess. Great weight may be attached to the testimony of the testator's own doctor or psychiatrist if they had the opportunity to examine the testator at the time the will was made. If, on the other hand, an expert extrapolates from the views of others, the court may attach little weight to their testimony, especially if it conflicts with reliable witnesses who knew the testator. Once proved, a diseased state of mind

585. Section 9, Wills Act 2007.
586. *See* B Atkin 'Will-making and Capacity' in I Reuvecamp et al *Mental Capacity Law in New Zealand* (Thomson Reuters, Wellington, 2019).
587. Section 10, Wills Act 2007.
588. (1870) LR 5 QB 549, 567: *Public Trustee v. Bick* [1973] 1 NZLR 301.

is presumed to continue, with the burden of proving that there is no longer any incapacity falling on the person who makes such a claim.[589]

405. Subject to a narrow exception, capacity must exist at the time of execution of the document. The exception is where a testator has instructed another person (usually their solicitor) while having the requisite capacity but, prior to the execution of the document, the testator loses the capacity to understand all the terms.[590] There is a presumption of capacity, and no proof is required unless the testator's capacity is called into question. It is the duty of the executors to show that the will is the act of a competent testator; where doubt exists, they must prove the testator's competence.[591] The issue of capacity is one of fact and the justice or injustice of the will may help resolve the issue.[592] The fact that the testator committed suicide shortly after executing the document does not raise a presumption of insanity.[593]

406. In *Loosley v. Powell*, the appellant argued that the trial judge had unilaterally added an additional factor to the *Banks v. Goodfellow* formulation.[594] It was argued that the trial judge had gone too far by requiring that the court be satisfied with the testator's rationale for deviating from any previously expressed testamentary intention: an unexplained deviation on their deathbed would negative testamentary capacity. The Court of Appeal disagreed that this was the effect of the High Court's judgment. It said that the rationale or lack of rationale for a change in testamentary intention is relevant as part of the factual matrix for assessing capacity. An irrational decision may undermine a claim of capacity, while a rational decision may support it. Rationality may therefore be a factor, as long as the court does not substitute its own views of the correctness or morality of the decision. Therefore, as far as applying the *Banks v. Goodfellow* test, the trial judge had not added a further step as she had merely recognized that the decision was irrational in light of all the circumstances, and this indicated a lack of understanding and inability to comprehend the effect of the changes.

407. A will made during incapacity is void, and, if the testator regains capacity after execution, the document does not become valid. A will may be valid but a subsequent codicil invalid if the testator lacks capacity at the time of executing the codicil. Once the testator's incapacity prior to executing the document has been proven, the party seeking to rely on the will needs to prove the will was made after recovery from the incapacity and is, therefore, valid. This does not necessitate a full recovery as long as the testator is aware to the degree specified in *Banks v. Goodfellow*.

---

589. *Smith v. Tebbitt* (1867) LR 1 P & D 398.

590. *Parker v. Felgate* (1883) 8 PD 171. Followed in *Loosley v. Powell* [2018] NZCA 3, [2018] 2 NZLR 618, and *Singleton v. Marshall* [2019] NZHC 2486, [2019] NZFLR 273 (upheld on appeal: *Marshall v. Singleton* [2020] NZCA 450, [2020] NZFLR 556).

591. *Banks v. Goodfellow* (1870) LR 5 QB 549.

592. *Harwood v. Baker* (1840) 3 Moo PCC 282; 13 ER 117.

593. *Burrows v. Burrows* (1827) 1 Hag Ecc 109, 162 ER 524.

594. [2018] NZCA 3, [2018] 2 NZLR 618.

408. It is essential that the testator knew and approved the contents of the will for it to be valid. The burden of proving the testator did not have knowledge or approve the document is on the person making the assertion. If the testator executed the will, there is a rebuttable presumption that the testator knew and approved the document. This may also be satisfied by proof that the will was read to the testator, but this is a question of fact for the court to determine, as the testator may not have appreciated the impact of the document. Where the circumstances give rise to a suspicion that the document does not express the testator's wishes, the court should not pronounce it as being valid unless the suspicion is removed.[595] A person may have moments of lucidity during a period where their capacity is in doubt, but the evidence must convince the court that there was a 'window' of capacity and that it coincided with the relevant time of will-making.[596]

409. A will (or the relevant clause of the will) which has been obtained by fraud or forgery will be set aside. The same result occurs where the testator has been subject to undue influence. Undue influence involves pressure which overpowers the testator's volition. As said in one English case, '[I]t is only when the will of the person who becomes a testator is coerced into doing that which they do not desire to do, that it is undue influence.'[597] In *Carrington v. Carrington*,[598] issues arose about testamentary capacity and the capacity to grant an enduring power. A former wife argued that her estranged husband had been unduly influenced to change his will and enduring powers. Katz J in the High Court held that the proper forum was the Family Court and not the High Court, all the matters raised, in so far as they were justiciable, being within the Family Court's jurisdiction under the Protection of Personal and Property Rights Act 1988. She also held that a court could not determine the validity of a will of someone still alive nor whether a person would ever have testamentary capacity in the future.

410. Where a person lacks capacity to manage their property, the court may appoint someone to be the manager of that person's estate.[599] Such an appointment does not, however, mean that the person lacks testamentary capacity,[600] but the court may direct that the person make a testamentary disposition only with leave of the

595. *Tyrell v. Painton* [1894] P 151; [1891–1894] All ER 1120 (CA): *Tanner v. Public Trustee* [1973] 1 NZLR 68.
596. The court was not satisfied of this in *Marshall v. Singleton* [2020] NZCA 450, [2020] NZFLR 556.
597. *Wingrove v. Wingrove* (1885) 11 PD 81.
598. *Carrington v. Carrington* [2014] NZFLR 571 per Katz J. *See also* the discussion of the case above: General Introduction s. 4.
599. Section 31, Protection of Personal and Property Rights Act 1988.
600. The same applies where a person appoints someone their attorney for property purposes under an enduring power of attorney. If the power comes into operation because of the person's lack of capacity, this does not automatically mean that the person lacks testamentary capacity: *Re TN* [2020] NZFC 7851, [2021] NZFLR 431 at para. [75].

court.[601] In the latter situation, or where the person lacks testamentary capacity under the ordinary rules, the court may authorize the manager to execute a will on behalf of the person.[602] The object in framing such a will 'is to give effect to what the testator with all his or her traits and foibles would have seen fit to do if now able to do it'.[603]

§2. Different Types of Wills

411. Sections 11–14 of the Wills Act 2007 contain the formal requirements of a will. The requirements include that the will be written (but there are exceptions in relation to privileged persons, *see* below, paragraph 416), and signed (or 'acknowledged' as described below, paragraph 418) by the testator (under the 2007 Act referred to as 'the will-maker') and witnessed by two people. Unlike other Commonwealth jurisdictions, New Zealand courts used to insist on strict compliance with the formal requirements. However, section 14 of the Wills Act passed in 2007 enables the High Court to declare a will valid even if the formalities were not complied with. The court must be satisfied that the document expresses the deceased's intentions. The power to validate an otherwise defective will has been used quite frequently and seemingly without controversy.

412. For a court to be able to validate a will, there are four requirements. First, there must be a document. Commenting on this requirement one judge said that 'the linkage to s 11 strongly suggests that the purpose of s 14 is to cure non-compliance with s 11, rather than a wholesale absence of a will'.[604] A document is defined in section 6 as 'any material on which there is writing'. This encompasses multiple documents being able to form one completed will,[605] as well as electronic wills, one court saying that 'it would be odd in this age for words represented by ink to constitute writing but not words represented by pixels'.[606] However, verbal wills will not meet this requirement. This precludes the Māori customary tradition of oral wills, known as Ohaki. If verbal wills have been recorded in writing, then this will meet the document requirement.[607] However, audio recordings have been held to not satisfy the document requirement.[608]

413. The second requirement is that the document appears to be a will. This requirement is concerned with the substance of the document rather than the form.

---

601. Section 54, Protection of Personal and Property Rights Act 1988. In *Foster v. Foster* [2014] NZFLR 931 (FC); *Wilson v. Wilson* [2014] NZHC 2766, [2015] NZFLR104 (HC on appeal) a wealthy elderly man began giving large sums of money to a dominatrix. Although his cognitive impairment was mild, the court appointed a property manager and required any new will to be made only with the leave of the court.
602. Section 55, Protection of Personal and Property Rights Act 1988.
603. *K v. Public Trustee* [1995] NZFLR 249, 257.
604. *Re Feron* [2012] NZHC 44, [2012] 2 NZLR 551, at [13].
605. *Winterburn v. Wilson* [2016] NZHC 1422.
606. *Re Estate of Drury* [2018] NZHC 230, [2018] NZAR 370, [2018] NZFLR 243 at [15].
607. *Re Feron* [2012] NZHC 44, [2012] 2 NZLR 551.
608. *Pfaender v. Gregory* [2018] NZHC 161, [2018] NZAR 161.

To satisfy this requirement, the document must therefore do one of the things described in section 8. The third requirement is that the document does not comply with section 11. This third requirement effectively clarifies that the court may not use the powers in section 14 to validate a will made without testamentary capacity or under undue influence. The fourth, uncontroversial, requirement is that the document came into existence in or outside of New Zealand. The only practical purpose of this requirement is that it clarifies that the document could have come into existence out of New Zealand.

414. In one case,[609] the will-maker had initialled the first two pages of the will but failed to sign the final page. The witnesses had properly initialled and signed everything. The will was upheld. The result was the same in another case where a schedule of intentions was prepared by the deceased (who died in the Haiti earthquake) but was not witnessed. The judge took into account the parties' lack of awareness of the technicalities of will-making.[610]

415. In another case that reached the Court of Appeal, the outcome was influenced by the fact that the deceased stated that he wanted to first contact two of his four children about the changed will, as the new will was detrimental to them.[611] The burden of establishing that the document was the deceased's testamentary intention lay with the son advancing it, and that burden had not been satisfied especially in the light of the father's desire to communicate with the other children. It was not validated. In another Court of Appeal judgment, a will was validated even though it had not been properly witnessed.[612] The real issue was whether the deceased woman could speak enough English to be able to understand what the terms of her will were and that she approved them. The court considered that nothing in the terms of the will or the circumstances aroused the slightest suspicion, and the will was thus validated.

416. Any form of words, written or oral, used by members of the armed forces on operational service or at sea, or by a seafarer at sea, or a prisoner of war, constitutes a valid will so long as it is witnessed.[613] These types of wills constitute a class known as 'privileged wills'.[614] A privileged person's will does not have to be written. If oral, it is referred to as a nuncupative will. The will takes effect only if the person dies within twelve months of making the will, or, in the case of prisoners of war, within twelve months after ceasing to be a prisoner of war.

609. *Re Wilkins (deceased)* [2010] 1 NZLR 832. See *Re Stewart (Deceased)* [2010] 1 NZLR 838.
610. *Re Rejouis* [2010] 3 NZLR 422. *See also*, for example, *Re Campbell (deceased)* [2014] 3 NZLR 706; *Re Feron* [2012] 2 NZLR 551 (the will was not validated because it was created from solicitor's notes after the person died and was therefore not a document that appeared to be a will within the terms of s. 14); *Re Estate of Murray* [2012] 2 NZLR 546; *Gladwin v. Public Trust* [2011] 3 NZLR 566; and *Re Brundall (deceased)* [2011] 3 NZLR 528.
611. *Marshall v. Singleton* [2020] NZCA 450, [2020] NZFLR 556.
612. *Sun v. Sun* [2021] NZCA 489 at para. [45].
613. Part 2, subpart 3, Wills Act 2007.
614. *Re Stable* [1919] P 7; [1918–1919] All ER Rep 299.

417. Other than privileged wills and the power mentioned above (paragraph 411) for the High Court to declare a non-compliant will to be valid, all wills must comply with the requirements of the Wills Act 2007. Section 11 requires that a will be written, but does not restrict the form or language used. If a will is partly written in ink and partly in pencil, it is possible that a court will treat the pencil writing as being deliberative and not final.[615]

418. A further requirement is that the will must be signed. Prior to the 2007 Act, the signature had to be at the foot or end of the document. This is no longer the case. The 2007 Act also allows for the situation where the will-maker is unable to sign. The will-maker, instead of signing, may 'acknowledge that a person directed by the will-maker signed the document in the will-maker's presence'. *See* above (paragraph 414) for cases where a will was validated despite a failure by the will-maker to sign.

419. The next requirement of section 11 of the 2007 Act is that at least two witnesses be present when the will-maker signs the will (or acknowledges it as described in the previous paragraph). The witnesses must state on the will that they were present and sign the will in the will-maker's presence. These rules do not require the witnesses to realize that the document was a will[616] or to actually see the testator signing the will or even the testator's signature. Likewise, it is not necessary for the testator to see the witnesses' signing. The relevant test is whether the witnesses could have seen the testator sign if they had chosen to look, or the testator could have seen the witnesses sign if the testator had chosen to look. If the answer to these questions is yes, the will is valid, and if the answer is no, the will is invalid (unless declared valid by the High Court under section 14). This means that a testator must complete the signing in the presence of witnesses. If they are not in the testator's presence for the completion of the signing, the will is prima facie invalid. If the testator has a direct line of sight to the witnesses (this was held sufficient in the past),[617] under the 2007 Act, this will only be sufficient if it can be said that the witnesses were 'in the will-maker's presence'.

420. As a general rule, a witness cannot derive a benefit from the will nor can that witness' spouse, civil union partner or de facto partner (or anyone else claiming through these people).[618] A beneficiary of a will is still capable of being a good witness and their signature will not invalidate the will, but a disposition to them will be void. This rule is subject to four exceptions:

(1) where the beneficiary is in effect a third witness and the other two are not beneficiaries under the will;
(2) where the disposition in the will is the repayment of a debt owed to the witness;

615. *In bonis Hall* (1871) LR 2 P & D 256; *In bonis Adams* (1872) LR 2 P & D 367.
616. Section 12(2), Wills Act 2007. *See also In the Estate of Benjamin* (1934) 150 LT 417.
617. *Casson v. Dade* (1781) 1 Bro CC 99, 28 ER 1010; *Upton v. Public Trustee* (1915) 34 NZLR 614.
618. Section 13, Wills Act 2007.

(3) all the other beneficiaries consent; or
(4) the High Court is satisfied that the will-maker 'knew and approved of the disposition' and 'made the disposition voluntarily'.

It is advisable that witnesses be literate persons of sound mind and of fixed abode, in case they are called upon to attest to the will. By attesting, the witnesses must witness the document, so as to be able to give evidence if so required. Where the witnesses actually place their signature is not important but, if the signature is in an unusual place, the witnesses may have to explain to the court the reason for the location of the signature. If witnessed on a separate piece of paper, the paper must be connected to the will. If the witnesses sign a duplicate of the instrument, the will is invalid.[619]

421. If the will refers to other documents that are not attached to the instrument being signed, it is possible for the other documents to be incorporated into the will. There are three conditions that need to be satisfied for this incorporation:[620]

(1) The document concerned must have existed at the time the will was executed.
(2) The document must have been referred to as an already existing document.
(3) The will must have described the document sufficiently to identify it with certainty, although parole evidence may be admitted to identify it.

The main effect of incorporating a document is to allow it to be admitted to probate, therefore, allowing public inspection of it. This also means that it is subject to the same rules of interpretation as a will. If secrecy is desired, the more effective way to obtain this goal is to set up a secret trust (*see* §5, Provisions in a Will).

§3. Joint Will and Mutual Wills

422. Where two (or more) testators' wills are contained in one instrument, the document constitutes a joint will. Ordinarily, a joint will is proved when the person dies and then again on the death of the survivor. A joint will is contrasted with a mutual will where an agreement between two people about the disposition of property is contained in two separate instruments; that is, both parties make their own wills in accordance with the agreement. If a mutual will is altered by one party after the death of the other, a person who misses out because of the failure to keep to the agreement may claim against the estate of the person who did not keep the promise contained in the agreement.[621] The agreement that led to the making of the mutual wills may be oral, written or electronic.

619. *In the Goods of Hatton* (1881) 6 PD 204.
620. *In re Karsten* [1950] NZLR 1022.
621. Section 30, Wills Act 2007.

§4. Revocation of a Will, Changes and Revival

423. As a general rule, a will is revoked by a subsequent marriage or civil union (but not de facto relationship).[622] There are exceptions to the rule. The principal exception is that a will is not revoked by marriage or civil union if it is made in contemplation of marriage or civil union.[623] The will may expressly say that it is made in contemplation but need not do so. It is enough if this can be clearly shown by the circumstances at the time the will was made (a rule created by the Wills Act 2007). Some further points need to be noted with regard to this exception. The first of these is that the will must have been made in contemplation of a particular marriage, not marriage generally.[624] The second point relates to evidence. In *In the Will of Foss,* [625] Mr Foss made a will in favour of his fiancée expressing the disposition to be to 'my wife (Mrs P. Foss)'. The court held that the will was not revoked by the subsequent marriage, as it had clearly been made in contemplation of the marriage. Terms such as 'my future wife' or 'my fiancé(e)' have been held not to be sufficient evidence in New Zealand.[626] Whether this is altered by the wider language now found in the Wills Act 2007 remains to be seen, but the parliamentary intention was surely to save a wider range of wills. In *Re Stirling (deceased),*[627] a man with a terminal illness became engaged to his partner and one month later began the process of making a will. This was signed two months afterwards, but it was not stated to be made in contemplation of the marriage. Later that same year, the couple married just before the man's death. It was held that the will was not made in contemplation of the marriage and was, therefore, revoked. In *Scott v. King,* [628] it was held to be arguable that the deceased's will was made in contemplation of the subsequent marriage because only two days passed between the execution of the will and the announcement of the marriage.

424. Where a marriage or civil union is dissolved, any provision for the former spouse or civil union partner is void unless the will expresses a contrary intention.[629] The other provisions of the will remain valid.

425. Section 16(a) of the 2007 Act states that the whole or any part of a will may be revoked by a subsequent will. Such revocation may be express or implied, but in either situation the testator must have intended this effect. Express revocation occurs when a later will revokes a will or part of it in express terms, or it contains a general clause revoking all previous instruments.[630] An implied revocation is when,

622. Section 18, Wills Act 2007.
623. Section 18(3), Wills Act 2007.
624. *Burton v. McGregor* [1953] NZLR 487.
625. [1973] 1 NSWLR 695.
626. *Burton v. McGregor* [1953] NZLR 487; *Public Trustee v. Crawley* [1973] 1 NZLR 695; *Re Whale* [1977] 2 NZLR 1.
627. [2008] 3 NZLR 693 (HC).
628. [2019] NZHC 1538.
629. Section 19, Wills Act 2007.
630. *Sotheran v. Denning* (1881) 20 ChD 99.

although no express terms revoke an earlier will, the two instruments are inconsistent. Alternatively, the court will find an implied revocation where the whole document shows an intention to revoke any previous existing wills. Under section 16(b), a will or part of it may be revoked by a document that contains a clear intention of revocation, and that satisfies the criteria for making a valid will. This is similar to what in the past has been referred to as a 'codicil'. Under section 34, a military or seagoing person of any age may revoke a will so long as an intention was shown.

426. Under section 16(e) of the 2007 Act, a will-maker may revoke a will by destroying it or destroying a part that is intended to be revoked. The legislation lays down no conditions for destruction. It is not necessary to mutilate a document to the point of its being completely illegible. What is required is the mutilation of a part of the will that is of such importance that the will should not be admitted into probate as a result. Therefore, it is possible to revoke the whole instrument or only part of it.

427. In *Re Everest,* [631] the testator successfully revoked part of the will by cutting out specific clauses and destroying them while leaving the rest intact. This was held to be a partial revocation only. For destruction to be an effective revocation, it is necessary to prove that the testator completed all that was intended to be done by way of destruction. In *Doe d Perkes v. Perkes,*[632] the testator tore his will into four pieces while in a fit of rage but was calmed down by the beneficiary before destroying it completely. The court held that he had not completed all he intended to do to revoke the will and admitted it into probate.

428. Under section 16(f), destruction can be carried out by another person as long as the testator directs the destruction and it is carried out in his presence. To revoke a will, the testator must intend the instrument be revoked by the act of destruction; the testator must also possess the same mental capacity as is required to execute a will. Where the will is destroyed by accident, the requisite mental element is absent and, therefore, it will not be held to have been revoked, nor will it be revoked if it has been destroyed due to a misunderstanding of its legal status.

429. A testator may also revoke a will by doing anything else that satisfies the High Court that there was an intention to revoke the will.[633] This represents a very broad power to recognize the intention to revoke and may raise doubts about some older cases. For example, in *Cheese v. Lovejoy,* [634] the English Court of Appeal held that, where a testator drew a line through the instrument and wrote 'revoked' on the back, the act was not sufficient to comply with old law. The testator went to his death assuming the instrument had been burned with the rubbish, but his maid had retrieved the will from the rubbish and produced it after death. This could arguably now fall within the terms of the 2007 Act.

631. [1975] 1 All ER 672.
632. (1820) 3 B & Ald 489.
633. Section 16(g), Wills Act 2007.
634. (1887) 2 PD 251.

430. The High Court also has a residual power under section 16(h) to declare valid a revocation that fails to comply with the necessary formalities.

431. According to section 15 of the Wills Act 2007, changes to a will may be made in the following ways:

(1) written on the will and signed and witnessed beside or near the change;
(2) described in a note, duly signed and witnessed;
(3) the obliteration of words 'in such a way as to prevent their effect being apparent';
(4) upheld by the High Court despite any formal failures; or
(5) done under section 34(2) by a military or seagoing person in any way that indicates the person's intention.

432. Under section 17, a will that has been revoked (or a part of a will) may be revived by following the same procedures as for making a valid will, by making a codicil containing the intention to revive, or by any means for military and seagoing persons falling within section 34(2). Where a will was partly revoked and then wholly revoked, revival does not apply to the provisions that were first partly revoked unless the revival makes it clear to the contrary.

433. Section 31 of the Wills Act 2007 empowers the High Court to make an order correcting a will so that it conforms to the will-maker's intentions. The will may contain a clerical error, or it may simply fail to give effect to the will-maker's instructions. The High Court may also, under section 32, use external evidence to interpret words in a will that are otherwise meaningless, ambiguous or uncertain.

§5. Provisions in a Will

434. None of the relevant legislation restricts the manner and form the testator may use to bequeath property. The testator may gift absolutely, impose conditions on the beneficiary and create a trust, even if this is a secret or half secret trust. A secret trust is where no trust appears on the face of the will, and a half secret trust is where the trust is apparent, but the beneficiaries of the trust are not. A secret trust is enforceable because it arises independently of the will and imposes a personal obligation on the legatee.[635]

435. There are five main categories of legacy. The first is a general legacy where the gift is expressed in general terms. The principal advantage in a general legacy is that it is not subject to ademption (i.e., taken away from the donee). However, if there are insufficient assets, it is the first devise to be subject to abatement.

---

635. *Re Young* [1951] Ch. 344.

436. The second category of legacy is a specific legacy. This is a gift of an identifiable part of the testator's estate. A specific legacy places a duty on the executor to preserve the gift as far as possible. If forced to pay debts from the sale of the specified property, the legacy is deemed and the legatee gets nothing.

437. The third category is the demonstrative legacy which is a combination of a specific and general legacy. This normally takes the form of a general legacy with some added direction. An example of this is a payment of a sum of money, with the bank account specified from which the money is to be sourced. There are two reasons why it is necessary to decide whether something is a demonstrative legacy. First, if the fund in question does not contain the necessary funds or is non-existent, a demonstrative legacy becomes a general legacy and is, therefore, payable out of the general estate. The next reason for determining if a provision is a demonstrative legacy is that it does not abate with general legacies unless there are not enough funds in the specified account.

438. The fourth category of legacy is pecuniary; these legacies may be demonstrative, specific or general gifts, although the term is normally used to describe a general legacy of money.

439. The final category of legacy is a residuary gift, that is, all property the testator has not specifically disposed of, or specific gifts that have failed for some reason.[636] This category also includes all property in respect of which the testator had a general power of appointment which has not been exercised (unless the will makes it clear to the contrary).[637] Any property which comes to the testator after the will's execution which is not included in any specific gift will form part of the residue of the estate.

440. A devise is a gift of land. This refers to the interest in the land that the will-maker had at the date of death.[638] In the unusual situation where land has not been brought under the Land Transfer Act 1917, it refers to the fee simple.

441. A testator may also grant annuities in a will. Again, these can be specific, general or demonstrative. A specific annuity is either specifically bequeathed in the will or charged against the specified property. A general annuity is paid out of the testator's general estate. The demonstrative annuity shares features of the specific and general annuity. The demonstrative annuity reveals a general intention to bequeath an annuity but specifies that the annuity is to be derived from a specific part of the testator's property.

442. In making gifts by will, the testator has a lot of freedom in the way in which dispositions are arranged. Thus, a gift need not be made outright to one person, but may be given to more than one person as joint tenants or tenants in common, or may

636. Section 29, Wills Act 2007.
637. Section 26, Wills Act 2007.
638. Section 21, Wills Act 2007.

be made subject to future or successive interests. For example, one person may be entitled to use an item for life with a gift over to someone else.

443. Gifts may also be subject to conditions. This freedom of testation is not absolute, and the powers in particular in the Family Protection Act 1955 (discussed in §6, section II) represent a considerable limitation. They come into operation only when the person has died, and someone makes an application under the Act, but they should be in the mind of anyone advising a person writing a will.

444. Conditions attaching to gifts may be of various kinds and will not always be valid. For instance, a condition may be declared void if it is against public policy or is uncertain. Conditions are divided into conditions precedent and conditions subsequent. The former must be satisfied before a bequest can be given effect to. However, if a condition subsequent is not fulfilled, this will end the bequest (which in these circumstances will normally be an ongoing one). A condition requiring that the donee not remarry is likely to be valid as a condition subsequent, unless it is interpreted as being in general restraint of marriage.[639] A condition that the donee is not to enter a de facto relationship is void for uncertainty.[640] Conditions relating to religion may be valid so long as they are certain.

§6. Restrictions

I. The Legitim

445. In New Zealand, there is no forced share as such in favour of family members, including the surviving spouse and civil union or de facto partner. Considerable litigation occurs, however, in relation to claims under the Family Protection Act 1955, discussed in the following section.

446. Surviving spouses and civil union or de facto partners may claim a share of the deceased's estate under the Property (Relationships) Act 1976. Prima facie, the survivor can claim a half share of that portion of the deceased's estate which is classified as relationship property. This share does not form part of the estate. The share is not, however, automatic. It depends on a claim being made. The survivor may do just as well or better under the will or rules of intestacy, in which case there is no advantage in applying for a share. If, however, an application is made, then, unless the will expresses a contrary intention or a court orders otherwise, testamentary gifts to the applicant are revoked. The choice of whether to elect to apply under the Act or to settle for what is given in the will is, therefore, one which needs to be made with care. For further discussion, *see* Part III, Chapter 3.

639. Compare *Re McKay* (1914) 33 NZLR 811; *Re Wilson* [1947] NZLR 847.
640. *Re Lichtenstein* [1986] 2 NZLR 392, cited in *Re Tucker* [2019] NZHC 2928 (condition excluding grandchildren 'living in a De Facto, civil union, gay or lesbian, lifestyle' held to be void for uncertainty).

II. Maintenance Provisions

447. There are two statutes that potentially place restrictions on a testator's freedom. These are the Family Protection Act 1955 and the Law Reform (Testamentary Promises) Act 1949. Both Acts allow the court to vary wills or alter the destination of property if the deceased died intestate.

448. In the case of a claim under the Family Protection Act, the court may make an order if adequate provision is not available from the estate for the proper maintenance and support of the applicant.[641] The court may, in its discretion, order that such provision as the court thinks fit be made out of the estate of the deceased for the benefit of the deceased. Although the Act talks in terms of proper maintenance and support, the court determines this question by considering the moral duty of the testator towards the applicant.[642] Further, in considering what is proper maintenance and support, the court is not restricted to looking at financial need but should take account of the importance of belonging to a family and playing an important part in the deceased's life.[643]

449. The people who may apply are the widow, or widower, surviving civil union and de facto partners, the children (including stepchildren but not *whāngai*, as discussed above in §3, IV) or grandchildren, and the parents.[644] The definition of 'stepchild' in section 2(1) is narrow. So, for example, a stepchild must be 'living' when the parent and the deceased got married, entered a civil union or started a de facto relationship (as the case may be) and not be born afterwards. In a variation on this theme, a majority of the Supreme Court held that a child en ventre sa mère at the time of the marriage of the mother to another man could not claim: the word 'living' cannot be expanded to include 'conceived but not yet born'.[645]

450. The courts have always considered that the widow has the strongest claim to the estate.[646] If the widow is the second wife of the deceased, her claim may not be as strong as if she were the only wife. Even where the widow remarries, this is no bar to a claim as her status is fixed at the time of the testator's death, but remarriage may affect the amount of any award. The position is the same where the widowed partner enters a de facto relationship after the deceased's death. The court does not have jurisdiction to vary a condition that the widow's benefits are to cease if she remarries. In the case of a separated wife, the grounds of separation may be a relevant circumstance for the court to look at, but the separation is, of itself, no bar to relief. Once the marriage has been dissolved, the ex-wife has no claim. The widower will have a claim only where it can be proved that the wife had a moral

641. Section 4(1), Family Protection Act 1955. Since the Family Protection Amendment Act 1991, the jurisdiction that used to reside solely with the High Court was extended to the Family Court.
642. *Allardice v. Allardice* [1911] AC 730 (PC).
643. *Williams v. Aucott* [2000] NZFLR 532 (CA) and *Auckland City Mission v. Brown* [2002] 2 NZLR 650 (CA).
644. Section 3, Family Protection Act 1955.
645. *Wood-Luxford v. Wood* [2013] NZSC 153; [2014] 1 NZLR 451; [2014] NZFLR 483 at [28].
646. *Rush v. Rush* (1901) 20 NZLR 249.

duty to support him. In the past, the widower tended to be at a disadvantage, but this is less true now, in the days of equality. The points just made should apply similarly to the case of a surviving civil union partner. However, a de facto partner can only claim if the relationship lasted three years (subject to two exceptions: where there is a child of the relationship or where the claimant made a substantial contribution to the relationship, and in either case, there would be serious injustice if an order was not made).[647] Further, a surviving de facto partner must have been living with the deceased at the time of death in order to be able to make a claim. In some cases, it may, therefore, be vital to know whether the parties have separated and thus whether the de facto relationship had ceased.

451. Children have a claim in so far as the moral duty of the parent extended to them. There is no claim for equal shares of the estate as the needs of children will often be different. Administrators may lodge a claim for infant children but have no duty to do so. Stepchildren of a deceased may not claim an interest in the estate unless they were being maintained wholly or partly, or were legally entitled to be maintained wholly or partly, by the deceased immediately prior to the death.[648] The Status of Children Act 1969, section 3(1) provides for ex-nuptial children to succeed equally with children born to a married couple. Grandchildren can apply only if they were living at the date of the deceased's death. Parents may apply only if they were being maintained wholly or partly or were legally entitled to be maintained wholly or partly, by the deceased immediately prior to the death or if the deceased left no spouse or child.

452. Relevant matters in determining whether to make an award will be decided on the facts of the case before the court. However, some considerations are always relevant. These include any provision already made for the applicant, and it is only where this is inadequate that the court will have jurisdiction. The court will take into account the opinions and wishes of the deceased.

453. Under section 11 of the Family Protection Act 1955, the court may receive evidence of the deceased's reasons for making inadequate provision for the applicant. The operation of this section is limited because the reason may be ignored if the testator forms a mistaken or unfounded belief. The testator's reasons are in any event only part of the backdrop against which an application is considered. So, for example, a moral duty is still owed to the surviving spouse even if the marriage was an unhappy one. Likewise, a child who has been estranged from the testator is still owed a duty. These factors may, however, affect the amount of any award. On the other hand, the character or conduct of the applicant may be such as to disentitle that person from an award.[649] However, this provision is rarely used and would not, for instance, disentitle a person who has been in prison, whose sexual conduct is queried,[650] or who is an alcoholic.

647. Section 4A, Family Protection Act 1955, as amended in 2001.
648. Section 3(1)(d), Family Protection Act 1955.
649. Section 5, Family Protection Act 1955.
650. Compare *Re Z (dec'd)* [1979] 2 NZLR 495 (widow living in a de facto relationship not disentitled).

454. The next three considerations for the court are all interrelated and can be looked at together. They are as follows:

(1) the applicant's age and state of health;
(2) the applicant's ability to earn a living; and
(3) the financial position of the applicant.

If the court has jurisdiction to make an order, the amount of the award will be influenced by factors arising after the death of the testator. If, for example, the applicant received finances from another source, this will reduce any potential award to the applicant. It is important to note that where the will provides for the widow, this is not regarded as providing for her children as she may remarry and have further children.[651] Arguably, this may apply in the case of a widower and, *mutatis mutandis*, to surviving civil union and de facto partners.

455. Another factor the court will assess is the applicant's standard of living. The court will attempt to maintain the standard of living the deceased has provided for the applicant where the estate is sufficient for this purpose, and there are no competing claims. In *Welsh v. Mulcock*,[652] Salmond J expressed reservations about this approach by saying that:

> It seems to me clear that the true measure of a testator's moral obligation is not necessarily to be found in the standard of maintenance and the way of life to which his family was accustomed in his lifetime. Testamentary provision in conformity with such a standard is not necessarily either obligatory on the one hand or sufficient on the other. It may be higher or lower than that required by natural justice and moral duty. It is no answer to a claim by a wife or child for a further testamentary provision that the testator in his lifetime, though possessed of ample means, accustomed his family to a life of penury, and that the testamentary provision made by him is sufficient to maintain them in the same way of life which they followed in his lifetime. He cannot, by failing in his duty to them while alive, reduce the standard of his testamentary obligations towards them on his death. Conversely, a testator who in his lifetime keeps his family in luxury is not necessarily under a moral obligation to make such testamentary provisions as will enable them to live on the same scale after his death even if he is financially capable of doing so. The most that can be said is that the way of living to which the claimant has been accustomed in the testator's lifetime is doubtless one of the elements which may be taken into consideration in determining the justice of a testamentary provision. For a reduction to a lower scale of life may impose upon the claimant a needless and unjustifiable hardship.

456. The court will consider any other sources of maintenance that are available to the applicant. Even if these sources are only opened up to the applicant after the

651. *Bosch v. Perpetual Trustee Co Ltd* [1938] AC 463 (PC).
652. [1924] NZLR 673, 686.

death of the deceased, the court may take this into account. In addition, the size of the estate may also be taken into account by the court.

457. In assessing whether to make an award under the Act, the court must consider the applicant's claims alongside those of others, especially beneficiaries under the will. The Court of Appeal has accepted, for example, that the testator may have owed a moral duty to a de facto partner who has been provided for in the will.[653] In the past, the claims of the estranged legal wife and children meant that the de facto partner's bequest could be considerably reduced to enable an award to be made to the legal wife. Now that de facto partners are included as claimants under the Act (since the passage of the Family Protection Amendment Act 2001), it is probably much harder to make this argument. The interests of other beneficiaries, such as charities, are generally treated as low priority.

458. Section 11A of the Act places a duty on the administrator to put before the court any relevant information concerning the testator's financial affairs. The administrator must comply with this provision unless imparting the information would breach a legal or moral obligation to keep it secret. In the absence of special circumstances, this will not allow a solicitor who drew up the will to claim solicitor/client privilege.

459. In *Black v. Black*,[654] the High Court explained that the enquiry into the moral duty and any breach involves a consideration of a number of different factors such as:

(a) the nature of the relationship between the testator and the claimant;
(b) the financial need of the claimant;
(c) recognition of familial connection and belonging;
(d) *inter vivos* contributions, if any;
(e) entitling and disentitling conduct;
(f) repair of parental abuse and neglect; and
(g) the size of the estate.

460. Because of the ambiguous nature of the 'moral duty', the outcome of a family protection claim is often hard to predict, although most applicants are likely to receive something extra. The point is illustrated by the Court of Appeal decision of *Williams v. Aucott*.[655] A woman left her estate to her two daughters, one getting 95%, the other 5%. The discrepancy was explained not as a lack of affection but as a recognition of the first daughter's poor financial position compared to the other's (who was married to a wealthy businessman). The High Court held that the testatrix had not provided properly for the second daughter who was entitled to 25% of the

653. *Re Sutton* [1980] 2 NZLR 50. The High Court had in effect excluded the de facto partner from the estate but the Court of Appeal reversed this, granting the de facto partner NZD 3,000 and another share held on trust for the child born to the testator and the de facto partner.
654. [2014] NZHC 1478, [2015] NZFLR 9 at [48].
655. [2000] NZFLR 532.

estate. The Court of Appeal agreed in part with this but reduced the second daughter's share to NZD 50,000 or approximately an extra 5% of the estate. A factor which influenced the court was the testatrix's apparent misunderstanding of the size of her estate, which was much larger than she thought when writing her will.

461. In *Kinney v. Pardington*,[656] the deceased's daughter, Erin, was awarded 70% of her father's estate.[657] This distribution was made on the basis of the court's assessment of the deceased's ill treatment of his daughter. The deceased had conceived the applicant in an extramarital affair, and, although he had acknowledged his fatherhood of the applicant, the court found that he had breached his moral duty in several ways, such as initially denying paternity, turning a blind eye to abuse suffered by Erin and failing to respond to requests for assistance in Erin's life when asked by the authorities. The consequence was that the applicant had experienced great suffering in her life. When this was balanced against the comfortable and financially secure lives of the deceased's two sons, the court found that it was just to award Erin the greater share.

462. This judgment can be contrasted with that of *Flathaug v. Weaver.*[658] In this case, the facts were similar, but the daughter, residing in England, was well cared for by her mother. The court awarded 7% of the estate in recognition of the fact that the disclosure of the applicant's true paternity would have been an emotional blow but also giving weight to the fact that the testator's decision to play no part in his daughter's upbringing was not one of neglect but of 'enlightened forbearance'.[659]

463. Where a family protection order is made, the administrator of the estate is bound to pay the amount ordered. In one case, this was not done, and it appeared that the administrator had dissipated the assets.[660] The judge issued an arrest order under the Contempt of Court Act 2019, although there was a short period during which the administrator had a final chance to pay the money.

464. The Family Protection Act 1955 is the area of succession law that gives rise to the greatest level of litigation in New Zealand. It has been criticized because of the uncertain nature of the outcome of any claim, with consequent delay in distribution of the estate, and because of the inroads it makes on a person's testamentary freedom.

465. The goal of the original legislation, the Testator's Family Maintenance Act 1900, was largely to provide for dependants. In days of little social security provision and low rates of women in the workforce, there was much justification for what

656. [2019] NZHC 317.
657. *Ibid.*, at [69].
658. [2003] NZFLR 730 (CA).
659. *Ibid.*, at [34].
660. *Connolly v. Eckhout* [2022] NZHC 293 per Campbell J.

was regarded as an innovative policy. Today, however, applicants who are financially well situated and who are unlikely to be a drain on the welfare state nevertheless have a good chance of success under the Act. Two official reports have recommended that the legislation be revised, and its scope narrowed significantly so that claims are more commonly based on need.[661] So far, the government has not made any policy decisions about these matters. As noted above (paragraph 12), the Law Commission has submitted its final report on succession to the government.[662] Unfortunately, on the crucial question of whether adult children should be able to claim, the Commission was divided. It leaves the government to choose between a wide discretion to make awards for adult children or a very limited power to assist children under 25, for example, still in education, children with disabilities, or those unable to maintain a reasonable standard of living.

466. Apart from the Family Protection Act, an estate may be the subject of a claim under the Law Reform (Testamentary Promises) Act 1949. Unlike family protection claims, anyone may apply under this Act. However, certain conditions must be satisfied. The deceased must have made a promise, express or implied, to reward the applicant. The applicant must have rendered services or performed work for the deceased during the deceased's lifetime. There must be a nexus between the promise and the applicant's actions.[663] Thus, services which would normally be provided as part of family obligations will not be enough, but a family member may have a claim if he or she goes beyond normal expectations and can show a promise in return. A de facto partner, who cannot apply under the family protection legislation, may, in appropriate circumstances, be able to succeed on a testamentary promises claim.[664]

§7. Interpretation of a Will

467. The primary principle in interpreting a will is to give effect to the testator's intention as disclosed in the will and any codicils.[665] This intention is generally to be ascertained from a consideration of the testamentary documents and, until recently, not by reference to some other intention expressed outside the will. Effect is to be given to this intention unless some rule of law prevents this. Words in the will should be given their natural and grammatical meaning, modified only if some more general intention on the part of the testator appears from the will as a whole. The testator's intention is to prevail even if it appears capricious or unreasonable. Only if there is some genuine ambiguity in the words is a more reasonable interpretation to be adopted.

661. *The Report of the Working Group on Matrimonial Property and Family Protection* (Justice Department, 1988) and Law Commission, *Succession Law: A Succession (Adjustment) Act* (NZLC R39, 1997).
662. Law Commission *He arotake i te āheinga ki ngā rawa a te tangata ka mate ana | Review of succession law: rights to a person's property on death* (R145, Wellington, 2021) at paras. [21]-[23].
663. Compare *Re Welch* [1990] 3 NZLR 1 (PC).
664. For example, *Chambers v. Weston* (1982) 1 NZFLR 377.
665. *See* generally Patterson 'Wills' in the *Laws of New Zealand*, especially paras 163–259.

468. Until the passage of the Wills Act 2007, in general, only the will and any codicils were evidence of the testator's intention. Extrinsic evidence, such as things which the testator may have said, was not generally admissible. Outside evidence was justified in some situations, for example: to help decipher the testator's writing or to explain some specialized language of a trade or business that the testator was involved in or to explain some facts or circumstances described in the will. This evidence, however, helped (and still should) to explain the will, not to justify some alternative testamentary intention. Again, if a gift is plain and unambiguous, no extra evidence is required, but if there is ambiguity, for example, who the donee is or what the subject matter of the gift is supposed to be, evidence of the surrounding circumstances could be used to clarify the position. Now, under section 32 of the Wills Act 2007, the court may have resort to external evidence to interpret words that otherwise make the will or part of it meaningless, ambiguous or uncertain. The external evidence may include the will-maker's testamentary intentions, but, as under the previous position, they cannot be used to change the testamentary intention. The court must look for some meaninglessness, ambiguity or uncertainty before invoking section 32.

469. Where there is an obvious mistake in the will, the court may correct the will under section 31 of the Wills Act 2007, so that the will-maker's intentions are carried out. This may apply to not only 'clerical errors' but also where the will 'does not give effect to the will-maker's instructions'. If there are two inconsistent gifts in the will and if the court cannot resolve the inconsistency by reference to the testamentary intention, then the last-mentioned gift prevails.

470. There are several presumptions which assist the court in interpreting wills. They tend to arise when the provisions of the will are not clear and when the construction of the will is in doubt:

(a) A presumption against intestacy. A person may die partly testate and partly intestate. If there is some uncertainty about whether this is so on reading the will, then the court will favour a construction which will allow all the property to devolve under the will.
(b) A presumption against illegality. A provision in a will may be struck down because it is contrary to a rule of law. If, but only if, the provision is capable of an interpretation which does not offend, then the court will favour that interpretation.
(c) A presumption in favour of children. A provision in favour of family members which is ambiguous will be construed in favour of the family generally, so as to include as many children as possible.

Chapter 3. Acts *Inter Vivos* Related to the Estate

§1. ESTATE PLANNING

471. A considerable amount of estate planning has occurred in New Zealand, primarily to lessen the incidence of taxation. An important factor for the wealthier sections of the community was the existence of estate duty (tax) which was levied on estates following a person's death. Certain items such as the home were exempt, and the duty applied only when the estate was of a certain size. Estate duty was abolished by the Estate Duty Abolition Act 1993, and, therefore, this factor is no longer relevant in estate planning.

472. Estate planning still occurs to try and minimize income tax. This may be done by disposing of income-earning property to family trusts or family companies. Income splitting between spouses is also possible. Under the Property (Relationships) Act 1976, the parties to an ongoing marriage, civil union or de facto relationship may enter into an agreement, or seek a consent order from the court, which has the effect of giving the less wealthy spouse or partner their share of the relationship property. Special provisions in the Income Tax Act 2004 mean that these steps do not fall foul of anti-avoidance tax rules. Once property has been disposed of in one of the ways just mentioned, it will not form part of the disposer's estate when that person dies.

473. Despite the predominance of freedom of testation in New Zealand succession law and freedom to dispose of property while alive as part of estate planning, in some situations, these freedoms may be circumscribed. In *A v. D and E Ltd*,[666] three adult children had been badly assaulted and abused by their father, the deceased, as they grew up. The daughter had been raped and sexually abused. During his lifetime, the father had disposed of the majority of his assets to a trust, thus minimizing his estate after he died. The children were excluded from the will and contemplated Family Protection Act claims (discussed above, paragraphs 447 and following). However, such claims were largely worthless unless assets could be clawed back into the estate. The children made several claims, but in summary, they argued that the father's conduct could be the basis for undoing the estate planning regime. The arguments were novel but successful. Gwyn J held that the father owed a fiduciary duty to the children while they were still minors, and he breached this with his abuse of them. The judge then held that the fiduciary duty continued into adulthood, in particular at the time when the assets were alienated. At that point the duty was breached. Further, the trustees were liable for 'knowing receipt' because the father's knowledge was imputed to the trust. The trust property was therefore held on constructive trust for the estate. The upshot of this was that the size of the estate was significantly bolstered. The broader result is that a person who engages in estate planning does not have a free hand when nefarious motives affecting members of the family lie behind the plan.

666. *A v. D and E Ltd* [2021] NZHC 2997.

§2. Donations

474. Where there is an *inter vivos* gift or a disposition of property without fully adequate consideration, the gift used to attract gift duty (tax) under the Estate and Gift Duties Act 1968. However, gift duty was abolished in relation to gifts made after 1 October 2011 by section 245(3) of the Taxation (Tax Administration and Remedial Matters) Act 2011. The duty still has to be paid for gifts made before that date, but there are important exemptions, including a general exemption of NZD 2,000 to the same done in the same year, an exemption for the maintenance and education of the family,[667] and no gift duty payable on gifts up to an aggregate of NZD 27,000 in a twelve-month period.

475. An unusual gift is a *donatio mortis causa*. This is a gift made in contemplation and on condition of death. If the donor dies, then the gift takes effect retroactively from the date when the gift was made and does not form part of the estate, but if the donor survives, then the subject of the gift reverts to the donor.

§3. Trusts

476. Trusts are commonly established *inter vivos*, and property held in the name of the trust does not form part of the testator's estate. Although estate duty has now been abolished,[668] there are still tax advantages and protection against creditors in creating such trusts. The common form of trust is known as a family trust. Typically, the settlor's spouse or partner and children will be beneficiaries, but the settlor may also benefit. Most of the case law has involved *inter vivos* disputes[669] and, as noted above, where one party has effective control and a 'bundle of rights', a property interest may arise.[670] These same issues may surface in an inheritance context.

§4. Insurance Contracts

477. Life insurance policies are commonly taken out in New Zealand. If the policy specifies a named payee, for example, a spouse or partner, then that person is entitled to the proceeds, a trust being created in favour of the beneficiaries and the money payable under the policy not forming part of the estate.[671] Otherwise, the policy will form part of the policyholder's estate and be distributed in accordance with the rules of succession.

---

667. Sections 71 and 72, Estate and Gift Duties Act 1968.
668. *See* above para. 417.
669. For example, *LR v. JR (A bankrupt) [Relationship property: bundle of rights]* [2011] NZFLR 797 (FC).
670. Above §4 Ch. 2, especially *Clayton v. Clayton [Vaughan Road Property Trust]* [2016] NZSC 29, [2016] 1 NZLR 551, [2016] NZFLR 230.
671. Section 75A, Life Insurance Act 1908.

§5. OTHERS

478. The testator may have entered *inter vivos* into a contract to make a bequest in the will. So long as the rules of contract have been satisfied, the contract is legally enforceable. It will be effective against the estate and takes priority over a family protection claim, but not over a testamentary promises claim.[672]

672. *Breuer v. Wright* [1982] 2 NZLR 77 (CA) and *McCormack v. Foley* [1983] NZLR 57 (CA).

Chapter 4. Acquisition and Administration of the Estate

§1. Probate and Administration

479. An estate cannot be administered unless probate has been granted or, in the case of intestacy, letters of administration granted. The High Court has jurisdiction in these matters. Jurisdiction can relate to a deceased person whether or not the deceased person was in New Zealand or left property in New Zealand.[673]

480. Probate involves the court determining what documents are testamentary[674] and appointing the nominated executors as the deceased's personal representatives. Letters of administration may also be granted in relation to people who die testate, but where, for example, they fail to appoint executors, the executor is unable to act, or the court passes over the executor. The latter may occur where the executor is insolvent or where there are other special circumstances.[675] A grant of administration is necessary before the assets of the deceased person can be paid or transferred to beneficiaries. In this context, 'administration' means probate of the will or letters of administration.[676]

An exception which allows dealings with the estate without the above procedures is where the deceased was the holder of limited government or local government stock not exceeding the 'prescribed amount', which, as at the time of writing, is NZD 15,000 and certain similar investments.[677]

481. Typically, where there is no controversy, probate is granted 'in common form', and this will usually be done by a court Registrar rather than a judge.[678] An executor can apply to the court without notice,[679] with an affidavit setting out the facts necessary to prove the death of the person and the validity of the will along with a promise to faithfully execute the will in accordance with the law. In *Re Crawford (deceased)*,[680] Mackenzie J said, '[t]he will for which probate is granted is the physical document actually signed by the will-maker and the witnesses. There is a well-established practice to deal with cases where probate cannot be granted of the will itself, because the original document is not available'. A scanned or electronic copy of the will is not enough.

482. Where the grant of administration is opposed or where the executor has doubts over such matters as whether the testator had testamentary capacity or had been subject to undue influence or whether the papers purporting to be testamentary

673. Section 5, Administration Act 1969.
674. Section 6(2), Administration Act 1969.
675. Section 6(2), Administration Act 1969. For an example, *see Re Estate of Berghan* [2020] NZHC 1399, [2020] 2 NZLR 585, discussed above (paras 384 and 397).
676. Section 2, Administration Act 1969.
677. Section 64, Administration Act 1969. For the 'prescribed amount' *see* the Administration (Prescribed Amounts) Regulations 2009, clause 4.
678. Rule 27.14, High Court Rules 2016.
679. Rule 27.4, High Court Rules 2016.
680. *Re Crawford (deceased)* [2014] 3 NZLR 38 at [7].

are valid or properly executed, probate 'in solemn form' must be sought.[681] In such instances, a notice of the proceedings must be given to interested parties. A caveat can be lodged against any application for administration, and where this has happened,[682] the court is likely to require an application in solemn form.

483. When a person dies, the executors are entitled to possession of the person's body and have a duty to dispose of the body. People frequently include in their will a request to be cremated but, while this request is not legally binding, it is normally complied with by those arranging the funeral. The Supreme Court ruled, in a case where the deceased's Māori family removed the body contrary to the non-Māori widow's wishes and buried him in tribal land, that the executor had a discretion as to the manner of burial.[683] However, over the years, the law has been developed by requiring 'the personal representative to take into account different cultural, religious and spiritual practices as well as the views of immediate and wider family. Such development is consistent with the relevant statutory context in New Zealand. It ensures that due weight is given by the common law to the tikanga concerning Māori burial practices, where they arise and are brought to the attention of decision-makers'.[684] Ultimately, therefore, the common law prevails over customary law.

484. Funeral expenses are to be paid from the estate and take priority over all other debts.

485. Once there has been a grant of administration, the executor has various responsibilities with respect to the estate. The executor is required to get in the estate, the estate vesting in the executor or administrator.[685] So, the executor should get in all debts which had been given on personal security. There is no necessity to realize real securities such as mortgages. An inventory of assets may need to be made and presented to the court if the court so requires.[686]

486. An executor is, as a general although not binding rule, given one year to ascertain the testator's estate and perform the necessary acts of administration before the executor can be forced to pay any legacies – the so-called executor's year. This applies even where the will directs payment within one year.[687] During this period, the executor has a duty to preserve the property as far as possible. If the property has to be sold to satisfy debts, a specific legatee is entitled to compensation from the general estate. However, the executor is entitled to recover the whole cost of the property's preservation from a specific legatee from the date of the testator's death until the property is handed over to the legatee.[688] In practice, this is

681. Rule 27.6, High Court Rules 2016. *See also* Rule 27.31, which distinguishes between common and solemn form.
682. Section 60, Administration Act 1969 and Rule 27.11, High Court Rules 2016.
683. *Takamore v. Clarke* [2013] 2 NZLR 733.
684. *Ibid.*, at para. [152].
685. Section 24(1), Administration Act 1969.
686. Section 44, Administration Act 1969.
687. *Bell v. Courtney* [1919] NZLR 170.
688. *Re Pearce* [1909] 1 Ch. 819.

done only when there is significant cost attached to the upkeep of the property. The executor has a duty to pay all taxes, testamentary expenses and debts. The executor is not liable to claimants who do not respond to the advertisement. In *Sadler v. Public Trust*,[689] the Court of Appeal dealt with a claim by the deceased's estranged daughter that the Public Trust as executor had breached its duty of even-handedness by failing to alert her of the death. It was held that the duty is to be reactive rather than proactive, but there are exceptions where, for example, it was known that someone wanted to make a claim against the estate or where someone seeks information (there must be no active concealment). There is no general duty to advise potential claimants of the death or even those where there it is suspected that there may be a claim.

487. The executor (or 'personal representative') has a wide range of powers which are basically the same as those conferred on trustees.[690] This is subject to any contrary intention in the will. This means that the personal representative can, among other things, alienate and charge estate assets, carry on the deceased's business and settle claims against the estate. The personal representative can sue and be sued on behalf of the estate, except that the personal representative cannot sue in defamation and claim for exemplary damages.[691]

488. An important duty of the personal representative is to distribute the assets of the estate in accordance with the terms of the will, a task which should normally be done within the 'executor's year'. This means paying specified legacies, managing annuities and paying out the residue of the estate to the residuary beneficiaries. If a testator provides in the will that the executor is to buy a legatee an article, the beneficiary is entitled to ask for the money instead. Where the gift is subject to a condition that the legatee must fulfil before receiving the legacy, the executor is not bound to notify the legatee of the fact even where the executor benefits as a result.

489. In *In re Lewis*, [692] this meant that where the executor was the residuary beneficiary and the condition imposed on the legatee was not fulfilled, the forfeiture of the legacy was held to be valid. The position may be different in the case of fraud on the part of the executor.[693] An annuity begins to accumulate from the date of the testator's death unless the instrument shows a contrary intention. The first payment is not due until the end of the one-year period unless a contrary intention is shown by the will. Normally an annuity will be for the beneficiary's lifetime; however, this can be varied by the terms of the will to shorten the length of time, impose conditions on receipt of the annuity or make it a gift in perpetuity.

689. [2009] NZFLR 937.
690. Trusts Act 2019.
691. Section 3, Law Reform Act 1936.
692. [1904] 2 Ch. 656.
693. Re *Bragg (deceased)* [1977] 2 NZLR 137.

490. In general, legacies cannot be paid to minors until they reach the age of majority, unless there is an express provision in the will to the contrary. The age of majority under the Age of Majority Act 1970 is 20. The minor is, however, entitled to maintenance out of the income of the legacy.[694]

694. See *The Laws of New Zealand*, 'Administration of Estates Part II' (LexisNexis, Wellington) paras 412 and 413.

Selected Bibliography

B. Atkin. *Living Together Without Marriage* (Wellington: Butterworths, 1991).
B. Atkin. *Relationship Property in New Zealand.* 3rd edn (Wellington: LexisNexis, 2018).
G. Austin. *Children: Stories the Law Tells* (Wellington: VUP, 1994).
R Fisher. *Fisher on Matrimonial and Relationship Property* (LexisNexis, online).
M. Henaghan et al. *Family Law in New Zealand.* 20th edn (LexisNexis: Wellington, 2021).
M. Henaghan & Atkin B. *Family Law Policy in New Zealand.* 5th edn (Wellington: LexisNexis, 2020).
B.D. Inglis. *New Zealand Family law in the 21st Century* (Wellington: Thomson/ Brookers, 2008).
C. Kelly and G. Kelly. *Garrow and Kelly Law of Trusts and Trustees* 8th edn (Wellington, LexisNexis, 2022)
LexisNexis Family Law Service (online).
LexisNexis Wills and Succession (online).
J. Palmer et al (eds). *Law and Policy in Modern Family Finance: Property Division in the 21st Century* (Cambridge: Intersentia, 2017).
W.M. Patterson. *Family Protection and Testamentary Promises.* 5th edn (Wellington: LexisNexis, 2021).
M. Peart et al. *Relationship Property & Adult Maintenance: Acts & Analysis* (Wellington: Thomson Reuters, 2013).
M. Peart et al. *Relationship Property on Death* (Wellington: Thomson/Brookers, 2004).
I. Reuvecamp et al. *Mental Capacity Law in New Zealand* (Wellington: Thomson Reuters, 2019).
L. Breach. *Nevill's Law of Trusts, Wills and Administration.* 13th edn (Wellington: LexisNexis, 2018).
Westlaw Family Law (Thomson Reuters, online).
The Laws of New Zealand, especially the Titles 'Administration of Estates', 'Children and Young Persons', 'Dissolution of Marriage', 'Family Property Arrangements', 'Husband and Wife', 'Matrimonial Property', 'Parent and Child', 'Wills'.

Selected Bibliography

Index

The numbers here refer to paragraph numbers.

Index

Index

Made in the USA
Coppell, TX
05 November 2026

11306034R00103